BENNY GREEN

*'When a great man dies, he leaves a
gaping hole behind him, which explains
why it takes the rest of us so long to get
used to the draught.'*

Benny Green, on the lyricist Yip Harburg

BENNY GREEN

Words and Music

A Biography
by Dominic Green

LONDON
HOUSE

To My Mother

First published in Great Britain in 2000 by
LONDON HOUSE
114 New Cavendish Street
London W1M 7FD

A catalogue record for this book is
available from the British Library

ISBN 1 902809 39 4

Edited and designed by DAG Publications
Ltd, London. Designed by David Gibbons.
Edited by John Gilbert.
Printed and bound by Creative Print & Design,
Ebbw Vale, Wales.

Contents

Acknowledgements

For so generously sharing their memories, I am very grateful to Lily Green Wexper and David Wexper, Jill and Peter Donker-Curtius, Dax Wexper, Robin Green, Andy Green, Kim Green, Betty Kanal, Kenneth Griffith, Lennie and Anne Bush, Kenny Lynch and Harry Klein, not forgetting the great Bernie Stanton.

I would like to thank Rod Dymott and Susan Herbert at London House for their support; Colin Webb, Benny's long-time publisher at Pavilion, as this book was his idea; and John Pawsey, who was Benny's agent, for believing in it. My dear friend Rob Cheek was as generous as ever with his encouragement and advice, and I will never forget the kindness shown to me by the JTQ and Scott Thompson.

John Fordham's excellent biography of Ronnie Scott, *Let's Join Hands And Contact the Living* (republished as *Jazzman*) was invaluable for the period 1953–6. Further good material came from Kenneth Griffith's autobiography, *The Fool's Pardon*.

To Mum, Jay, LG and Tasha, I can only say that without your love and your many contributions to this book, it wouldn't have happened. And, of course, my thanks and love to Maja, inspirational pep-talker and ruthless reader of manuscripts.

Prologue: Langley House

I can pinpoint the day on which I realised that my father was not like most others. It was a summer afternoon in August 1974, and my parents had taken my two brothers and my four-year-old self to a garden party at the baronial home of John Dankworth and Cleo Laine. As we entered the Dankworths' capacious garden, we saw that at its far end a temporary stage had been built, and that a jam session was in progress. Without a word, my father strode off towards the music that rolled up the garden, his back leaning to the left as he lugged the mysterious, battered brown case that he had brought with him from home for some unknown purpose. Laying it down at the side of the stage, he produced from its red velvet depths the glinting elements of an apparently ancient saxophone. Then, in a process that the retreat of childhood has made no less magical, he screwed the curved pieces of brass together, walked on to the stage and placed his legs squarely either side of a microphone stand, before leaning back and taking a deep breath as he put the mouthpiece to his lips. Suddenly there came from the horn of the saxophone the sweet and thunderous torrent of melody that I would come to know as jazz. After a couple a numbers, he left the stage. I remember little else about the afternoon, other than having my photo taken with Bill Oddie, but I know that it was on that day that I first understood that my father had a life outside our home, and what he did in that life. It was also on that day that I decided to be a musician when I grew up.

Before that day, I'd had only shadowy intimations of the true man that lay behind the punter of footballs and reader of bedtime stories that I knew. My earliest memory of him dates from the year before. The two of us are sitting on the steps in the circle of the Mermaid Theatre, watching an afternoon rehearsal of *Cole*, his musical about Cole Porter. At three, I was too young to realise most fathers don't spend their time writing musicals. My illusion was compounded by the presence in the cast of Una Stubbs. Two of my limited circle of infant contemporaries were her children, and they didn't seem to be any more surprised by it all than I was.

As I grew older and realised more and more that my father was by all accounts a polymath and professional encyclopaedia, I also came to understand that, by his own admission, his life broke into two segments. Firstly, there were the 34 years before he married my mother. In this period, he seemed to have been raised in a world rendered so distant by its antiquated poverty that I could only imagine it as a scene from *Oliver!* But despite these hardships, this was also the world of fond memory, of feckless uncles brought low by gambling, of his Russian-born grandmother's kitchen, of his first encounters with literature and jazz. These first 34 years were also those of his career at the business end of a tenor sax, a period of distant travels and outrageous yarns that had clearly set my father apart from other men. After all, he couldn't drive, despite having spent several years living on tour buses.

The second period was the more familiar of the two. This was his life as a writer and family man. It began with his marriage in 1962, took in the appearance of my elder brother Justin (1965) and sister Gaby (1967), swept past my own entry in 1970, and those of my brother Leo (1972) and sister Natasha (1976). In this scheme, he left the house as little as possible, spending most of his days hammering at an old Bluebird typewriter, which he assured us was the best you could get in the Sixties, even it if was made in Germany. Apart from the odd foray at a wedding, the saxophone stayed in the hall cupboard, although he did toot 'Happy Birthday' on a toy version of it for our birthdays. This instrument, a soprano as it turned out, was that rarity, a family heirloom, having been in the possession of his Uncle Henry. The sound it produced suggested that at some point in his curateship, Henry had stamped on it. Other than that, as a musician my father had reached a status familiar to freelancers everywhere, that of the musician who doesn't play.

The setting for these years was our home, Langley House, the 'big house' of a village on the A41 just beyond Watford, although some of its earlier scenes had been played out in Wembley, in a semi down the road from the flats where my grandparents lived. My childhood was an idyll only marginally infringed upon by the usual sibling frictions, and my father was only ever kind and entertaining, with the rare knack of talking to a child without making it feel inferior. There were six of us in total, living a life all the more enjoyable for its relative seclusion. On Sundays, my mother drove us all down the A41 for lunch with my grandparents, David and Fanny, and David's surviving sisters and their husbands. I now realise that those impossibly wizened faces into which so many salt beef sandwiches and cigarettes were disappearing so quickly were the last survivors of the extended family that had filled my father's mythical childhood in the back streets of Marylebone.

It was quite obvious to me that whatever my familiarity with the more recent half of my father's life, the key to who he really was lay in the earlier half. The problem was how to find out the mysterious process by which he had become the musician and writer I knew. Although his parents worshipped him, it seemed that their adoration had never allowed them even to acknowledge that their son had ever grown up, that his life had ever changed, or that he had acquired a personality independent of them. For a man who could give you a potted biography of the life and rides of Gordon Richards, my grandfather had a strange amnesia when it came to his only child's formative years. My grandmother, whose idea of art would have been an eight-foot-high bronze of her beloved son in the act of eating lokshen pudding, could offer even less, only variations on the theme of my father's divinity in a thick Leeds accent. His aunts and uncles only retailed thinly veiled anecdotes from their own lives that masqueraded as being about my father, as if his unfeasible success in the public arena had rendered his early life irrelevant but for those episodes in which he had learnt something crucial from them.

The father that I knew was a country-dwelling author who hated smokers, was besotted with his wife, doted on his children, and had few friends. The man that he appeared to have been in the first 34 years of his life was quite another person. He was a musician who lived in the West End, smoked heavily, and was an only child who, though unlucky in love, had an extended family of crowd-sized proportions, and a wide cast of friends with rococo personal habits. Who was this earlier incarnation, and how had he metamorphosed into the man I knew? Although externally he appeared to be the father from the second phase of his life, so much of who he was had its roots in the first, inaccessible time. The great exception to this was my mother, whose arrival had precipitated the biographical rupture in question.

When we asked her what our father had been like when she met him, my mother was quite forthcoming. They had met on a TV show being filmed on a boat. He was unhappily single and was playing in the band, she had just left RADA and was dancing. When he proposed to her, he accidentally poured lemon tea over her crotch. He lived in a damp basement in Cleveland Street with his parents. He once came to meet her at Euston Station in a beret, vest and braces, which she thought was very bohemian. Her mother liked him, and they had married a few days after her twentieth birthday. He was 34, it snowed, and they went to Switzerland on honeymoon, where the beret came in handy, as did the galoshes that his mother had made him bring along. His first book was published within six months of getting married.

This was informative, but to my juvenile mind it didn't explain how he had navigated such a profound change in the direction of his life. It seemed to me that my mother was as ignorant of his early life as I was. In fact, I was entirely wrong in this; she knew all about it, but had taken the sensible precaution of saving the more complex material until we were old enough to understand. Meanwhile, I was perplexed.

Fortunately, my father came to the rescue. As I skimmed through the regular articles that he wrote for all manner of papers and magazines, I noticed that regardless of the subject, there was always a strong autobiographical content to his writing. Almost guiltily, I began to fillet out the personal detail from his work, and was able to construct from this a pretty accurate, if idealised impression of his own childhood. But this was only the surface of things, and a polished one at that. His emotions remained hidden behind the topic at hand and his humorous touch. It was not that my father was uncommunicative. For a man of his generation, he was more warm and honest with his children than most, and we grew up knowing that we were loved by a man of exceptional talents for little other reason than the fact of our existence. He found in his own children the companionship he had missed as an only child. But he was less prolix about his feelings when it came to his early life, that veiled time of childhood, youth and jazz.

Luckily enough, I was able later to meet that hidden man on the more level field of adulthood, when the musical efforts of my brother Leo and I re-awoke in my father his own love of playing jazz. I was a student defaulting on his literature course when I began to play jazz guitar, and when I returned home at the end of one term and announced my progress, his face was a mixture of surprise and pride. Shortly after my graduation in 1991, I found myself playing on stage with him. I can only assume that what drove him to offer me the gig was an extremity of paternal generosity, as at that time my ability on the guitar was well below professional standard. We played the standards that I knew from the repertoire that he would whistle as he wandered around the house looking for a particular book, 'Dream', 'Love Me Or Leave Me', 'There'll Never Be Another You' and 'Slow Boat To China'.

I staggered through their complex chord changes, marvelling at the ease with which he cast lazy Lester Young phrases in the wake of the beat, and hung in the air like the smoky curlicues left behind a steamship. He controlled the arrangement of each song through the arcane sign language that cues each member of the group as to what will happen next, would execute comic dances to accompany the drum solo, and had that elusive iron grasp of exactly where in the whirl of beats and chords he was at any moment, a casual, instinctive skill born of years of careful bar-counting. Once again, I felt like that four-year-old boy, awed by the unlikely talents of his giant father.

Over the next seven years, we played dozens of engagements together, travelling hundreds of miles up and down the country, and even crossing the Atlantic on the *QE2*. It would not be an exaggeration to say that those were the years in which Leo and I really got to know our father as a friend. We met not as father and sons, but as citizens of the democracy of the jazz musician, a kind of hip freemasonry through which my father moved with the effortlessness of a grandee. One Sunday afternoon, we had trekked up to Scarborough, where his sextet would be supporting that of his old friend Ronnie Scott. Having set up my amp on stage, I was wandering around the backstage labyrinth looking for the dressing room when suddenly a roar of laughter resounded down the corridor, and then another. I tracked it to its source. At the far end of the dressing room, Ronnie and my father were telling stories to the younger musicians who formed their groups. Everyone, the raconteurs included, was laughing, my father's face beaming. I saw the punning, surreal humour that I had grown up with in its natural state, an easy-going fraternal gathering of like-minded musicians.

Having long considered himself a devotee of a criminally underrated art form, I think it came as a surprise to my father to receive such interest from young players, or that the callow exploits of his and Ronnie's youth had become the stuff of legend, as the pioneering of Modern jazz in Britain. As he passed his working life in a state of inspired disorder, it fell to Leo and me to book his rhythm sections, and we usually hired our own contemporaries, which led to a pedagogic backstage situation that pleased all parties. One of our regular haunts was the Pizza Express club in Maidstone, a fine building converted from a bank, where we played beneath a giant photo of that most elegant of tenorists Coleman Hawkins sipping tea, and whose manageress Jan would indulge my father with extra slices of apple pie in the interval. There would be eight of us: my father; a three-piece rhythm section of our friends; the singer Maxine Daniels, whom my father knew from the old days; the young tenor player Ray Gelato; and Leo and I. The conversation would be that strange mixture of bawdy anecdote and rocket science unique to jazz, shifting smoothly from the sexual

11

habits of Art Baxter to analysis of Hawkins's handling of the key change at the bridge of 'Body and Soul'. Often, we would be so absorbed in our talk that Jan would have to come in and drag us back out on to the stage, as the natives were getting restless in our absence.

Onstage, his powers returned with each gig. The passing of the years had meant that his style, which he would modestly belittle as a mere pastiche of the great Lester, had become a rarity. Like many of his interests, his playing was from a gentler age, the time before jazz had ditched melody in favour of intrepid harmonic adventure. Musicians and punters alike would listen rapt as his sonorous tenor would gently carve out the melody of a ballad, as if a musical species previously thought extinct had been found alive and well in Hertford-shire. On the faster numbers, he would casually toss out great chunks of inspi-ration, constructing an edifice of burnished melody that made following his solo with your own a daunting prospect, his creation echoing in your ears long after the audience had finished applauding it.

The high points of the show were when the three tenors (he, Leo and Ray) would stand shoulder to shoulder, swapping lines in the way of amicable compe-tition known as 'cutting heads'. As the rhythm section stoked the fire, each man picked up the melodic tail of the last one's phrase, turning it into a new one before passing the baton on to the next. As the improvisations became more and more extravagant, the pressure would increase, until their whirling relay would reach a climax at the point where melody meets cacophony, a delirium of honking and squealing saxophones. As Leo and Ray have told me, my father could more than handle himself in this demanding situation, making up for any shortness of breath with the cunning of a fox, able to put a challenging spin of rhythm or melody on the tail of a phrase like a demon Test bowler.

We often had with us a drummer called Bobby Orr, a grandstanding swinger who had toured with the great Benny Goodman. When Bobby was on the gig, part of the show would always feature his other great credential: he could play excerpts from *The Marriage of Figaro* and *The Flight of the Bumblebee* on his teeth with a pencil. One night during a two-week stand at Pizza On The Park, while Bobby was performing his solos and bringing the house down in the process, my mind wandered to the subject of how it was that my father's playing was so good, even though he had barely played a chorus in 30 years. It dawned on me that all that whistling around the house had not been as aimless as we thought. It was like the steam that emits occasionally from a dormant volcano.

His mind had never stopped analysing changes and constructing melodies. Disturbing the sediment of thirty years of writing, his original talent emerged from the depths of memory, untarnished by three decades of neglect. In his head, he had never stopped being a musician, he had just stopped pumping the tread-mill of the professional circuit. Every morning in bed, while 'looking for work', Benny would run a chord sequence in his head, his hands working the keys of an imaginary saxophone.

But despite the sold-out clubs, good reviews and praise from musicians, he was oddly dismissive of his own playing. By his own admission, this was not just because his embouchure was not what it once was and his fingers were a little rusty. This self-doubt had been a feature of his early musical career, and he would often castigate his youthful self for having been so shy and self-conscious about his ambitions. Even at the height of his playing, when he had played bari-tone in Ronnie's legendary nine-piece and had even deputised in Stan Kenton's Orchestra, he felt that he was perpetrating a kind of confidence trick, that he was a journeyman interloper among real talents. Certainly, in mixing it with players such as Scott, Lennie Neihaus and Tubby Hayes, he was playing with saxophon-ists of rare skill, even genius, who were not only better than him, but were among the best in the world. Then again, he was not unaware of his ability. One night after a gig, he told me of how he and Ronnie would trawl the afterhours clubs in the small hours, looking for groups to sit in with. With puzzled pride, he said that on one of those occasions, and only on that night, he had kept up with his friend and inspiration.

Not least because he was still so unsure of his sax playing after such a long lay-off, my father's trademark anecdotage formed the backbone of the show, with each song being prefaced with a scene from the lives of its composers, or a comic moment from his own youth. As in the writing that I had read as a child, stories of his family and his childhood came up again and again. But as I grew older and came to know him better, I began to wonder if that self-doubt was another, less charming legacy of that lost extended family, to whom emotional subtlety seems to have been quite alien. After hearing black American soldiers playing jazz in dull moments of the First World War, his own father had decided to become a jazz musician, one of the first in Britain, and his brother Henry had followed him. Both of their careers ran aground on the rocks of indolence and family mockery, forcing them to earn a living as compulsive gamblers with a sideline in tailoring. After my father's death, I went looking for clues about the musical seed in my family, and went to my Great-Aunt Lily, last of the nine Green siblings of Marylebone.

Lily told a story of how, long before my father was born, Dave and Henry had secured themselves one of their first professional engagements, at a West End dance hall. The two saxophonists began to play, only to receive a storm of heckles. The barracking came from their many cousins, who lobbed at the stage such plaudits as 'Stick to tailoring!' They had come to watch Dave and Henry only for the sport of ridiculing them. When, as an adult, I discussed with my father the perilous path of making your way as a musician, another narrative emerged, one quite different from the jollities of his writing. It seems that many of his uncles and aunts had taunted his aspirations as a musician, had regarded his dreams as being futile as those of his own father, who was a disappointment even by the standards of his own feckless family. Only then did I realise why it was that my father, who had been so florid about his family in print, did his best to shun them in later life. I think he still felt the smarts of their casual demolition of his teenage hopes.

In his later years, he added to the mountain of journalism about his family some extended pieces, which he hoped to collect one day into what he called 'the family history'. Of course, there are obvious questions to ask here, which, to my frustration, I never got round to asking him. Why, instead of writing his own autobiography, was he concentrating on this collection of long-dead obscurities? What sort of family history is one that excludes its most famous member, the author, from anything other than a child's walk-on part? To these, there is linked another question, one regularly posed by his children, his wife and his publisher, all of whom realised the value of his extraordinary life. When would he write his autobiography?

The subject of the unwritten autobiography became a familiar one at our family tea on Sunday afternoons. With generous folly, my father would open to the floor the question of how he was going to keep paying the bills. We would make the usual suggestions, such as, given that a decent interval of five years had elapsed since the death of his agent, surely it was time to get a new one? We would then proceed to several indecent suggestions, before my mother would mention an autobiography, the writer's equivalent of cashing in your insurance policies. Reaching for the moral support of a generously buttered crumpet, my father would consider it, but refer us to 'the family history', which he clearly considered covered the topic of his own life.

To be fair, he had a point. His reminiscences of his family not only described the world that he came from, they also contained many of his formative experiences. For him, his account of the people and circumstances of his early life were enough, and gave what seemed to him to be bountiful reasons for the subsequent shape of his character. If you knew him, it was possible to pick out this character and its feelings from the narrator-shaped hole at the centre of the writing. By following the contours of his stories, you could escry the outline of his own personality. But this was not explicit enough for a reader, and perhaps not explicit enough for his own children, whose imaginations had developed a thirst for these tales due to our early exposure to their most comic moments. We wanted to see more of this intriguing earlier Dad, whose shadow the present Dad was either unwilling or unable to shake. We wanted to know not only what had happened, but how he had felt about it. But the present Dad felt that he had dealt with this past as much as he wanted to, and was not to be pushed into any further excavations. Perhaps unreasonably, we felt deprived by his refusal to casually denude himself for our entertainment. In my selfish frustration, it sometimes seemed to me that the old cliché was true – that autobiography is as much an act of covering up as it is one of revelation.

In what turned out to be the last eighteen months of his life, a protracted delay in a flat-buying chain deposited me, my fiancée and our cat on the parental doorstep, 'for a few weeks'. Those few weeks turned into nine months. Retrospectively, I realise that what at the time was an inconvenience was actually another of those lucky privileges that I enjoyed in my relationship with my father. It was an unexpected chance to spend more time in each other's company than we had in ten years. Not only did we share our interests, we both had insomniac tendencies. When I returned at two or three in the morning from a gig, he would often be up in his dressing-gown, saying 'Fancy a cup of tea?' with the mock innocence of a man about to flout his wife's dietary regime with a quick slab of bread and jam.

On those nights, we talked about everything that mattered in our lives, of love and work, art and ambition. Just as having his own children had allowed him to focus his memory of his childhood, so seeing me making shaky progress into my adulthood brought out memories of his own early steps in that other, earlier life. By this time, he knew that the end of his life was not far away, and I think that knowledge sharpened those long talks for both of us. After nine months at Langley, I was lounging around one day when the phone rang. It was one of those life-changing moments that were legendary occurrences in the life of the early Dad, moments that the modern Dad had always told us would come. I was offered a long American tour, and accepted like a shot. When I left for the airport with my guitar and an overnight bag, our parting had the emotional nature of a provisional farewell for good, as neither of us knew how long he would hold off the cancer. By a twist of fate, Leo had left for America on another tour only days before, and over the next weeks we crisscrossed each other's path, both wondering whether we would see our father again.

When I got back a month later, I went straight from Heathrow to the hospital, where he had been brought to the edge of death by an infection that made another operation inconceivable. To the astonishment of the doctors, he recovered within days, and was back at Langley within two weeks, minus his spleen. He lived for another six months, never stopping work. His last newspaper article, on George Gershwin, was written five days before he died. When he went into hospital with another, final infection, in his bag was his script for the following Sunday's Radio 2 programme, ready to be recorded the next day. He drifted away over the next three days, with all of us around him. At one point, I had to go down to Greenwich to play a gig. I explained that I had to go to work for a few hours. He smiled, and said, 'That's jazz, baby.' As he slipped away in a deep sleep, his fingers would flex sporadically on an imaginary saxophone, or he would occasionally raise his eyebrows in his familiar way of greeting a loved one. In his last moments, he was back in his early life.

After the funeral, we began the task of filing the contents of his study. We found libretti for musicals that were never set to music, proposals for books that had never been commissioned, annotations to half of the Savoy operas, and numerous empty cartons of Mr Kipling's apple pies. Cuttings and scripts came out by the box- and cupboard-load, to be piled up on the floor, and catalogued by topic. Again and again, we came up against the same problem. An article that began with a description of Charles Dickens's domestic arrangements (See under: Literature), would take a sudden diversion into my great-grandmother's basement kitchen (See under: Family), before depositing the disorientated reader in the Long Room at Lord's (See under: Sport, Cricket). Or a tale from his days on the road (Autobiography) would elide into one about Gilbert & Sullivan (Musical Theatre), by way of a bout with Gene Tunney (Boxing) and Bernard Shaw (Literature). It was impossible to separate the intimate details of his life from the historical events of the world around it. This unique blend of the esoteric and personal gave his writing a universal touch, despite the often obscure literary, musical or sporting subject matter. As nothing was excluded in the quest for material, he touched on the full breadth of human experience from the profound to the everyday, or, as that great anti-Semite T. S. Eliot so fatuously put it, 'Spinoza and the smell of cooking'.

Reading him now, I am unsure whether he was a compulsive autobiographer who set his own life in the wider frame, or an historian of the popular arts who rooted his passions in his own experiences. Perhaps he equivocated here, too, as with his playing. This material was autobiographical, but it did not constitute an autobiography. Added to it was the jazz-based novel he had written after his marriage, which was strongly autobiographical, and a third, more problematic book from the Seventies, *Swingtime In Tottenham*, an episodic story of his days rowing in the galleys of Jewish wedding orchestras, which was as close to auto-biography as you can get without actually naming the guilty parties.

Surveying the mountains of print that ranged over the study floor, I came to the conclusion that he had documented in one form or another all of the salient people, events and influences of the 34-year grey area that had made the man I knew. It also occurred to me that in the course of that blessed adult friendship we had shared, I had discovered many of his true feelings about those years. I first got to know him through his writings, and this book is as much a commentary on them as on the close relationship that developed as I grew older. What follows is my father's account of himself, and my reading of him, which is as subjective as his own rendering of the world in which he grew up. He was my mentor, and my best friend. By its very nature, such an account cannot be balanced, and I make no pretence towards either accuracy or inclusiveness.

I feel that the real Dad lay somewhere between the father I knew as a boy, the musical co-conspirator of my youth, the *flâneur* of my early manhood, and the pieces of Croxley Script that piled up inexorably by the old Bluebird, each with their own reading of his life. Somewhere between the man I called 'Dad', the son whose mother had named him 'Bernard', the husband that my mother called 'Ben', and the public figure that the world outside Langley House knew as 'Benny Green'.

When we said our emotional goodbye as I left for America, he pushed a letter into my hand. Reading it as I drove away, it seemed like a benediction for the rest of my life.

17

'Good luck on your extraordinary trip. I hope you see fabulous sights and play some great music.

'While I'm on the subject, the conversations I have had with you over the past months have been all memorable. We have talked, sometimes in the middle of the night, and I shall never forget a word.

'Anyway, enjoy the explorations, eat like an empirical scientist, laugh a lot – and then come home.'

I shall never forget a word, either.

Dominic Green, London, 1999

A Marylebone Childhood

Greenwell Street 1

Benny Green was born on December 9th, 1927. As the *Manchester Guardian* for that day records, more serious matters were afoot while my father was adapting to his new surroundings. In New York, a first edition of *The Pickwick Papers* was being auctioned to a prescient bargain hunter for a mere $16,300, (£3,260). Meanwhile in New Orleans, the promising young trumpeter Louis Armstrong was recording 'Struttin' With Some Barbecue' with his Hot Five. Through the day of his birth, books and jazz, the twin tracks of my father's life, run in a pleasingly novelistic fashion, ready to carry him to his inevitable future. However, the narrative becomes more complex from then on, as life doggedly interferes with the straight plotting of art and biography.

I suppose it is inevitable that in the life of this most paradoxical of men, the contradictions begin to accumulate with his first moments. The man who was to be many people's idea of a Cockney was born not in London, but in Leeds, and was named not Benny, but Bernard Green. His mother Fanny, not trusting her London in-laws, had gone home to her mother's to have her first baby. Although no one ever mentioned it, I can only presume that his father David was also there, although his concentration may have been badly knocked by the calamitous international news lurking on the *Guardian*'s front page. The day before, Australia's government had banned nocturnal dog-racing, while in Spain they'd banned it altogether. How was a man to earn a living?

Benny's parents had met the year before, when my grandfather Dave had been playing with a jazz orchestra in Leeds. Given the subsequent tangent of his career, this engagement represents the height of Dave's success on the saxophone, not counting the time when he prevailed on the great Sidney Bechet to play on Uncle Henry's soprano. Fanny Trayer was, at 23, five years younger than Dave when they met in that long-demolished dance hall. My grandmother's character, or what was left of it after she had been trained for domestic slavery, had a dangerous combination of attributes. She was ambitious in a small way, and ignorant in a broader way. I think that the suave metropolitan saxophonist she met that night would have seemed a good catch, a well-travelled man earning good money in a glamorous profession, at a time when money was tight in the family after the death of her father, a tailor who was so tall that they couldn't find a coffin to fit him. To this day, dark rumours circulate in the older strata of the family that some coercion was involved in the way Fanny kept hold of her catch, including a feigned pregnancy. In the way of their generation, their marriage was to be more functional than contented.

They married in London in December 1926, setting up home in the madhouse that was the home of Benny's grandparents, Number One Greenwell Street, a three-storey house sliding into slumdom in the streets behind Fitzroy Square. Originally built for the rising petty bourgeoisie of the nineteenth century, the area had been leapfrogged by the same mad scramble for the suburbs that had generated it. By the Twenties, much of it had sunk into teeming decrepitude, its population predominantly composed of Jewish and Italian immigrants and their families. Living amid this Victorian poverty in the relative comfort of an entire house were Dave's parents, Joseph and Deborah Green, he a master tailor, she his drudge. They had met after Joseph's arrival from Russia in the 1880s, when he had taken lodgings in Spitalfields with Deborah's family. Their marriage produced nine children in all, ranging from the inspirationally demented to the dangerously half-witted, most of whom seemed to be a source of profound puzzlement to their parents. All of them, and almost all of the men that the girls married, were gripped by the Jewish vice, gambling. Their names, and the names of their spouses, read like the rhyme scheme from a Victorian comic song: Ginnie, Katie and Sam (and then Barney), Davey, Simey, Lewis, Minnie and Albert, Henry and Edith (and then Doris), Eva and Frank, Lily and David.

In this menagerie, Dave had some status, by dint of birth if not merit. Although he was the third-born, he was Joseph and Deborah's first son, and when Benny was born, he was their first grandchild. From his earliest days, Benny was doted on by a familial horde, led by his grandmother, with dozens of aunts and uncles in train. Even after Benny's parents had moved around the corner to a basement flat in Cleveland Street, the focus of family life was always his grandfather's house, and it was to that house and its improbable cast of sad clowns that he returned perennially in his writing. His earliest memory is of their warm embrace. His grandfather Joseph was doing well enough as a master tailor to rent a summer pied-à-terre in Brighton, to which the family and its extended array of cousins would decamp:

> There is a small boy and the small boy is me, and I am in a larder and the
> larder is in my grandmother's kitchen and the kitchen, to say nothing of

my grandmother, is in Hove, and Hove is in England and England is clearly one hell of a big place, for according to my Aunt Ginnie it stretches out beyond that point on the sky where the railway lines disappear, although with my Aunt Ginnie you can never be sure she isn't talking about something else. Anyway, I am in this larder because I have a desire to play with a string of onions dangling from a hook on the inside of the door, which gives you some idea of what kind of child I am. My grandmother, who spoils me horribly, tells my grandfather that my taste for onions suggests that I will grow up to be a greengrocer, an observation that causes my grandfather to respond with the thought that if my father's career is anything to go by, I won't grow up to be anything at all.

Brighton was to recur in Benny's life, its childhood hold on his imagination cemented by later passions. In 1948, having dutifully fulfilled his grandfather's prophecy and avoiding any paid work for the first 21 years of his life, he returned there for his first professional engagement as a musician, playing for the dancers at Sherry's Ballroom, a setting with the requisite seaside loucheness for it to feature in Benny's second novel, *Fifty-Eight Minutes to London*. His wife, Toni, whom he had met on the Thames, turned out to hail from Bognor Regis, half an hour from the racier delights of Brighton. As children, we would spend our summers at Bognor with our maternal grandmother. Book-hunting trips to Brighton were a feature of our weekends, when the bibliophiles among Benny's offspring would spend the morning trailing him up and down the rickety staircases of second-hand bookshops, through the narrow Lanes and out on to the Front. As we strolled on, he would indicate the site of Sherry's, or the ballroom at the end of the pier, in whose band Justin's godfather Bernie had worked, which one stormy night later had fallen into the sea, a fate that now seemed imminent for the whole crumbling town.

That a novel about his rites of passage in Brighton would take as its title the precise time that it takes to return to London is a testimony to where Benny's heart lay. If it is possible to anchor his emotional sense of himself in one place, then that place is the domain of his grandmother Deborah, the basement kitchen where the boy Benny was sent when his mother was out working, and his father was just 'out':

My father's mother, Deborah Slovis, was a shortish, dumpy old lady with a disposition so genial that even her own children quite like her. By the

23

time I became aware of the world, she had already settled into the final role of her career, an obese matriarch swathed in long, shapeless black dresses which somehow gave her the aspect of a pantomime charlady. Never dressing in any other colour, never venturing out into the street, half-crippled by arthritis, rendered stoic by the loss of too many children, she remained a cheerful, affectionate, lovable old woman in whose lively brown eyes the twinkle was unquenched by the hardships imposed on her by an indifferent world. In my early years, I spent a great deal of time alone with her in the great subterranean kitchen of the house in Greenwell Street, observing her style as she shuffled across the rush matting from table to stove, stove to sink, sink to table. I was her first grandchild, indeed the only one she survived for long enough to enjoy, and the novelty of my status rendered me a protected species. On those occasions when my father was tempted to give me a corrective clip round the ear, she would forbid any such measure, saying that whatever misdemeanours I might have committed, they were nothing compared to the chaotic disruption of the whole neighbourhood he had wrought in his time.

One afternoon, while out in the long, narrow strip of yard which ran along the front of the house and was known as 'the area', I was competing against a ghostly host for the world javelin championship, and inadvertently flung a long pole through the kitchen window, making such a racket of shattering glass that half the family came dashing down into the basement to see if anything interesting was going on. The moment my father took in the situation, he decided that he must express his disapproval, not because I had smashed a window, but because I had smashed someone else's. But before he could formulate a plan, the old girl had made her move. I can see her now, standing between us, shouting, 'Davey, leave him alone', an instruction somehow so ludicrous that it never failed to clear the air by reducing all three of us to self-conscious laughter. She was, looking back on it, one of my best friends, an approving relative so ancient that I could not imagine how many years she had seen.

From this kitchen there also came an unlikely source of musical sustenance, one to which Benny the author would return 50 years later. Floating through the

Eastern European cooking vapours were refrains from his grandmother's memory of the music halls of her nineteenth-century youth:

> As she worked at the sink, or fed the cat, or sat contentedly at the vast deal table, peeling potatoes or slicing apples, she would hum or sing. They were not the melodies I knew from my regular visits to the local picture palaces, or from my crude empirical experiments with the portable gramophone in the parlour cupboard, but seemed to be in some quaint way airs from another time, music in retrospect, a vocal analogue of the twin portraits on the back wall of King Edward and Queen Alexandra. It comes back to me that once, as she was serving me a bowl of steaming barley soup, she was singing something about dilly-dallying on the way. And another time, when the early winter dusk was gathering outside the window over the sink, and the sad winter rain drummed on the dustbin lids in the yard beyond, she made a cryptic reference to one Dolly Daydream ...'[1]

From the basement, 79 stone steps rose through three floors to the leaky skylight at the top of the stairwell, passing en route the five bedrooms into which the house's eleven-plus occupants compressed themselves at night. The ground floor of Greenwell Street was divided into two rooms. In these, there lay two fiercer presences, which were closely linked in the mind of the young Benny. In the rearmost room was his grandfather's tailoring workshop. In the room that faced the street was the polar bear:

> The great glory of the house in my time was the Parlour. Its very title hints at the habits of a vanished past, and so did its trappings. On the hearth was a polar bear rug, whose grim head, with its fierce, staring eyes and terrifying fangs, seemed to a small boy to have mysteriously retained the power of attack even after death. On rare state occasions when the fire was lit, those eyes winked at me in the lambent glow of the flames, and I must have been at least seven years old before I mustered the courage to straddle its back and cover the Arctic wastes to the far wall.
>
> Behind the polar bear was an upright piano which nobody ever played but me, a bookcase filled with an Edwardian edition of Chambers'

Encyclopaedia which nobody ever looked at but me, and a two-piece telephone which everyone was allowed to use but me.[2]

It is a scene from Edwardian London, the showpiece of a house whose furnish-
ings would have been familiar to a parvenu from an H. G. Wells novel. Many
years later, when Langley House was being refurbished by my mother, she
installed my father in the study of his dreams, with shelves built to fit his
records and collection of *Wisden* cricket almanacs. To mark this watershed,
the Bluebird was replaced with an electric typewriter. Soon afterwards, my
mother told us that the room which had previously been his study, where he
had typed away while we watched children's television, was henceforth to be
known as 'The Parlour'. Of course, we children considered that to be an affec-
tation, but my father, who normally had a hawk's eye for social posturing,
loved the idea. Only now do I realise why, and the particular evocations held
for him by that name.

While Greenwell Street's parlour was usually closed, after that strange
Victorian fashion of not using the best room in the house for any other purpose
than intimidating your guests, the workshop was much busier. Here was the den
of Benny's Russian grandfather, the endlessly industrious Joseph:

> My paternal grandfather, the one with whom I reached some sort of
> friendly understanding, must have left the loony Romanovs to their
> own deplorable devices around 1875 ... He was a tailor, a real one, not
> one of those huckstering front-men who stand behind the counters of
> Savile Row displaying the impeccable manners of genteel tricksters,
> but a man who could actually make clothes, loved to make them, took
> pride in making them, and was, at last, a sort of virtuoso in the art of
> making them. You could put my grandfather in a room with a roll of
> cloth, needle and cotton, a few pins and a slab of tailor's chalk, and a
> few days later he would emerge from the room asking who had stolen
> his cutting shears. But give him a few more days and he would re-
> emerge wearing the cloth, by now transformed into the perfect
> ensemble.[3]

Joseph was working at 80 despite chronic cataracts in both eyes. But even
amid his ceaseless work, the house's twin allegiances were fatally evident:

Here he stitched away the days of his long life, adapting effortlessly to the changing demands of the period, shaping liveried finery for butlers and footmen in his prime, and turning in his old age to greatcoats for admirals and generals.

The rest of the brood, however, was less interested in making its jackets than in losing its shirts. Never in my life have I known any family group so committed to the arcane study of why one horse runs faster than another. Racing form books lay scattered among the cotton reels and pressing irons. Fashion plates from the *Tailor and Cutter* alternated on the walls with portraits of horses and jockeys ... In that household, the patter of little feet meant an Apprentice race for two year-olds.[4]

For a family more attuned than most to the value of a photo finish, it is surprising that there exists only one photograph of Benny's grandfather, master of a house which his children so busily undermined. It is a pose from the studio of an unknown snapper. Joseph looks every inch the successful immigrant, with his best three-piece suit, his fob watch, and a half-smoked cigar in his hand. He stares out with fierce probity over the promontory of his ample moustache. The dignified effect is sabotaged only by the contribution of the photographer, who has stood Joseph behind a thigh-high piece of Gothic masonry which, as Benny observed, makes his grandfather look as if he has been preserved for future generations in the act of climbing over a wall.

Much of the 'friendly understanding' that Benny reached with Joseph must have been founded on mutual incomprehension. When, one Saturday afternoon in 1935, Benny rushed into Joseph's workroom and scrawled the words 'Aston Villa 1, Ted Drake 7' all over the walls in tailor's chalk, his aunts' ire at this act of vandalism was cooled by the illiterate Joseph, who 'said that small boys should be encouraged in the pursuit of literature and, if I was capable of writing on the walls, they should all be proud of me'.[5] For Benny's part, nothing was as perplexing as the events that followed the opening of the Paramount Cinema in Tottenham Court Road. To drum up business, the owners distributed free passes among the burghers of the neighbourhood. The opening presentation was to be *The Last Days of Pompeii*:

The entire family turned out to see him on his way, and I can visualise him now, in his black Homburg hat and the brown overcoat with the

27

velvet collar which he had made for himself in 1921. He had a flower in his buttonhole, a carnation I think, and as he sauntered off to his assignation with a celluloid disaster, he looked like some boulevardier from some lost age, which I suppose in a way he was.

Next morning, I rushed around to the house to find out what he had made of it all. When I asked him, he said, without looking up from the morning coat destined for the overfed contours of Lord Wotsit, 'Not bad. I think I'll go again next week to see what happened.' This seemed to me so wonderfully, beautifully, unbelievably sublime that I gawped at him, as any small boy would at a man who thinks 'The Last Days of Pompeii' was a serial.

About six months later, he returned to the Paramount to see something about the Wild West, and he recognised one of the cowpunchers as a man he had seen walking the streets of Pompeii. The next time I had a chat with my grandfather he told me about this, and said, with an air of triumph, 'You see! He got away!'[6]

For all his hard work and respectability, Joseph could not have been surprised at his children's galloping mania for gambling, as he himself enjoyed more than the odd punt. In this, his main handicap was linguistic, as for him English came an unplaced fourth behind Yiddish, Russian and Polish. However, with the famous ingenuity and persistence of his people, he eventually found a way round this trifling obstacle:

His life was a touching allegory of the old belief that what the human being desires he can, if he desires it passionately enough, bring about.

So far as his desires were concerned, these numbered four: enough tailoring work to keep himself busy; chicken-and-rice; a bottle of whiskey; and the ability to stay in the horse-racing swim. The first three may be satisfied easily enough without the trouble of learning to be literate. But the fourth desire, to follow the horses, necessitates an intellectual grasp which is sometimes not acknowledged by the puritans. As a brief example, here are the names of the Derby winners in the years 1933 to 1939, those years in which I observed the members of my family with an intensity never subsequently approached. 1933: Hyperion, 1934: Windsor Lad, 1935: Bahram, 1936: Mahmoud, 1937: Midday Sun, 1938: Bois Roussel, 1939: Blue Peter.

My grandfather, as a dedicated punter residing in a hornets' nest of
punters, came to know each of these seven lumps of exalted cat's-meat
as he knew his own children. He pronounced their names constantly, and
rightly regarded them as aristocrats. He bandied their names about
without a thought, and that is how a semi-literate Russian immigrant
came to terms with Greek mythology (Hyperion), ancient Persian history
(Bahram), the Ottoman Empire in the 18th Century (Mahmoud), elementary French (Bois Roussel), and the laws pertaining the British maritime
practices (Blue Peter) …

My grandfather, hampered as he was by his own illiteracy, somehow
found a way round it, and came in the end to a command over the names
of the runners and riders in each day's racing sheet. As to how he did, I
cannot say, and neither can anyone else, least of all my grandfather, who
never did learn the corrupting art of describing the nature of his own
intellectual accomplishments.[7]

Having seen the plentiful misery wrought by his family's compulsive gambling,
Benny never placed a bet in his entire life. But he never could shake an affection
for his family in the regular moments when they were gripped by flights of optimism and threw fate to the wind, along with all the money in their pockets.
Whatever the flaws of its occupants, it was the Runyonesque romance of their
betting dreams, the exoticism of their language, and the womb-like comfort of
Deborah's kitchen that drew his mind back to Number One Greenwell Street long
after the house and the entire street it sat in had both been so thoroughly demol-
ished that they might never have existed. For Benny, as for many people, the
passage from childhood to adolescence was also one from Edenic innocence and
safety to the harshly 'indifferent' world outside:

Once upon a time, the myriad rooms of the house had been packed with
a bewildering congeries of temperament and prejudice. To me as the
small nephew of the occupants, each room had represented a unique
and fascinating expression of human personality; behind its doors I
discovered neurosis and blockheadedness, slapstick virtuosity and
spectacular social pretension, reckless generosity and Gradgrindian
parsimony, Panglossian optimism and Gummidgean despair, wondrous
naîvety and flowering cynicism.[8]

29

In September 1971, after the last inmate, maiden Aunt Ginnie, had finally decamped to a suburban nursing home, Benny went back to the house one last time before it was pulverised to make way for a Forte hotel:

> And so, knowing this was my very last chance, I grubbed around in the debris of my own past.
>
> I found precious little. A couple of volumes from The Sportsman's Book Club, forgotten in a cupboard, and, in the tiny loft in the roof, one of my grandfather's tailor's dummies, with its pouter-pigeon chest caved in and a deep wound in its side from which the horsehair dangled. Nothing else, at least nothing tangible. But the houses we grow up in can sometimes become private museums with invisible exhibits, and as I trailed through the rooms, forcing a door here, ripping the wallpaper there, the waves of nostalgia clouded my judgement.
>
> Whether or not houses take on the personalities of those who live in them I am not sure, but perhaps the walls retain the echoes of vanished voices. Before long the basement kitchen will probably be part of a subterranean hotel car park. They will be mixing cocktails where the upright piano used to stand, and rubbernecking tourists will overlay the bedroom where on a Saturday morning in 1937 I received the miraculous news that Oxford had at last managed to win the Boat Race …
>
> I wonder if ever in the future I will be obliged to spend a night at the hotel they are building. That really would be the final crushing irony. Because after all, it is true that, be it ever so humble, there's no place like childhood.[9]

Cleveland Street 2

Time for a walk. We begin in the top left corner of the West End, on the corner of Warren Street and Cleveland Street, facing south towards Oxford Street. To our left, at the far end of Warren Street, is the turmoil of Tottenham Court Road. Behind us is the even greater tumult of Euston Road, and behind that Albany Street and the stucco Nash terraces that fringe Regent's Park. Over to our right lies Portland Place, the western boundary of our travels. Amid the noise and dirt of these arteries, Cleveland Street is a backwater, with only occasional eddies from the main road to disturb our contemplation, running a crooked path down to Newman Street, whose more solid buildings lead you to Oxford Street.

By the lofty standards of Fitzrovia, to which this undignified street clings, Cleveland Street has made little contribution to the world outside. Only two events of wider significance have occurred in it. In one of the houses on its western side, a would-be painter named Samuel Morse lived between 1812 and 1815, before returning in disgust to America and inventing his famous Code, whose one hundred and fifty-five years of usefulness finally expired on the day I write these words. The other event of note occurred in 1889, when, during a raid on a homosexual brothel operating at Number 19, Lord Arthur 'Podge' Somerset was caught *in flagrante* with a teenage post boy, one of a trio procured for the purpose, who went by the piquant names of Swinscow, Thickbroom and Newlove. From this small but prurient beginning there soon grew the 'Cleveland Street Scandal', whose tabloidesque subplots came to include an exotic and depraved cast: the notorious male prostitute and blackmailer Charles Hammond; the future Lord Esher; Oscar Wilde, who was to publish 'The Picture of Dorian Gray' a few months later; and, most sensationally, Queen Victoria's wayward grandson Prince Eddy, who admitted slumming it, but rather weakly offered he had thought he was attending a striptease bar, not a brothel. Out of Samuel Morse, 'Podge' Somerset, Prince Eddy and Oscar Wilde, only Samuel Morse gets a blue plaque.

In the eastward progression of the streets that run north-south in parallel to Portland Place, there is an incremental modesty with each step taken towards Tottenham Court Road. Portland Place is a ceremonial avenue, an extension of

Regent Street after it has rounded Broadcasting House, and the grand approach to a Regency palace that was never built. One step eastwards, in the shadows of Great Portland Street, the mansions of Portland Place have been replaced by mansion blocks, with offices on the ground floor, and half a dozen redbrick storeys above them. Further east, we come to Great Titchfield Street, a more private place than the highways on its flanks, where the traces of a local neighbourhood have not yet been washed away by high rates and the flight to the suburbs. Among the wholesale outlets for the rag trade are Italian delicatessens, and restaurants which fill at lunchtime with braying voices from the nearby BBC. There are more of the same mansion blocks, but a little meaner, a little more cramped.

Another step to the east, and we come to Cleveland Street, on the border between the boroughs of St Marylebone and St Pancras. Here, the imagination must fill in the gaps in the physical fabric. For by one of those strange concatenations of aerial bombardment and town planning, the westward side of Cleveland Street that we are standing on now has been entirely redeveloped, and is now a random straggle of sub-modern building blocks, dwarfed by the Post Office Tower. But the eastern side is entirely intact, albeit equally straggling as it meanders towards Oxford Street. The houses here are of a plain type, two- and sometimes three-storey terraces whose limited parlours have been adapted for service as newsagents or sandwich bars. It is easy to imagine them fifty or a hundred years ago, and easy to imagine what the west side of the street used to look like.

Across the road from the corner of Cleveland Street and Warren Street is our first port of call. It is a modern block of flats, built for the student nurses of the nearby University College Hospital. On the ground floor are housed offices memorialising that pioneer of contraceptive modernity for the urban poor, Marie Stopes. In memory of the site's previous occupant, this ugly building is called Howard House. If it had a basement, I could point down to it from the street, and indicate precisely where Benny grew up. As it doesn't, I can only gesture vaguely at the pavement, and note that somewhere to the left below street level is the location of what used to be 22 Howard House, and that somewhere below the modern brick and concrete, there lies the geography of the first 34 years of his life.

Whatever the architectural virtues of the first Howard House, its basement was a cramped and unsanitary place. When Benny wanted to describe its pervasive damp to his children, he referred us not to his father's eternal bronchitis, but would merely hold one of his old paperbacks under our noses. The passage of twenty years on a dry shelf above ground had done nothing to remove the sour, earthy smell of Howard House, whose aroma floated out of the book like a miasma from a Victorian slum. The lives of the flat's occupants seem to have been conducted in almost subterranean darkness, with electric lights burning almost continuously to add to the sliver of natural light that filtered through the railings from the street above. When Benny first took Toni back to meet his parents in the summer of 1959, she was appalled that people lived like this, and even now the memory of where Benny grew up distresses her.

After descending a flight of stone stairs and entering the flat, she moved past the bathroom and along a narrow, pitch-dark corridor, lit at the end by a bare bulb. Although by that time the bathroom offered such amenities as a bath and hot water, for much of Benny's childhood the flat had no bath, no central heating and no hot water. Benny and his parents would wash their bodies in cold water while standing at a sink, with supplementary visits to the local baths. The flat had two rooms. There was a kitchen, which doubled as his parents' bedroom, in which the sole furniture was an oven, a table, a bed and a wardrobe. There was a living room, with a street-facing window, the top quarter of which showed the world above ground, although only up to calf-height. This room doubled as a bedroom for Benny's Aunt Rose, a sad figure who worked in the same sweatshop as Fanny.

The living room had a windowless alcove, thin but deep, perhaps five feet by eight, which could be curtained off from the main room. This was Benny's bedroom. This space's depth was not much greater than the length of the bed, and its width was only broad enough to accommodate the bed, a bookcase and a careful occupant. The bed itself was so narrow that even after he had moved into a colossal *bateau lit* at Langley House, Benny stayed abnormally still at night, sleeping flat on his back, as if a movement to either side might tip him overboard, or bump him into the wall. To Toni, it seemed more like the nest of a mole than the private space of a human being. To the pampered ears of Seventies children, the decay, poverty and intolerable physical closeness of Howard House were almost inconceivable. Only marginally more conceivable is that the Rachman who was the ultimate landlord of this shameful squalor was the Duke of Westminster.

Although he described his grandfather's house from basement kitchen to leaky skylight, Benny wrote only cursorily about Howard House. I think that some of the shame that he felt should have attached itself to the good Duke instead became attached to him. Often on the receiving end of snobbery, he realised that to publicly announce just how degraded were the circumstances in which he had been raised would have tainted him, would have further circum-scribed the ambition of a man already handicapped by a strong Cockney accent and a foreshortened education. But privately he made sure that we understood the epic journey he had navigated across English society, from slum tenement to country house, poverty to wealth, anonymity to fame. The very completeness of that transformation had ultimately cut him off from all of his contemporaries, both family and friends, yet he could not break an emotional attachment to the streets in which he had grown up, just as he could not shake the person that he had been.

He was at once repulsed and attracted by its memory. In 1948, when Benny was 21, he found himself marooned on Selsey Bill in a holiday camp dance orchestra. Away from London for the first time, he suffered from insomnia, disturbed by the incidental noises of rural nights. So deeply was his character entwined with Howard House, and so deeply part of the fabric of city life was he that the nocturnal cacophony of Cleveland Street had become a prerequisite of falling asleep:

> In my years in St Marylebone I became so conditioned by the nocturnal effects of the Industrial Age that I could sleep through the most persistent and disturbing sounds. My bedroom looked directly on to a T-junction, which meant that no vehicle could venture across the border to or from St Pancras without spectacular changing of gears. On wet nights the tyres would swish through the slush in the gutters, the gears would grind, and I would benignly slumber on.
>
> When the burglar alarm in the factory across the road went awry and started to clang in the absence of burglars, as it did roughly once a week, I had become so resistant to its message that I slept through the racket without noticing anything ...
>
> What really mattered was not the number of decibels being thrown up, but the way in which they were thrown up. After twenty years of being lulled to sleep by the sound of distant buses droning down the Marylebone Road; of taxis keeping their engines throbbing right outside the bedroom window while the drunken fare searched his pockets for

money; of cats squealing at fire-bells; of the heavy tread of the policeman covering his beat between the Albany Street and Tottenham Court Road stations; after twenty years of this, I had gone to work in the countryside – only to discover that a terrible alien racket was making it impossible for me to sleep.[1]

After exhaustive investigations of the local fauna, the source of this noise was revealed to be the cricket *Orthoptera gryllidae*, which rubs together its forewings to produce a high-pitched whistle that attracts the opposite sex:

> I spent the rest of that week sleeping fitfully by day and reading at night, marvelling all the time that I, a child of the Euston and Tottenham Court Roads, conditioned from birth to sleep the sleep of the just through the orchestrated chaos of London night life, I a veteran of the Blitz, who had listened to the wail of the air-raid warnings and merely turned over on my other side and returned to sleep, I, who had slumbered through wars and the spilling out of the drunks from The George & Dragon down the street every night of my life, had been bested by a small insect, which knows so little of what's what that when it is sexually excited it rubs its legs together.[2]

There were other noises in the night in Cleveland Street:

> Ever since I remember, Rose and I shared our front room. And if her weekly contribution to the rent brought a welcome element of insurance into my parents' lives, it lent a certain carnival flavour to my own; a tendency to dyspepsia, caused, in my opinion, by a hopeless enslavement to hot curries and chocolate creams, had endowed my Aunt with a most exotic subliminal existence. Not to put too fine a point on it, Rose mumbled in her sleep, usually inchoate protestations against the injustices visited upon her by day in the tailoring factory just round the corner. From time to time these really rather sad outbursts of spectral demagogy would swell into startling aural coherence.
>
> One of the earliest breaches ever made into my innocent schoolboy faith in universal order was on the night when she began ranting about the arrival upstairs in the street of a pack of hungry wolves. The idea

that Cleveland Street in the small hours could be invested by wolves struck me as so improbable that my conviction that Rose was a bit of a loony dates from this night. But an entertaining and soft-hearted loony. Feigning sleep in my own bed, I watched in wonder as Rose sat up in hers, eyes wide but unseeing, making a loud announcement consisting of the single reiterated phrase, 'The wolves are after me'.

My first thought was that Rose, whose vast bulk had always disposed her in the past against even a vicarious sporting career, had somehow got it into her head that she was about to be offered terms by Wolverhampton Wanderers, a football club which was creating a great stir at that time with its youth policy and the eccentric stratagems of its manager, a certain Major Buckley.[3]

Running down Cleveland Street was the usual selection of neighbourhood shops, endowed with unlikely exoticism by a child's mind. In 1978, after one of Callaghan's ministers had promised to bring domestic life back to the inner cities, Benny was roused to a typical reverie, a mixture of satire and nostalgia in which the Government would rebuild faithfully the site of his childhood, beginning with the destruction of the 'accursed' Post Office Tower, 'preferably while those responsible for it are sitting inside, enjoying their last supper in the revolving restaurant'. He remembered the vanished landmarks that stood amid so much neighbourly poverty, knowing that it was a lost world, but basking in the sense of a Thirties childhood that its memory brought back:

Then of course, they will be re-redeveloping Cleveland Street, the greatest and most noble cause of all. That they will reconstruct our old flats, even down to the last ill-fitting coal-hole cover, goes without saying. What interests me just as much is that they will be sparing no expense to bring back that wonderful comprehensiveness which those little backstreets accidentally and yet so completely acquired, through the years between the burial of William IV at Windsor [1837], and the death of Ramsay MacDonald at sea, where he had spent most of his life [1937]. Closing my eyes and opening my mind, I can evoke, I hope with perfect accuracy, the sequence of mercantile events as they unfolded themselves along the western flank of the street. This sequence is vitally important, for when the Minister finally gets around to honouring his word, he will want to know all the details of our ravaged, pillaged, sacked little city in order that he may be able to produce reasonable facsimiles.

The Oil Shop, on the corner of Cleveland and Carburton, sold no oil as far as I know, but it did sell just about everything else, from Reckett's Blue to six-inch nails.

Then there came a haberdashery whose proprietress was like something out of a censored chapter from a Brontë novel. She was the crucified victim of a terrible nervous disorder which manifested itself in the violent shaking of the head every four or five seconds, the periodic slapping of her own face, and the muttering of a certain wonderfully proscribed four-letter word. Unfeeling urchins would enter that emporium and ask for two and a half miles of pyjama cord just for the sheer pleasure of watching the head convulse and the hair, corrugated by the ruthless engineering of a Marcel wave, come tumbling over the forehead, and then that muttered blue pencil of an expletive. Goodness knows what was wrong with the poor lady, but at least she had two compensations in her affliction; first the attentions of a doting husband, and second, a share in the most memorable haberdashery since the one which employed the adolescent H. G. Wells.

Then came a newspaper shop which smelt of old peardrops. There were several of these shops on the street, and why they didn't all run each other out of business, I never will understand. Their smells, interiors, stock and business approach were all distinct and individual, and I recall of the peardrop parlour that whichever newspaper or comic you asked for, they always seemed to have arranged affairs so that they had every other one, but not yours. A couple of doors along was another paper shop which smelt of the owner, who used to put Anzora on his hair, and worked up a nice little corner in trade by taking in Small Ads and displaying them down the side of his window. Things like sewing machines, unwanted kittens, awls for lacing footballs, secondhand pipes, back numbers of *Dalton's Weekly* or *Woman's Own*, old bedspreads, perambulator parasols – these were the kind of items you might pick up through his window. When he moved out and closed the place down, he didn't bother to clear his window quite completely, and for months after he had gone, there remained, among the cardboard effigies of Gold Flake and Kensitas, and the empty jars once brimming with peardrops and lime juice nibs, a piece of paper asking if anybody was interested in picking up, at a real bargain price, a typewriter with 'only two kys mssng'.

Next door was an establishment of real distinction. It was a concern called J. Bazin and was dedicated to the proposition that letters and signs were not only beautiful, but also essential things without which nobody could exist. In that beautiful window were capital L's two feet tall in spangled purple glass, whole families of small e's in bright red. A great yellow X hung suspended from the ceiling as though awaiting the starting whistle for the last celestial game of Noughts and Crosses. There were pink S's in magnificent serpentine scrawl, square O's, round O's, and even a letter i with its dot connected by a wire of such hairline delicacy that on winter evenings, when the light was fading out of the sky, the two component parts appeared to be held together by nothing more than the faith of the literate.

A little further on was an ancient café. The condensation of a million urns of tea effectively screened its operations from the outside world, but if you happened to pass when someone was going in or out, the ghost of long-dead toad-in-the-hole would reach out and try its hardest to pluck you inside.

An old blackboard, tilted against the wall, announced the day's Bill of Fare, which never changed, although oddly the chalked writing did. But the surface of the board was so greasy with age and rain and accretions of local soot, that nobody could read any of it anyway. By a quirk of treacherous memory, it is that blackboard in my mind's eye which announces to me the big news of a certain day in 1937, 'Death of Sir James Barrie', although in fact Barrie's death must have been trumpeted on the placards of the newspaper shop a few doors along; what the blackboard announced that day was not the death of a writer, but the proximity of beans on toast for 3d and cocoa at a penny a cup.[4]

Coming out of the front door of Howard House, we turn right, passing almost immediately the George & Dragon on the corner of Cleveland Street and Greenwell Street, a few yards from the house of Benny's grandfather. Crossing Greenwell Street, at the next corner we come to Clipstone Street, the utterly unprepossessing site of Benny's primary school, which along with his grandfather's house was to be the second great fund of his childhood memories:

> In the jumble room of my memory, that vast private sanctuary with the elastic-sided walls, there hangs a mental picture of me emerging from the schoolhouse door after my first day of education, to find my father leaning against the playground wall, awaiting my reemergence with a reassuring smile. It is September 1931, and I am nearly four years old; very possibly this is my first coherent memory. Details obstinately endure. One of my father's shoelaces is loose, and he is holding a newspaper in his right hand, possibly that morning's edition of *The Sporting Life*. The mid-morning sun casts a flattering sheen on the nap of his bowler hat, and over his head, like a rusty halo, is the iron ring which the older girls use for their netball goal. As I run towards my father, the asphalt is bumpy under the soles of my sandalled feet. We start to walk across the yard towards the street, but after a few paces the picture fades and merges into the oblivion of the past.[5]

It is worth pausing on the corner of Cleveland and Clipstone to consider how exactly Benny's father came to be leaning against the schoolyard wall that morning, totemic racing paper in hand, when most of the other children's fathers were at work. Ever unconventional, Dave had arrived at a division of labour between himself and Fanny. In this unique domestic scheme, she worked, and he didn't. This meant that Fanny spent her working life running off ladies' clothes for a pittance in a nameless sweatshop, where it was so hot in the summer that on their breaks the women would rush to an outside standpipe, and run cold water on their wrists to stop themselves from fainting. By a stroke of poetic justice, a large proportion of the profits from her workshop were squandered by her boss, another obsessed gambler, and found their way into the pockets of her husband, his brother Henry, and several equally wayward brothers-in-law, who would collectively bet it away. For the rest of his life, Benny would speak with unquenched bitterness of watching Fanny's employer strolling up Cleveland Street, smoking and idling as he frittered his money on the horses, while around the corner Fanny and Aunt Rose worked away from eight in the morning in a noisy, airless factory.

Her meagre gleanings from this hard labour paid the rent for her family's damp basement flat, for their food, and for her subs to the Funeral Society. Clearly holding out little hope for this life, Fanny chose to concentrate her savings on a spectacular entry into the next. It goes without saying that when she died in 1990, her headstone was still unpaid for, despite a lifetime of contributions. It also goes without saying that with the blinkered stoicism of her generation, she rarely complained about the profound inequity of her life. I don't think she had ever expected anything else, and had grown up grateful for the not inconsiderable mercy that the site of her drudgery was not some boggy Russian *shtetl*. Stocky, with the flaxen hair common among Russian Jews, she was still serving Dave, Benny and all of us with improbable vigour when she was 80, although by then she had been deprived of her life's only consolations, the proximity of Benny and her cigarettes. If her tale of Victorian domestic enslavement wasn't such a common story, her life would be a martyrology, in which she plays Nancy to Dave's Bill Sykes.

In Benny, his mother's plight produced an irreconcilable split in his emotions. He was deeply attached to his mother, and reserved a particular contempt for the type of boss that her employer represented. She in her turn had invested him with all the hopes of her own frustrated life. But he was also deeply attached to his father, and could not bring himself to blame Dave for placing the onus for winning the family bread so firmly on his wife's bowed shoulders, not least because of Dave's own unconditional approval of his son, which easily matched Fanny's in its ardour. It was only later in his life, through the gently suggestive agency of my mother, that Benny came to realise that he himself had also been party to the sacrifice of his mother for the family good, as Dave had never expected Benny to go out to work the day after he left school, and had encouraged him to take a more leisurely route to employment.

Perhaps because of these mixed feelings, his parents' marriage is not one of the many topics addressed in Benny's copious autobiographical writings. While he reminisces about his childhood, his parents' individual and corporate feelings remain veiled. His mother is only an incidental character, contributing cameos to the comedy of family life, such as when she leans into the pickle barrel at the local shop, and loses her wedding ring in its briny depths. Meanwhile, his father, while remaining emotionally oblique, has a vivid life on the page, a picaresque of madcap schemes and barely legal get-rich-quick scams. This bias reflects the emotional balance of Benny's upbringing. As it is for many boys, his relationship with his father was the dominant influence of his childhood, and Dave, generous and unconventional father that he was, was a complex man. In fact, so complex that his influence overhangs the subsequent life of my family like some brooding but beneficent spirit, a man whose wrestling with an insoluble predicament defined the parameters of my father's life, and the lives of his grandchildren. Without Dave, Benny, and by extension his wife and children, would have been unrecognisable.

By stark comparison to Dave, in Benny's writing, Fanny rarely steps from two dimensions to three. It is a misfortune which she seems to have reflected in her actual life, always negating her own character for the needs of others, always protecting her only son, always enduring the casual cruelties of her husband. When Leo and I were children, we both associated her with the picture on the sleeve of one of her favourite records. It was of Sophie Tucker, arrayed in all her feathered pomp, the statuesque and sentimental Last of The Red Hot Mommas. I realise now that in life Fanny was closer to the martyred old lady of Tucker's 'My Yiddishe Momma', who forgoes everything for her child.

'How few were her pleasures,
She never cared for fashion styles,
Her jewels and treasures,
She found them in her baby's smile.'[6]

Davey 3

They say that a person's memory begins not with blurred recollections of our own childhood, but that larger, more nebulous sphere known as 'living memory'. It is this 'living memory' that gives us sharply focused vignettes of life before we were born, that are transmissions from our parents' and grandparents' own memories. An accumulation of 'living memory' eventually coagulates into a family history, encoded on every descendant as irrevocably as a big nose or bat ears. If memory is the cornerstone of identity, then living memory is its foundation. Sometimes, another person's memory can be more influential than your own.

I can remember clearly the horror I felt when as an eight year-old, I had asked my eighty-year-old Grandpa Dave what the First World War had been like. Perhaps inspired by the remains of our Sunday roast, he responded by demonstrating how to twist a bayonet when removing it from a man's stomach, so as to disembowel him. Indeed, the spectre of Dave's two years at His Majesty's Pleasure in Flanders hung over all of us, even though the episode had ended nine years before Benny's birth. If it is possible to locate a single factor that threw Dave and Benny (and the rest of us) off their predestined path of tailoring and beyond normal society, then this was it.

Alongside the benign influence of Benny's Yiddishe grandmother and doting mother, there was this darker and more crucial influence in the 'living memory' with which he grew up. The outrage that Dave felt at being sent on a bicycle to sure and pointless dismemberment in the Ypres Salient produced in him a profound psychological reaction. If he had been an intellectual, he would have called the man who returned unable to believe his luck at still being alive an Existentialist, or more likely a Nihilist. If he had been a psychologist, he would have realised that for the rest of his life, he was to exhibit the alienated, aggressive behaviour of 'post-traumatic stress' syndrome. When Dave hung up his cycle clips and was demobbed in 1919, he decided that as he had no right to be alive, no one else had any right to expect anything of him, and that he was going to enjoy his improbable remission for everything that it was worth.

He was progressing quite successfully down this path of wanton self-gratification when he met Benny's mother, who had the iron will of Field Marshal Haig, and stymied his musical career in a strike whose twin pincers were pregnancy and tailoring. Unfortunately, she also had Haig's tactical subtlety, and the manner in which she tried to outflank Dave's sociopathic attitude to his fellow man did nothing to ameliorate his anger. Dave died when I was twelve, and as he was very concerned that his grandchildren would remember him, I knew him quite well. He was a wonderful grandfather, the sort who would sneak up behind you and ring a bell in your ear to check that you weren't deaf, and taught you how to eat whole lemons while filling out Pools coupons, but even a child could feel the bitter frustration in him. He had an unfocused loathing of the whole world.

Dave was a man in a cruel predicament. In his cranky way, he had developed the idea that happiness lay in the pursuit of his desires, but he lacked the talent, education and discipline needed to make anything of this aesthetic. He was a saxophonist who abandoned his art, a tailor who forgot to put pockets on a jacket, a gambler with the longest losing streak in racing history. For his failures, he blamed the world, his siblings, the Tote, and the hapless Fanny. Maybe in dark moments of self-knowledge he blamed himself. Certainly, he never blamed Benny, who both he and Fanny came to regard as the only successful product of their whole lives.

When searching for psychological reasons why Benny turned out as he did, I return time and again to his father's life in the decade before Benny was born, a period that Dave talked to Benny about exhaustively, and which Benny talked to us about with equal passion. Dave had entered the fray in France an Edwardian jingoist, and had exited it believing in nothing. Against this trauma was weighed the precious gold of modern civilisation, panned from the slaughter: two new-fangled American inventions. The first was the safety razor, the second jazz. After the war, the now clean-shaven Dave had set his clarinet against the world, but, following a promising start, he had crashed badly. In fact, the manner in which he had lost was so heroic in its profligacy that to all of us in his wake it served only to magnify his raging individuality, however bitter the taste of his failure.

More gentle by nature than his turbulent father, Benny inherited none of Dave's bitterness, but all of his individualism. In Benny, Dave found the ally he needed against the cruel world, yet soon acknowledged that his son's freakish talents meant that he would easily outstrip his father. Many fathers would have involuntarily held back their sons at such a juncture. Dave took the more intelligent course of encouraging and supporting Benny throughout his extended childhood and adolescence, although this did not mean relinquishing his paternal claim on Benny. When Dave gave his collection of instruments to the teenage Benny in 1941, it was a poignant passing of the familial baton, as much an acceptance of his own failure as a support of Benny's promise, which might yet validate Dave's own wasted life.

To his credit, Dave did exercise some discretion in the frittering of his natural intelligence. His mania for gambling had made him into a sports fanatic, with the true obsessive's memory for form – not that it made any difference. The only obstacle to his armchair pursuit of sporting excellence was the child-minding responsibility that fell to him while Fanny was out enjoying herself at work. He solved it by the simple expedient of taking Benny everywhere with him:

Christmas morning, 1936: one of those bitter winter days when the breath streams from the nostrils in twin plumes, and people stamp their feet on the pavements to generate some heat; in tomorrow's papers there will be the inevitable report of the Canadian who went out without any earmuffs and came back without any ears.

My father and I, being representatives of that small elite of Western civilisation generally acknowledged to be the highest point yet reached on the evolutionary graph, are spending this freezing morning standing in the open air with 44,998 other lunatics. We are inside an arena called Highbury Stadium watching twenty-two grown men running around in coloured shirts. The Arsenal players wear red shirts, the Preston players wear white shirts. Both sides wear blue legs and purple noses. I, being nine years old, am very happy. My father, being frozen solid in the shape of a disenchanted parent, is neither happy nor unhappy, but just immobilised.

We stand behind the goal defended by Arsenal. A player in a white shirt, called Maxwell, suddenly thunders towards us, flinging himself bodily through the air to make contact with the ball. He reaches it with his head, but I sigh with relief as I see the ball is flashing outside the Arsenal citadel. The ball continues flashing past the Arsenal citadel, and goes on doing so until meeting a solid object, which happens to be my face.[1]

The long hours he spent with his father meant that not only did Benny acquire a lifelong taste for sport and the statistical trivia that attends it, but also that his relationship with Dave developed an unusual closeness, despite Dave's irascibility. Although the moments that were written about were often classically filial, such as watching his father shave, the relationship that Benny described to us, and the aspects of it that he tried to bring to his own fathering, were almost fraternal. Put simply, Dave, Benny and Benny's children were all co-conspirators in the noble art of avoiding gainful employment in any field outside that of personal gratification, a skill handed across the generations with the same loving care that the baffled Joseph had wasted when he taught Dave how to be a tailor.

Dave first appears in Benny's writing in his memory of the first of the four uprootings of his life: his move from his grandparents' house in Greenwell Street to 22 Howard House. Inevitably, the story revolves around a bet that Dave loses:

> I was five, and my father, a complete master of child psychology, shrewdly bet me I couldn't go round the block forty times on my tricycle without stopping. By the time I had won the bet, the removal had been effected, and I moved into our new camp with the healthy callousness which only very small children ever seem to possess. To me the whole thing was no more than an elaborate cabaret contrived by doting parents for my exclusive benefit. When, on my twenty-first circuit of the course, I crashed into a vaguely familiar-looking man with a kitchen chair under each arm and a coal scuttle on his head, I thought it one of the most sublimely comic moments in history. Twenty-four hours afterwards, I had completely recovered from my cycling marathon, but it took my father weeks to get over his misfortunes.[2]

Dave's appearances retain this essentially comic nature throughout Benny's life. This is not surprising, as Dave had a more than healthy sense of his own absurdity, which he imparted generously to Benny. I remember a similar scene to the one that follows, with the roles of Dave and Benny taken by Benny and me, in which the solemnities of masculine ritual are mocked by the ineptitude of their execution:

> One morning in my eighth year, being in need of a laugh and not feeling disposed to travel very far in search for it, I decided to watch my father

having a shave. At about ten o'clock, having read the morning newspaper, whose contents he always absorbed in order of cosmic impor-
tance, starting with the racing news on the back page and gradually
descending to the anticlimactic twaddle of the world news on the front,
he rose and began preparing for his ablutions, while I, seeking an unin-
hibited performance, pretended to be absorbed in the contents of my
trouser pocket ...

First my father boiled a kettle of water, and poured it into the basin.
Then he rubbed a white deposit into his face and lathered it with the
hot water to the required fever pitch, using for this operation a brush
whose small print on the end of the handle proclaimed it as genuine
badger hair ...

Having achieved the required lather, which made him look like a
cross between King Lear and Eddie Cantor, my father began to scrape
away at the soap and bristles with a silver safety razor. All went disap-
pointingly well for a couple of minutes, during which I became acutely
conscious of the ticking of the clock on the mantelpiece which said
twenty-three minutes past four, the wheezing of the cat asleep in the
armchair, and the faint rasp of the blade as it swept across my father's
face. At last it swept a shade too emphatically and a thin red line opened
up on his chin. My father let the razor fall with a plop into the basin,
pursed his lips and peered at his reflection in the mirror on the door of
the cabinet fixed over the sink. With an expert eye he took in the situation, assessed the damage and summarised it as any rational adult
would. 'Bugger it', he said, and took immediate remedial action by
applying to the cut a small square of alum stone. Then he saw that he
had smeared the top of his vest with a compote of gore and cream.
'Bugger it', he said again, a shade more emphatically this time and
began to remove the mess.

By the time he had removed it completely it was all over his chest,
and the cut on his chin had begun oozing again. He began reapplying
the alum stone, which he accidentally dropped into the soapy water in
the basin. 'Gord blimey', he observed sagely, adding 'Bugger that',
before resuming operations. He cut himself twice more before the
shave was over, once on the lobe of the left ear, and again on the lobe
of the right ear. Being a thoughtful child, I asked him why, if there were

no whiskers growing on the lobes of his ears, he had tried to shave them. He answered: 'One day you will understand.' (Sure enough, one day I did.)

After he had mopped himself dry, changed his vest, stemmed the flow of blood, removed the flecks of shaving cream from the wall, and rinsed out poor old Badger, he asked me what I thought. I said it looked fine, but why was he only growing half a moustache? He spun back to his reflection and saw that in his haste to be done with the job, he had forgotten to clean up the right side of his upper lip. With a few more 'Bugger it's and 'Gord blimey's he started all over again and in no more than another fifteen minutes or so, had done. Then he mopped himself dry again, changed his vest yet again, stemmed the flow of blood again, removed more flecks of cream from the wall, threw the towel away and rinsed out poor old Badger again, and seemed satisfied with his handi-work. Again he asked me what I thought.

This time I gave the matter much deeper consideration and while he was awaiting the verdict he said that if I didn't say something soon, he would need another shave. (This was a family joke connected with his detested brother-in-law Nat, who my father persisted in relegating to the animal kingdom by calling him Gnat, with an audible 'G'. Gnat's whiskers were so prolific and his complexion so unwholesome that his chin and cheeks had long ago turned into a muddy green colour as a result of incessant shaving. My father used to say that Gnat shaving himself was like the men painting the Forth Bridge, which I took to mean that by the time he had perforated the lobe of one ear, it was time to perforate the lobe of the other.)

Then, having pondered the bad news that one day, in the hardly fore-seeable future, I, too, would be obliged to perform this dangerous ritual, I spoke my thoughts.

'It looks fine,' I said to my father. 'But I think that when I grow up, I will wet my face, put the cream on, and then wipe it off with the towel. Why risk cutting yourself?' My father laughed over that for the rest of that year and took it as yet another example of the infallible logic of the child's mind, which, incidentally, he seemed to hold in much higher regard than the adult mind. (This may have had something to do with the prevailing intellectual climate in his family.)[3]

Benny's boundless love for his father casts a warm light on these scenes, as perhaps it should. But all material for a writer is double-edged, and what is said often outlines in relief the contours of what is unsaid. In the unspoken private narrative of his shave, the safety razor that Dave applies to his beard is itself a consolation prize from the Great War, which evokes a different 'thin red line' from the one on his chin. When Dave died in 1983, his three grandsons divided up his meagre legacy. There were his medals, his Army kit bag, his watch, some ties, a few broken cigarette lighters, and several dozen of those short Biros that come with the compliments of Ladbroke's. There were also hundreds of disposable safety razors, unopened in their packaging. They spilled out of every cupboard and drawer in his flat, like fragments of hope gathered against the crushing insanity of the trenches, which had continued their black work of destroying all meaning for Dave long after his return to civvies.

Dave's real life was not the gentle comedy of an unworldly man ever confused by his surroundings. It was the cruel farce of a man who, regardless of how much he values his own life, knows how little that life is worth in the grand scheme, and can only shrug at his helplessness when life itself becomes a black comedy. As a 75-year-old man, Dave, perhaps beginning to disbelieve his own memory, became obsessed with finding a replacement for the Overseas Medal that marked his war service in France, and which had become lost sometime after Dave, 'eager to resume his interrupted life, [had] tossed [it] into the chocolate box that served as a receptacle for his cuff-links and shirt-studs'. Benny recorded the saga that ensued.

Dave chases the medal through 'the pleasant byways of military bureaucracy', from the address on his demobilisation papers (the War Office, unfortunately converted into a bomb-site); to the Citizens' Advice Bureau; the Ministry of Defence; and the Badges and Medals Office, where a porter directs him to the Headquarters of the Suffolk Regiment, before running them to ground, care of the Army Medal Office, Droitwich Spa, Worcestershire. Fighting a spirited rearguard action, the Medal Office sends to him an affidavit which must be signed by Dave in the presence of a Commissioner of Oaths, in order to satisfy the Army that Dave really is who he claims to be. This accomplished, and £1.64 sent off to a lieutenant-general at Droitwich, the medal eventually arrives. Or rather, it doesn't:

> One evening, I went round to view this elusive trophy, to find my father even more at peace with the world than I expected. He had the

demeanour of a man who has just heard the best joke in the world for the first time, and was thankful for the poetry and romance that were still to be found if only you persisted in looking for them hard enough.

'It's magnificent,' he said. 'It may not be war, but it's magnificent.'

'What is? What are you talking about?'

'Droitwich, the British Army, that porter, the whole lot of them.'

'Why? What's happened?'

'They sent the wrong medal.'

And then I saw, lying in the palm of his hand, a shining medallion whose brightly burnished, pristine face was an instantaneous reminder of a flowered, oval chocolate box whose oddly assorted contents had beguiled a few wet afternoons for me forty years ago. I took the medal from him, hardly able to believe it wasn't a piece of milk chocolate wrapped in gold foil. But it was the real thing alright; the inscription on the back read 'The Great War for Civilisation, 1914–1919'.

'That', explained my father, 'is the Victory Medal. Same as this one', and he took from his pocket another medallion identical to the one I was holding, except that its surface was tarnished, the impression of its lettering faded; there was also a dent in its side which I must have put there in childhood, flinging it up in the air as part of my training to become an England slip fielder.

'They were supposed to have sent me the Overseas one. They've sent me this one by mistake. I'm the only man in England with two Victory Medals.'

After basking for a few days in the rare glow of having been decorated twice for the same deed, an honour which in the normal course of events only comes the way of generals, he sent the medal back to his friend the lieutenant-general at Droitwich, with a request for the other medal, the right one, the one he had been asking them for all this time.

Droitwich reply that, 'as the second medal was a more expensive item to produce than the other one, a further remittance of 54p was required, otherwise the authorities would, with the very deepest regret, be obliged to withhold the replacement'. Sensing ultimate victory within sight, Dave sends the money, and receives his Overseas Medal. Benny goes round to admire it, and then the conversation turns to less martial matters:

Thoughts of the military, however, could not have been hiding very far beneath the surface of his mind, because later that evening he produced a creased and faded sepia photograph which I dimly remembered examining once or twice in my medal-flinging days. It showed him standing in a private's uniform, the overcoat of which had clearly been designed by and for a baboon. The photographer had placed him in the forefront of a two-dimensional clearing in a two-dimensional woodland glade, amongst whose foliage were copious hints of a two-dimensional baronial hall. After the medal had arrived, he had dug out this old scrap of evidence just to reassure himself that he hadn't imagined the entire episode.

'I was just thinking,' he said. 'It's funny how they never asked me for an affidavit in 1916 when they shipped me off to France.'

'I suppose it was that people were more trusting in those days,' I replied.[4]

The story is a comic redaction of the tragedy into which Dave had been roped in 1916. It is a demonstration of military insensitivity, in which stupidity is compounded by a mean unwillingness to recognise Dave's service. It is also a recognition by Benny of the existential burden that was Dave's inheritance from that service, which went as unrecognised by his family as it had by the War Office. Dave's sister Ginnie appears to have had a particular lack of sympathy for her brother, and was later to tar Benny with the same contemptuous brush as Dave:

Her indifference to me probably had something to do with the fact that I was my father's son, for she regarded my father with unsisterly contempt, dismissing him not simply as a lazy man, which she might have tolerated, but as a maddening amalgam of lowlife and soppy dreamer, a hopeless gambler who fooled around with music to the detriment of the family fortune, who frittered away priceless time reading books and who even made one abortive attempt to write one. To define him once and for all, she produced from her rusty arsenal of vituperation the epithet 'silly bugger', the implication being that by some obscure process of genetic causality, so was I. The roots of their mutual animosity had been planted long before I was born, and may well have had much to do with the vexed question of my father's Army gratuity. When, after planting him in the Ypres Salient and leaving him there for three years to no apparent purpose, the Government, with a generosity characteristic of an administration busily constructing a land fit for heroes to live in, awarded him the huge sum of £180, or three shillings per day for the vacation in Flanders. The modesty of this award some-what disappointed my father, who, having noted that his Commander-in-Chief had received £100,000 for doing a great amount of damage to his own side, understandably felt that £180 was a niggardly tip for a man who had done hardly any at all.

Most men confronted by such a windfall would have resorted to a deposit account at the local bank, but my father, who regarded banks and all who sailed in them as only slightly higher on the evolutionary scale than the commissioned nitwits who had just misspent his youth, opted for the disused copper in one of the attic rooms. His version of subsequent events was that Ginnie had helped herself at regular inter-vals until there was nothing left, hers that the money had been frittered away in the course of my father's regular visits to Sandown Park and Hurst Park.[5]

If Dave shaped Benny, then the war shaped Dave. From out of the frustrations of Dave's life there came not only the passions of Benny's life, but also the ambi-tion that drove Benny forward. Dave, who sought to dodge the tag of 'failure' by not trying at all, always exhorted Benny to be something in his life, to be the big man that his father had never been, to prove to the gallery of mocking aunts and uncles that not everything that came from Dave was a joke, to show that Dave had been right not to 'stick to tailoring'. I think Dave passed on the materials that might transform Benny's life in full consciousness of their potential effects, as I know Benny did to us. Benny understood retrospectively what had been going on amid all that idling and banter, although I am less sure that he realised at the time.

When, as a successful man in his fifties, Benny wondered with modest surprise how his abilities sprang from such an unassuming gene pool, he was tempted by the idea of some lost poet or composer among his unknown ances-tors, 'perhaps some bearded screwball who wrote for the Moscow magazines or newspapers, or composed passionate poems on cowhide and kept sending them to St Petersburg'.[6] In the absence of any genealogical evidence, Benny realised the truth. Dave, a man whose life fell off the scale of conventional achievement, had provided not only the environment, but also more than a half-share of the heredity that had made his son's strange life and unfeasible success possible:

I am a musician and writer, two occupations fairly uncommon, and as a combination, very rare. An accident of circumstance, or the working-out of some obscure genetic conspiracy I know nothing about? My father was a musician before me. He taught me to play and presented me with two saxophones and a clarinet when I was thirteen. Is that heredity or environment?

It comes back to me that when I was about eight or nine years old, my father used to try writing short stories which he hoped to sell to one of the London evening papers. Although he never got as far as sending any of the tales to any of the editors, he impressed upon me almost without realising it the special, almost mystical nature of the act of picking up a pen and a sheet of paper. Again, is that heredity or environment?[7]

Uncle Henry 4

We were on the corner of Clipstone and Cleveland Streets, considering the bowler-hatted figure of David Green. The next landmark in the geography of Benny's childhood is just around the corner. Turn right at Clipstone Street and then first left, and you find yourself at the northern end of Hanson Street, which by some unlikely miracle of bombs and town-planning has retained some of its original houses. It was here that the dashing Henry Green, sportsman bachelor and the most cherished of Benny's aunts and uncles, plied his esoteric trade, always wearing a bespoke overcoat with bottomless pockets, whatever the weather:

In those days the northern half of Hanson Street was a rickety Victorian rookery in which the twin ranks of houses, parted only by a narrow roadway, were lent a rakish air by the angle at which their clusters of chimney pots would stand against the sky. Each house leaned on the next, as if to save itself from collapsing altogether. About halfway down on the eastern side of the street, every day bar Sunday, from eleven in the morning till five in the evening, come sunshine or snow, Henry stood in the doorway of one of these houses taking bets and keeping a weather eye open for any vagrant policeman unaware of the delicate treaties which had been brokered between Henry and the police station in Tottenham Court Road.

The decrepitude of the houses and their niggardly proportions were an immense professional asset, because if the approach of the Law was spotted, he could duck inside the house, cross the tiny back yard, vault the wall into an adjacent back yard, walk down the side alley of a local draper's shop, and emerge into Cleveland Street with the air of a respectable burgher enjoying a morning saunter. I think he enjoyed these scuffles. They lent an air of adventure to what was essentially a routine job as unvarying as that of any office clerk at his desk.

The families who lived in the house where he conducted his business affairs were envied by everyone else in the street, for Henry's rent of £1 a week, split among the occupants, rendered their straitened lives virtually rent-free. Indeed, I found the whole enterprise entirely praise-worthy, and was always proud to be part of it. Whenever a street book-maker was arrested, the size of his fine usually went in proportion to the amount of stake money he was holding at the time. I was therefore a useful device for the unloading of his small change. Whenever the need struck him, he would hand me a carrier bag as I passed his business premises en route to lunch at my grandfather's house. I never looked into the bag, but I knew from the jingle of coinage inside that I was smuggling contraband across the frontiers of legality. I was the perfect courier, above suspicion and entirely honest, and although I was never tipped for my services, the point was entirely academic, because throughout my childhood Henry was forever showering gifts on me.[1]

As a child, Benny adored Henry. In Henry, Benny found an inspiring spirit, who had kept his boyish obsession with sport well into adulthood, and had even made it the focus of his life, whatever the sniping of Aunt Ginnie. The story of Benny's relationship with Henry is one aspect of the story of his growing up, a parable about how idols are revealed to have feet of clay. For while Benny's adulation of his father never allowed him to assess Dave critically, the greater distance between uncle and nephew allowed him to judge Henry more freely. In later life, Henry would come to occupy a different symbolism for Benny, a perhaps harsh one whose ramifications still echo in the family.

Ironically, it was that very same distance between uncle Henry and nephew Benny that had been the foundation of Benny's admiration. By stark contrast with Dave, Henry seemed the paradigm of the successful man, able to reconcile his adolescent pursuits with the exigencies of making a living. Six years younger than Dave, Henry had not been brutalised by the Great War, and was more sensitive to Benny than Dave was. In his turn, Benny idolised Henry, both for his juvenile sporting exploits and the caddish poise of his bachelordom. Still with traces of awe for his sophisticated uncle, Benny would tell us how on Saturday evenings, Henry would appear in Greenwell Street's basement kitchen, immac-ulately turned out in black tie and evening dress, with pomade on his hair and cologne on his freshly shaven face, ready for a night on the West End. No such event would be complete without first making a stop at one of the area's many cinemas. Henry would leaf through the evening paper, and run through the list of films currently showing. So wide was his knowledge of the world outside Greenwell Street that as he read out each name, he would say 'Seen that ... seen that ... seen that'. But Henry's true charm lay less in his veneer of worldliness than in the generous naïvety beneath it:

> He was engagingly boyish in his enthusiasms. When one of the cigarette companies began issuing cards of footballers, he instantly switched brands, bought the matching album for tuppence, and each evening in the basement parlour would stick newly acquired cards in their places. I always witnessed this ceremony, but was requested not to take the album down from its place on top of the wireless. When the day came, he stuck in the last elusive card and handed me the finished work as though it were a priceless manuscript, which for me was exactly what it was.[2]

The precise limits of Henry's worldliness lay somewhere in the region of the driving seat of a car. Benny, a man who was later to demolish a fence as part of his own ill-fated attempt to learn to drive, once entrusted his life to Henry, who had promised to drive down to Chelsea, to watch their beloved Arsenal:

> It was usually my father who took me to Highbury, but once or twice Henry filled the breach. One of these occasions gives a perfect demonstration of the qualities which I, a small boy, admired in him, and which the rest of the world, labouring under the riotous illusion that it was mature, regarded as proof of a reckless nature. The occasion was an afternoon mid-week match between Chelsea and Arsenal, and as if this were not joy enough, we were to travel to Stamford Bridge by car. Pound for pound, Henry was probably the worst driver in the whole of the metropolis. His motoring career, brief though glorious, was strewn with the wreckage of old bangers whose glistening exteriors flattered only to deceive. To sit alongside him in a car was certainly a perilous enterprise, but I was much too young to be fearful of danger.
>
> For this jaunt he had borrowed a friend's car, an uncomfortable relic which made peculiar noises every time Henry changed gear, noises supposed to warn of crises to come. We both laughed about the noises, and were halfway along Piccadilly before I noticed that the weather was

beginning to change, and it was getting foggy. The traffic thickened, the fog became deeper and progress slowed almost to walking pace. By the time we inched into the King's Road, we were at the heart of an irate cavalcade of buses, taxis and cars carrying all the other crackpots headed for the stadium.

Henry kept looking at his watch and assuring me that the fog was not thick enough to cause the cancellation of the fixture. Soon, a plume of thick black smoke began furling out from the car bonnet, adding to the surrounding fog, and forcing me to admit, for the first time that afternoon, that we might be late for the start. We jerked forward a few inches at a time. Henry was finding some difficulty now in controlling the car, saying that everything was heating up. The kick-off time came and went, and the awful realisation came upon me that we were fated not to see any football that afternoon. Then the car refused to start when it was required to, and Henry suddenly reached a decision.

'Come on,' he said, and got out of the car. I followed him in wonder as we began guessing our way back to Sloane Square station. He took me to tea somewhere as a consolation for having missed the game, giving no further thought to our car, abandoned in the middle of the traffic in the King's Road. 'What will the owner of the car say?' I enquired.

'Don't you worry about that,' he replied, and then added mysteriously, 'It's not his car, anyway', and ordered more cream cakes.[3]

Henry's boyhood prowess as an inside-right had given way to a passionate gambling habit, by way of a flirtation with the saxophone. The habit was funded from the proceeds of illicit street bookmaking; his daughter's first memory of an outing with her father is a trip to Tottenham Court Road police station, to 'bung a flim' to the sergeant. So committed was he to a good wager that he would liven up dull moments on his patch in Hanson Street by betting against himself, by challenging the local urchins playing street cricket to three of his underarm leg-breaks, the prize being a threepenny bit if he failed to bowl them out. Having passed the day in bowling practice and betting-slip collection, there came the reckoning of the day's trade:

At five o'clock each afternoon Henry would, so to speak, leave the office and go home to my grandfather's house. There he would fling hundreds of bits of paper on to the parlour table, closely followed by a mountain of small change, and start to work through the results.

Within the hour he knew his fate for the day. But he announced it in an inaccessible argot. Thrusting his account book aside, he would rise from the table saying, 'See a tanner', or if it had been a bad day afternoon, 'Be a score'. One day it dawned on me that he was not saying 'See' or 'Be', but 'C' or 'B', and that these letters stood for 'Cop' and 'Blew' – that is to say, win and lose. The family understood all this perfectly. It was well versed. Henry and my father were more passionately devoted to the game than any bishop to his see. They viewed the whole of life through a pair of binoculars. Everything was measured by racing.[4]

I experienced at least one other, more alarming manifestation of this inability to see the world in anything but sporting colours. My route from school back to my grandmother's kitchen for lunch took me through the street where Henry's pitch was located. One lunchtime, I had reached the corner of Hanson Street when I was set upon by a boy twice my size. In no time a ring of interested spectators had formed, and I found myself wishing I was anywhere but here on this day at this time. But even as I started to panic, the thought occurred to me that Henry was no more than twenty yards away, and, realising my plight, would surely rescue me. The thought steadied my resolve, and I stuck out my left hand and began taking evasive action. Out of the corner of my eye, I could see him approaching, and I told myself I was saved. Then he leaned over the ring of boys and announced to the street at large, 'I'll take seven-to-four the little 'un.' He then proceeded to study my technique and to shout encouragement. He would probably have counted me out too had not the Law arrived and the contest broke up. Once the danger was over, I burst into tears with the strain of it all, at which Henry delivered the phrase for which he was famous all over the borough. Giving me his handkerchief to mop up the damage, that handkerchief, crisp and freshly laundered and smelling of home, he asked, 'Wotcha crying for, ya big mug?'

He must at some time have said 'Ya big mug' to everyone in the district, from close acquaintances to perfect strangers, from the family doctor to the local shopkeepers, and even on one famous occasion to a Magistrate unfamiliar with the workings of the Totalisator. Whenever he said it to me, it was a gesture of affection, the closest he was able to manage in that strangely inhibited family to express any emotion.[5]

Perhaps it was inevitable that as Benny grew older, his worship of Henry became tempered by perspective and pity. As Dave had always known, the assured and dapper man of the streets was essentially a naïf. But Benny, with a child's adoration of a favourite uncle, did not realise this until later, and the realisation was tinged with the pain of disillusionment. The moment came in 1937, when Henry's gay bachelordom was abruptly terminated and his usual companion, Bertha, was supplanted from her place in the passenger seat of his red Lagonda. The fun-loving faction among Henry's family, the ten-year-old Benny included, had adored Bertha, 'a tall, leggy brunette with what the romantic novelists used to call romantic eyes' and a 'kind of reckless abandon in pursuit of the good life'. But they disliked her replacement, Edith, who not only disapproved of what you might call his profession, but also had social ambitions that were implicitly critical of Henry's family.

Before proceeding with the unexpurgated account that Benny was working on when he died, I must make a gesture towards impartiality. Benny's version of events is that of Henry's aggrieved siblings. I have checked it with the last surviving witness, Great-Aunt Lily, but cannot vouch for her accuracy either, as she continues to staunchly fight the Green corner despite her 87 years. After all, the family always did have an eye for the long shot, and 'obliged to choose between the magnetism of Bertha and the quietude of Edith, they might well have plumped for the dark stranger'. Certainly, the family's memory of Edith was not as vicious as their memory of her successor, Doris. Rather than the problem lying in Edith's failure to match Bertha's racy precedent, I think that it was what Edith and her family represented to the Greens that so enraged them, smacking as it did of aspirational hypocrisy, snobbery and the manipulation of a gentle nature. For Benny, his heroic uncle's marriage to Edith revealed the object of his unqualified worship as all too human, and he saw Henry's fall from glory as a harbinger of the similar fate that later befell many of Benny's friends, of the happy man brought low by an ill-advised marriage, of youthful hopes consumed on the pyre of upward mobility:

But what of Henry, the handsome, all-conquering Henry, the fast bowler and goalscorer? The moment Edith turned up, the proportions of our back street world were drastically amended. As Edith loomed larger, so Henry was diminished. Under the outer skin of a casual masculinity, he was a mere marshmallow, and made no attempt to resist Edith's campaign to improve him. The first job to be done was to elevate his professional situation. Edith considered it unspeakably vulgar for a man to spend his days lounging in a slum doorway collecting the sixpences and shillings of those members of the proletariat who considered themselves au fait with the machinations of the sporting peers and the conspiracy of crooked loons in their employ.

Edith's position was not an easy one. She succumbed to the temptation of his bookmaking profits, but knew them to be filthy lucre. It was a dilemma she resolved as best she could. Her broad stroke of realism told her that Henry was good for nothing but gambling, but at least it could be made to look a little more respectable. In no time at all, Edith had him out of the street and into an office, had transmuted him from street bookmaker to commission agent, had varnished him with a coat of respectability which, as it turned out, never did sit very easily on his broad shoulders.

Much to my horror, Henry was completely taken in by all this idiotic posturing. He took to wearing stiff new Trilbies on family state occasions, and drifted steadily out of the Greenwell Street orbit into a new world of bridge schools and charge accounts, of limited companies and unlimited folie de grandeur. Gone now were the attendances at the big fights; crushed forever the impulse to gather up a few allies and leg it to the races. The late night suppers after the cinema were ruthlessly killed off. Life was a serious affair, and Henry would have to wipe the smile off his face.[6]

Henry set up an office in nearby Margaret Street, but his voyage into respectability soon ran aground on some familial rocks:

The big mistake he made in becoming the proprietor of an office was to take as his partner his brother-in-law Albert, another hopeless case who could never resist the siren song of the starting prices. Each partner staked his wagers secretly, with the firm's money, so that whenever one of them won, the other lost, so that the very best the firm could hope for was to break even. In addition, nepotism was at work, nibbling away at the foundations of the enterprise. One of the clerks hired to sit at the telephone inscribing bets from callers was a brother-in-law of Albert's. Another was a cousin of Edith's. Between them, these predators filched great swathes of capital by slipping into their piles of tickets a few winning wagers of their own, ascribed to some strictly hypothetical customer. It was in this style of one of his favourite writers, Damon Runyon, with each partner cheating the other and half the staff robbing both of them, that Henry's career as a prince of the betting ring collapsed in thunderous clouds of debt and recrimination.

From muttered dismissive asides from my father, I began to realise as I grew into adult awareness what had happened to Henry. He had married into a family of blackguards. It may seen absurd to say this of a man whose entire adult life had been insured by payments to the local constabulary every Saturday morning, and who had featured at least twice in the regular *Evening News* feature, 'Courts Day By Day', but Henry had fallen among thieves. It is true that never in his life had he fallen among anything else, but in the innocent rascality of his bachelor days there was nothing of the predatory ugliness which was the dominant characteristic of Edith's relatives. In his days in the streets, the thieving was petty, and much redeemed by the generosity with which he dispensed the profits. If he was not quite a Robin Hood, he was known in the back alleys of his bachelor days as a soft touch. Now he was introduced into a school of skullduggery which skipped adroitly just this side of the law, and once or twice over on to the other side. My father, who alone of the family had perceived the fundamental naïvety of Henry's nature, always believed that Edith's family corrupted him; certainly they changed his personality very much for the worse.[7]

To be fair to Edith and her family, it should be noted that the partner who secretly gambled the firm's money was not one of Edith's family, but Henry's; not only that, but one of the thieving clerks also came from the Green element in the firm. On the other hand, the other clerk, Edith's cousin Stan, subsequently went to prison for doping racehorses, so Edith's family were not as respectable as she may have liked to think. Personally, I find Dave's protestations of his brother's relative innocence a little hard to digest. After all, Henry was a man in the habit of selling half shares in his business with such regularity that Benny's Uncle Frank, the only uncle not gripped by gambling and consequently an utterly marginal figure in this narrative, once quipped, 'Here, you'll never guess what happened to me this morning. I was walking along the street when I bumped into a man who was never Henry's partner!'[8]

I asked Henry's daughter Robin about her father's involvement in a collapsed betting shop, but she replied with something about John Aspinall and Lady So-and-So, which would suggest that Henry had been involved in more than one fiasco of this nature. The truth presumably lies somewhere between the accusations flung by each family at the other, and between Benny's unfeasibly high expectations of the uncle he knew as a boy, and the real life of the man who married Edith for love, and whose opinion about all of this no one seems to have got round to asking.

Benny kept rewriting the chapter of 'the family history' about Henry, inveterately chewing on the contradiction between his childhood adoration of his uncle and the diminished figure he knew as an adult. He recognised that his interpretation of Henry's life was a personal one, and that he may have been expecting too much for his uncle to perform the rest of his life with the same wall-hurdling, flim-bunging brio as in his youth. He also recognised that his mourning for the old Henry was really a mourning for the unknowing certainty of his childhood, in whose narrow world Henry was a colossus:

> It may well be that my crude schoolboy sensibilities at the time the change [in Henry] occurred were not capable of digesting adult events, and that what I took to be a calamitous change of personality was nothing more than the commonplace of a young man finally and not altogether willingly agreeing to grow up and begin the pursuit of gravitas ... The fact that my emergent schoolboy view of the world happened to coincide with the crowning years of Henry's ascendancy and his sudden diminution to a nondescript certainly coloured my own view of the whole business, but I can only describe it as I remember it. I confess that what I had conceived to have happened to my uncle filled me with compassion tinged with bitter disillusionment at the ways of a trumpery world.[9]

There is a coda to the story of Benny's relationship with Henry, one that touches on just those feelings of disillusionment. Perhaps fittingly, it occurs just around the corner from the site of the consolatory tea they had shared on the day of the foggy Chelsea-Arsenal game. In the early Seventies, Benny spent three nights watching his wife Toni in a play produced by the theatrical boyfriend of Henry's daughter Robin:

> In pursuit of his dream, he staged a short run of a limp melodrama about a day in the life of a betting shop. The production took place in the upper room of a public house in Fulham. My attention was distracted seconds before the action was due to start. There at the bottom of the single typewritten sheet which constituted the programme lay the wonderful device, 'Technical adviser: Henry Green'.
>
> Certainly there could have been no man alive who knew more about the minutiae of life in a betting shop than Henry, but the thought that this omniscience had brought him into what are often laughingly defined as the Fine Arts was too much for me to take in at a glance. For the next hour and a half, while the dialogue droned on, I sat there in awe at the ways of the world. Here was this man, whose only previous connection with the theatre had been the occasional musical show he had half-watched in the days of his single state, suddenly flung up into the higher reaches of theatrical authority. His status had magically changed, if only for a few hours, from back-street to backstage, and I relished the idea.
>
> During the interval, I spotted him standing by the door, and waved him downstairs to join me for a drink. We chatted easefully till it was time for the drama to proceed. This time he sat next to me, persistently turning and chatting to me in a voice audible across the room. I had neither the heart nor the courage to shush him, and the evening somehow ended. I was happy to report to myself that he seemed to have aged hardly at all; had he not been smothered in one of my old over-coats, he might have passed for a man in his fifties. A few days later, he awoke in the middle of the night, said something to his wife, turned over and died. He was seventy years old.[10]

This Sporting Life

5

Every Saturday night, Joseph Green's tribe gathered in Greenwell Street for the closest that it came to any form of ritual observance, a card school. As with most of the family's more arduous tasks, the labour was divided upon lines of gender. While the men sat smoking and gambling in the front parlour, the women worked in the basement kitchen, sending relays of omelette sandwiches upstairs, whilst Benny floated between the two, an almost unseen observer. In December 1936, Benny's grandmother Deborah interrupted the revels by having a heart attack 'after a Saturday evening spent in happy concentration breaking up firewood'.[1] She was carried up the 79 steps to bed, but never came back down. When he saw her body, Benny's father Dave fell in a cold faint. It was a watershed in the lives of all the family, the passing of an era as much as a mother and grandmother. In fitting style, Deborah's death was marked by a final rallying of the Edwardian old guard who were the elders of her side of the family:

> To this day I am unsure who my great-aunts and great-uncles were, what they did, where they lived, where they went and why. My father, a connoisseur of eccentricity in its more harmless modes, later told me that this one was a self-confessed scoundrel and that one generally acknowledged to be very slightly off her head. But I cannot say for certain which of the inmates of this parrot-house of consanguinity constituted cousins of the deceased, or in-laws, or old friends, or old enemies, or nieces and nephews. The house that day was nothing more than a wild gallimaufry of cloche hats and bombazine, pot bellies, blue serge and watch chains, jade ornaments and elastic stockings, gold rings and gold fillings, avuncular hands slipping sixpences into my embarrassed pockets, booming old ladies taking my cheeks between gloved fingers and telling me I was 'Davey's boy'. There were Annies and Toms and Sarahs and Joes and Lilys and Lews, but which was which I had, and have, no idea.[2]

Once the obsequies had been observed and Deborah installed in a cemetery in distant Streatham, Joseph's family pulled together, and set off in a familiar direction, but with new vigour. Off the matriarchal leash, Dave and Uncle Henry carried Joseph with them on a scheme that must have had the virtuous Deborah revolving in her grave. The front parlour, that cornerstone of the family's respectability, was converted into a bookie's office:

> A ticker tape was installed, a second phone added, and the encyclopae-dias dispossessed to make way for editions of the Sporting Chronicle Handicap Book, Whatever became of the piano and the polar bear remains one of the great family mysteries, but certainly they never survived the changeover.
>
> My recollections of the parlour ... have a distinctly Runyonesque flavour, of desperate men craning over the ticker tape as it spluttered out its pregnant messages; of my uncle recklessly scribbling down the names of horses on the fading wallpaper, with its fantastical motif of bulbous pineapples growing on a lattice frame; of the Edwardian chairs which had once accommodated the broad and eminently respectable bottoms of assorted great-aunts, groaning now beneath the weight of strangers with unlit cigarettes in their mouths and 'systems' on their brains; of local sportsmen sprinting down the street and through the ever-open front door in a despairing attempt to reach the sanctuary of the parlour before the 'Off'.[3]

Despite his sons' demolition of the work ethic in the front parlour, Joseph continued stitching and cutting in the back workshop, making the only occasional foray into the illegal gambling den that had been his parlour. The illegality of it does not seem to have bothered anyone, least of all the local constabulary, who were 'bunged a flim' in the handshakes that greeted them when they passed every Saturday morning. These payments allowed the uncles to continue in business, and to be tipped off when it was their turn to go through what Benny called the 'ritual dance' of arrest and fines. I don't know whether Joseph knew that all this sporting mayhem was illegal. For a man whose 'entire stock of political philosophy' was 'It's a free country',[4] the iniquity of a law which allowed only those wealthy enough to own a telephone to gamble freely may have been too abstruse to consider. But he was aware that his sons, abetted by his sons-in-law, had veered off the path of conscientious tailoring, and was a little perturbed at the results:

[Joseph] was a compulsive worker and frowned on too much self-indulgence in others. Not that he was a Puritan. He showed enough passion at the regular Saturday night card games to convince me that Dostoevsky could have extracted a reasonable short story out of him, a story which underlined his magisterial way of banging down the last trump in a hand of Solo which put you in mind of a tycoon buying an oil well. But that was strictly Saturday night stuff.

As to the goings-on of his children, who so obligingly provided for me a scintillating portrait gallery of avuncular – and that includes my aunts – eccentricity, my grandfather was disenchanted. It was not that he was opposed to playing the horses. He enjoyed playing them himself from time to time. But his sons were making a religion out of it, and my grandfather did not believe in making a religion out of anything, not even religion.[5]

By this time, Dave had stopped playing the saxophone professionally, as the rise of large, organised big bands in the Thirties had made musicians who couldn't read music redundant. As a tailor, he had been a further disappointment to his father by showing a talent only for one-armed jackets with detachable linings. But gambling seemed to be the only act in which Dave found complete fulfilment. Even Joseph must have noticed the seamless way that gambling mobilised in Dave the mental agility of a would-be writer and the musician's aptitude for spontaneous mathematics in the welter of form and odds that occupied almost all of his mental activity. He was a natural gambler, and like most natural gamblers, a natural loser.

Fanny's absence at work gave Dave enormous liberty to pursue his heart's desires, some of whom had two legs rather than four. On such excursions, the constant company of Benny served as a perfect alibi. Benny remembered being taken as a six- or seven-year-old on a bus and tram odyssey to an industrial workshop in some distant corner of north London, where a drummer friend of Dave's called George Franks worked. Fanny disapproved of Franks, quite correctly believing that he was a bad influence, not that Dave needed much influencing. Benny was left with Franks, and played among the brushes and drawing equipment for about half an hour, until Dave reappeared, and they went home. Another time, Benny was with Dave in the large Woolworth's on Oxford Street, when one of the shop girls called out, 'Hello, Davey!', all smiles, and patting

Benny on his head. Neither Fanny, or for that matter Benny, ever received solid proof of Dave's infidelities, but both knew what was happening.

If Dave had lived in a suburban cul-de-sac, then everyone would have known what he was doing. But in the turmoil of Cleveland Street, he was just one of many people scurrying about on unknown but probably unedifying errands. Some of them were what are usually known as pillars of the community, as in the case of the esteemed Doctor A, 'who carried around with him the spirit of Hapsburgian Vienna, pickled, as it were, in the preservative of his own immaculate punctilio'.[6] Dr A. was a particular friend of the family, not because they needed treatment, as they were an unusually healthy bunch, but because of his Hapsburgian eye for a fine horse. Being a better class of punter, the doctor would transact his bets undercover, by dropping in to Greenwell Street:

> A consulting detective would soon have noticed that illness suddenly afflicted my grandfather's house on Derby day, Oaks day, St Leger day, Two Thousand Guineas day, and so on, ranging right across the racing calendar from the Lincolnshire to the Manchester November handicap, and that once the flat racing season was over the family health improved just as suddenly, owing to the fact that Dr A. knew nothing and cared less for steeplechasing.[7]

Given Dr A.'s standing in the community, it was apt that on the occasion of one of the neighbourhood's rare brushes with celebrity, it should fall to the doctor to be its representative. Walk due north from Henry's pitch on Hanson Street, cut through Clipstone Mews, and you are in Carburton Street, a tributary connecting stagnant Portland Place to the great flow of human life on Cleveland Street. It was here in 1937 that one of British cinema's most important car accidents took place. In a time when a car was an unusual sight on the back streets, the excitement of two of them driving into each other was an important event, especially when news spread through the district that one of the passengers was a divinity from the screen:

> Here was the great Merle Oberon, the beauty who had appeared in 'The Private Life of Henry VIII' and 'The Scarlet Pimpernel', who was married to that Hungarian colossus among film-makers, Alexander Korda, who even now as she lay there on the cobbles of Carburton Street, was in

mid-portrayal of the wicked Lady Messalina in the much ballyhooed production of 'I, Claudius'. No wonder there was panic in the streets. The famous beauty must be saved, must be rushed to the nearest hospital. But wait, was there not a doctor's surgery fifty yards away? Yes, there was. To the surgery with her![8]

Although none of Miss Oberon's rescuers knew it at the time, all was not well on the set of Korda's production of *I, Claudius*. Filming was falling expensively behind schedule, as its star, Charles Laughton, 'continued to be bullied and harangued' by the director, a certain Joseph von Sternberg, whose idea of putting actors at their ease was to throw another understudy on the fire. Persecuted by Sternberg, wracked by his own professional humility, Laughton had been staggering around for weeks trying to find 'the key to his portrayal' of the stuttering, limping emperor, with little success. Eventually, some bright and despairing spark gave him a copy of Edward VIII's abdication speech, 'and it was there, in the halting unprofessional oratory of an ex-king's renunciation of his responsibilities that Laughton heard his Claudius'.[9] But by this time, Korda's finances had run down to such an extent that 'he needed a plain old-fashioned miracle, some get-out, some escape clause, some Act of God that would extricate him from the web of intrigue, enmity and sheer unproductivity which Laughton, Von Sternberg and the Robert Graves novel had flung him':

At which point there occurs an unfortunate and terrific accident in Carburton Street, after which there is brought in to the homely surgery of Dr A. none other than Messalina herself. And moreover, Messalina alias Mrs Alexander Korda. What did Dr A. care that his princess was made of pure celluloid and that she had been born Merle O'Brien Thompson? Here was that news from the great world he had always half-expected, a moment for him to savour when his striped trousers, his carnation and his punctilio came into their own. It might be his destiny to minister to the wants of people whose private lives held no glamour for him, like young Green, for instance, whose father had once come into this surgery and asked him if there was anything you could give a greyhound to make it run faster, an enquiry which had drawn from Dr A. one of his better responses, 'No, but I can give you something to make the other five run slower.' Dr A. could accept his modest station, so long as once, just once, he could bring all his unexpressed urbanity into play. And now, here in his surgery was, of all things, a princess in distress, a princess whose prince was busy looking for a miracle. Dr A. rose to the occasion with all the aplomb of a veteran courtier.

And that was how Alexander Korda's abortive attempt to create a masterpiece finally floundered in the improbable purlieus of my own backyard ... As for Dr A, he, after his brief hour of glory, reverted to type, except that after that day, whenever you entered his surgery, your eye would be caught by the photograph in the silver frame, placed in a strategic position on his desk. It showed a lady of serene beauty, her hair arranged in the sort of plaits that put you in mind of a harvest loaf. In the bottom right hand corner was a scrawled signature which might or might not have read Messalina O'Brien.[10]

As *The Times* reported in November 1979 in its obituary of Merle Oberon, '... she was to have been the star in one of Korda's most ambitious and expensive projects, a version of the Robert Graves novel *I, Claudius*, with Charles Laughton in the title role. But in March 1937 she was seriously injured in a road accident and unable to work for six weeks. The delay was fatal for the film, which had to be abandoned with the shooting only partly completed ...' Reading her obituary one morning at Langley House, Benny suddenly realised what had really happened:

It all came flooding back to me in reverse, like a movie run backwards; Korda's deep regret at having to abandon the picture because of a serious injury to his leading lady, the photograph on the desk, the confusion in Carburton Street, the clamouring onlookers, the electric atmosphere of melodrama in the air, the whole district straining to catch a glimpse of romance, among them a small boy craning out of his grandfather's first floor window and seeing a seriously injured princess walking to the surgery of the local doctor. Not every Balkan intrigue is recorded in the official histories.[11]

More predictable incursions from the glamorous world outside came from Uncle Henry, one of whose friends was the reigning champion of the Lightweight boxing division, Dave Crowley, who now faced challenges from two teenage prodigies:

Enormous public interest gathered about these world-shattering issues, and when my father told me we were to be Henry's guests at Harringay Arena to watch Crowley meet the challenge of an apprentice blacksmith called Eric Boon, there was joy unconfined in the household. On a December night, our party of three attended the arena to watch the great challenge match. I had never been inside a boxing stadium before, and was somewhat daunted by our distance from the ring, but I quickly adjusted. The main bout had attracted so much interest that it became the first sporting event to be shown as it was happening in a West End cinema. The contrast, between an artist and a slugger, was finally won by the slugger in the thirteenth round, when Crowley was counted out. It seemed vicariously to be a defeat for my uncle too, but I soon discovered that he had overcome sentiment to the extent of wagering on Boon at odds of six-to-four against.

For days after, I could see the gladiators in the ring, Crowley dapper in a purple dressing gown, Boon looking more like a schoolboy than a contender. But before the clamour had died away I learned that we were to go back to the same arena to watch the new champion meet the challenge of the other teenage prodigy of the age, Arthur Danahar. Again it was a protracted battle between the slugger and the artist, and again the slugger prevailed when the fight was stopped after fourteen rounds.[12]

In later years, Benny's brother-in-law in Bognor Regis, our Uncle Mike, was a kindred spirit in matters musical and sporting. As a young man, Mike had been a semi-professional clarinettist, and had even pursued his enthusiasm for boxing to the extent of having his nose extensively resculpted in amateur bouts. In the Seventies, having built up a confectionery business, Mike was looking for a manager for one of his seafront emporia when he heard that one of his childhood heroes was down on his luck. It was Arthur Danahar. Physically, he was sprightly, but even to an eight-year-old, his mental powers seemed a touch impaired. In a moment of lucidity, a gravely serious Arthur explained to Benny the secret of his success.

Apparently, a reckless doctor had once advised Arthur that the parts of the skull on which a boxer was most likely to be hit, the front and the temples, were much thinner than the part on which he was unlikely to be hit, the top of his head. Arthur had digested this information, and had then based upon it a technique that made him a champion. Every time a hammer blow was heading for the front or side of his head, Arthur ducked a little, and it landed on the thick top of his skull, with little obvious result. This left Arthur free to counter-attack, and led to him acquiring a reputation as a fearless fighter, who could take terrible punishment and never be counted out. Of course, the doctor who had tipped him off about his cranial density had neglected to mention the long-term consequences of repeated sledgehammer blows to the top of the head. By the time I met Arthur, he was well on the way past oddity to full-blown eccentricity, although it was not the typical glassy-eyed slurring of the punch-drunk. It was the harmless mania of a children's entertainer, a constant stream of winks, nudges and gibberish which, as the cunning Uncle Mike may have realised, was the ideal sales pitch for retailing candy-floss and rock to small children. As far as anyone was ever able to establish, Arthur seemed entirely happy despite his palpable insanity, and he eventually died in his Spanish villa after a long retirement.

With the death of his grandmother, Benny was unleashed along with the rest of the family. He became what his hero Sherlock Holmes would have called a 'street Arab', at large throughout the day with a gang of equally untrammelled contemporaries. But the change of atmosphere in Greenwell Street had touched everybody's lives. Instead of his beloved grandmother, Benny now fell under the supervision of his eldest aunt, Ginnie, a woman rendered bitter by having spent her own childhood nannying her numerous siblings, while her mother staggered through another pregnancy. It was Ginnie whose mania for tidiness extended to throwing away any scraps of paper that Benny had left lying around, even if they were covered in his writing. It was also Ginnie who, as part of her unending programme to purge the house of any items of emotional significance, announced that she had sold her father's overcoat for a good price, only for it to transpire that his gold watch was still in the pocket. With her mother dead, Ginnie now became the chatelaine of the house:

> For five days a week for two years, she served me the same iron rations, a Vienna stewed in its own dark juices, and a tablespoon and a half of what my grandfather used to call smashed potatoes, and a small dish of strawberry blancmange. That was the table d'hôte of my schooldays. Never just one spoon of potatoes, never two, always one and a half;

never raspberry blancmange or blackcurrant blancmange or even no blancmange, always the same quivering scarlet mass. I did not feel particularly hard done by in the strict calorific sense. I knew there were classmates like Benson, who had once revealed under close cross-examination by the stern but caring Mr Murrell that he lunched each day on a slice of dry bread and a small cube of cheese, and whose subsequent flirtation with malnutrition manifested itself, it seemed to me, in the milk-white frailty in the backs of his knees.

It was not that I was hungry, simply humiliated. My Aunt made no attempt to hide the fact that she was dispensing charity, and the fact that the charity was not hers but my grandfather's made the chore no less of a cussed nuisance to her. She would slap the potatoes on to the plate with a gesture of swift contempt for the spoon, against whose adhesive surface the potatoes insisted on sticking. She would fling down my blancmange, or 'afters', as it was known in our closed society with such vehemence that it became a policy of mine never to begin eating until its quivering declivities had achieved their milky, porous stasis, as though only in repose could the dish be said to be rinsed of venom. And no sooner had I concluded my business with the plates than they were whisked from my possession and tossed in the sink, where they would be drubbed maliciously with an old slop-rag wrapped round the head of a wooden spoon, and left to dry out until the next day. (The two plates, by the way, were always side plates, as if to remind me that this was not a proper meal I was eating, and ought not, therefore, require much time to eat.)[13]

If the fall of Uncle Henry had notified the young Benny that the world outside had different demands from his own dreams, then the death of his grandmother was a full-scale intrusion by that world into the securities of childhood. But while these domestic dramas were being played out, Benny was also meeting the heirs to that world, his peers. An only child, he found a new social focus in the extended world of school, and, in the latter years of his primary schooling, an inspirational figure who was to replace his grandmother as the latest in the line of influential women who so shaped his life.

Clipstone Street 6

From the site of Merle Oberon's car crash on Carburton Street, we turn south. We now stand at the head of Great Titchfield Street, the north-south artery of the neighbourhood which runs all the way down to the distant frontier with Soho at Oxford Street. Every other Friday morning for the last 22 years of his life, Benny went to Broadcasting House on Portland Place, to record the next two instalments of his 'Art of The Songwriter' series for Radio 2. In the years after Leo and I had moved out of Langley House, we would meet him in the lobby at 12.30 p.m., and would cut through Riding House Street to the junction of Great Titchfield and Foley Streets, which had once been the focus of the area's street market. Here we would decamp to the Montebello, one of the neighbourhood's many Italians, where we would be joined by a floating cast of friends of all three of us for a long lunch that would run late into the afternoon.

It was an odd mixture, with young musicians like Dave Lagnado swapping Marx Brothers lines with Benny, while friends from Benny's childhood would tell us of seeing Django Reinhardt and Stephane Grappelli's group playing sets between films at a Mile End cinema in the Thirties, as Brian Kennedy told us his latest adventures from the road, and Ray Gelato cast an expert eye over the menu. After the party had broken up, Leo and I would walk with Benny back to Euston station, letting him steer us on a circuitous stroll through the streets of his childhood that would stimulate a host of stories to add to the ones with which we had grown up. Never far from our minds on these field trips in the family history was the legendary calamity known to all of us as 'The 1938 Baby Derby', one of the more notorious episodes of Benny's childhood.

Ginnie's predicament of being a surrogate parent in the absence of Fanny and Dave was not unusual, although it was more common for the surrogates to be only a few years older than their charges. After the installation in Great Titchfield Street of a new-fangled electric clock, known as the Great Timepiece, one of these babysitters, surely inspired by the example of a gambling parent, had the idea that the clock was an ideal starting and finishing point for a race that could mobilise the many prams that the elder siblings of the neighbourhood had to push:

The race was to consist of one circuit of the block, start and finish at the Great Timepiece, no bumping and boring, any contestant finishing the race with either more or less bodies on board than when he started to be disqualified, any passenger falling out during the race to be put back, forcibly if need be, and, let us admit it, even if not be, before proceeding, the prize to be four back numbers of *The Hotspur*, donated by old man Frumkin, from his paper shop without his knowledge, a packet of glass marbles, one roller-skate and a pennyworth of lime juice nibs.[1]

Come the day, the jockeys and their prams lined up. Being an only child, it fell to Benny to be Clerk of the Course. Having cast an eye over the runners, many of whom had modified their prams for the occasion, by appending family crests, black flags, watering cans and water pistols to their mounts, the race was on. From his vantage point under the Timepiece, Benny could hear the uproar as the prams rounded the block:

There was Nordy, for instance, that petulant Slav with the enormous boots. Having no brothers or sisters, Nordy had borrowed one of Rademsky's, a situation which had tempted that gentleman to crash broadside into Nordy's pram and deposit everyone connected with it into the ripe fruitarian gutters of the market.

Spurred by this victorious joust in the very first seconds of the race, Rademsky had then worked up a tremendous burst of speed, stepped up on to the foot-rest with the maniacal idea of free-wheeling triumphantly through the district with black flag flying and kid sister howling hysterically, and had sailed straight through the front door of the doctor's surgery in Candover Street, thus achieving more in the way of stimulating the doctor's practice in five seconds, than the doctor had been able to do in the previous five years.

Meanwhile, Nordy, still dazed but semi-recovered, had put the pieces back together again, flung his passenger back on board and gallantly started off down the course, desperately trying to make up a leeway caused in part by the crash and in part by the weight of his own boots. Sadly, in his eagerness to overtake his rivals, Nordy overlooked one small technical aspect of his performance, which was to look where he was going, and had no sooner worked up speed than he smashed into an old lady emerging from the local delicatessen, laden with an armful of artery-hardening delicacies.

Nordy's pram instantly disintegrated, leaving Rademsky's sister laughing in the gutter while her jockey took up the pursuit pramless. The old lady, having picked herself off the pavement, began screaming that she was dead, a claim that certainly seemed to be substantiated by appearances, for in running over her Nordy had burst open a two-pound bag of flour, which had settled like a bedsheet over his victim and caused her to look distinctly spectral.

It is only fair to add that later Nordy denied the whole business, insisting that there had been no old lady, that the pram had fallen apart of its own accord, that it was her fault for not watching where he was going, and that anyway it was only a one-pound bag of flour.

Meanwhile, I had had time to observe that if more than two leading runners were to come into view together, there was bound to be a spectacular collision, as the pavement on my corner narrowed slightly and could not take more than two riders abreast. In the event, three riders appeared, one small child being deposited on the pavement and several wheels flying about at interesting tangents. At last two wrecked vehicles went lurching down Great Titchfield Street towards the Great Timepiece and immortality.

Speigalgass, in his 1934 de luxe model, passed the post first but was disqualified later when it was discovered that the small child cowering in terror under the blanket belonged to a passer-by; apparently there had been an enormous pile-up halfway down Candover Street and in their haste the drivers had grabbed the nearest midget to hand before resuming the race. (Speigalgass was eventually absolved from accusations of kidnapping but by the time he was disqualified he had already eaten the lime-juice nibs.) The victory eventually went to Daveneberg's 1929 model with the pneumatic tyres and the watering-can modification between the front wheels.[2]

The maniacs behind the prams were Benny's classmates at Clipstone Junior Mixed. Surprisingly, the school building from which we saw the four-year-old Benny running towards his bowler-hatted father was one to which he would return with enthusiasm. For a boy raised in the ways of anti-authoritarian belligerence, Benny's love of his primary school, and the unanimously positive things he wrote about it, would seem paradoxical. To deepen the perplexity, his passion for Clipstone Junior Mixed was matched only by his loathing of his secondary school, Marylebone Grammar. The explanation lies not in the school, but in the teacher: the wonderfully named Miss Daisy Head, one of those rare, inspirational mentors who often unknowingly alter the lives of their pupils. If anyone gave structure to the mental liberty that Dave cultivated in his son, it was she, whom Benny later eulogised as having given him 'almost the entire basic kit of knowledge which I carry around with me to this day':[3]

> I can see her now, her hair, the colour and texture of straw, in slight disarray, and her aggressive chin reddening with the effort to equip us for the world beyond the classroom windows. Miss Head believed passionately that education was the answer to all evils, the implication being that if only Eve had known her thirteen times table, we would all still be in the Garden of Eden. If anyone in this world ever had a vocation, Miss Head was that person and teaching that vocation. Never a moment was wasted. She would spray facts at us like a sniper raking a battlefield. Even while marching us into assembly she would inform us that the pavement edges were made of granite, that hygiene was the secret of happiness, that Constantinople was now Istanbul, that there were 360 degrees in a circle, that Constable's 'The Haywain' was the world's greatest painting, that it was wrong for a healthy man to lie abed in the morning, that George VI was a constitutional monarch, that pollination was performed by the wind, that our numerals were Arabic – and, of course, that a hundred pence made eight and fourpence.
>
> One bright summer morning not very long before the start of the last War she was striding out towards our school with that brisk step of hers when she suddenly came across me in the act of throwing an uncooked King Edward potato into the local off-licence. Without any faltering in her stride she said, 'Good morning, Green. And what is the chief airport of northern India?' to which I responded with the wildest of guesses and answered, 'Karachi'. I think it was this incident which finally convinced her that I was certain one day to become Prime Minister of England.[4]

Daisy Head's ambitions for turning her class into model citizens faced several natural obstacles, not least the poverty in which many of her charges lived, and the cultural gaps that lay between her and her class, and between the class and their own parents. Her pupils were the progeny of refugees from all over Europe, and consequently the languages they spoke at home were often not the one they spoke at school, producing a Babel of 'Hyman Kaplan' proportions. Benny's class was a polyglot assortment, half-Russian Jews, and half a motley of Irish, Belgians, Italians and Greeks, with a leavening from the Spanish Civil War:

Roughly half the population of our school consisted of embryonic Portnoys who had found themselves being born British only through the unwelcome attentions a generation earlier of assorted numskull Cossacks. And because academic standards in our school happened, in some altogether miraculous way, to be freakishly high, there existed among many of my classmates that comic-tragic fact of the immigrant life, the unbridgeable gulf of culture between parent and child. What point could there possibly be in the school sending parents the child's term report when the parents couldn't understand a word of it? How was the pupil to extract an excuse-of-absence note, even on legitimate grounds, from a father who could only write one in some obscure and possibly extinct middle-European dialect?...

One outcome of this kind of thing was a cosmopolitan classroom flavour undreamed of by County Hall, a world in which the teacher might easily have to ask the pupil how many z's there were in Leszczynski, or whether eastern Roumelia existed anymore. One afternoon during the 1938 Munich Crisis my form mistress asked us all to tell the rest of the class what our fathers had done in the Great War, and I remember distinctly that the replies ranged from 'Deserted from the Russian infantry' to 'What war?' Of course, the logical end of this was the alienation of one generation from another. When any of our number won a scholarship and graduated at eleven to a new school, he would almost certainly find himself six months later sitting at home writing an essay on the implications of Hamlet's indecision, while sitting there in the same room with him were parents saying things like 'Yes, I got three children and one girl.'[5]

By way of counterbalance, Miss Head 'had a very modern attitude to learning, which manifested itself in attempts to relate the facts to the living presence', teaching the geography of Canada by mapping the royal tour of 1939, and even transporting her class to London Bridge by river-bus, for which occasion, 'Appropriately enough, Miss Head's vocabulary took on a suitably nautical flavour when she called out, "That boy on the starboard bow, stop spitting in the water."'[6] Of particular didactic use was nearby Regent's Park, in which practical proofs could be demonstrated of the difference between a rose bush and an oak tree, or the inequity between the two halves of a lime tree leaf. Returning in 1961 for a last stroll around the park before marrying and moving to Wembley, Benny found it pleasingly unchanged, although it did remind him of an incident when he was reminded of another obstacle that sat between him and respectable citizenship:

> The émigrés still gather in the restaurants of the Botanical Gardens on spring afternoons, performing their unwitting parody of a crowd scene from 'The Count of Luxembourg', and the mid-morning crocodile of schoolchildren still gets taken on nature walks, although perhaps not to be confronted by the dilemma which once faced me, when, in the middle of a lecture from Daisy Head on the difference between rooks and crows, I spotted my father sitting on the grass scrutinising the contents of 'The Sporting Life', he having the punter's presence of mind to tip me a conspiratorial wink as I passed.[7]

Taking a class of budding anarchists on a field trip was a potentially hazardous business, in which both teacher and pupils ran serious physical risk. It was one of these forays that produced one of Benny's favourite quotations, 'Prot et Marbel', which as he noted, sounds like 'an epigram from Juvenal, or something fairly indecent from the footnotes to Gibbon's *Decline and Fall of the Roman Empire*'. Inspired by a joke made by one Jack Podemsky, a child with the body of a man and the brain of a chicken, about 'the Pharaohs being unkind to their mummies', Daisy Head set loose the barbarians of Class One in one of the world's great storehouses of knowledge. (In the interests of Podemsky's modesty, Benny preserved his classmate's anonymity by telling absurd stories of Podemsky's ignorance, but with their anti-hero's name changed to 'Rademsky'.)

One day Daisy Head, calculating the distance between Clipstone Junior Mixed and the British Museum, must have realised with a flush of exultation that not even a crocodile of thirty-one unruly midgets could very well commit many serious acts of violence or vandalism over so short a distance.

And so one Olympian morning many years ago, Daisy Head, who had once taken us up the Thames on a paddle steamer and down again on a fireboat, who had dragged us into Regent's Park Zoo to show us our great-great-great grandfathers slumbering behind the bars of the gorilla cages, who had described the map of Britain to us as an old spinster riding the pig of imperialism towards Ireland, this intrepid, compulsive, inexhaustible educator lined us up in the playground and issued notebooks and pencils, with instructions to enter anything we saw of unusual interest. This advice was received with varying degrees of asininity, especially from our prize exhibit Rademsky, whose academic accomplishments were such that giving him a notebook and pencil in the hope that he would enter therein things of unusual interest was rather like handing a pair of ballet shoes to a weightlifter and requesting him to perform a pas de chat. Off we marched ...

After giving us a potted history of the Phoenician mercantile navy, an analysis of Lord Nelson's handwriting, an exposition of the development of the Greek city-state and a thumbnail sketch of the evolution of the knife and fork, Daisy Head finally steered us into the Egyptian Room, by which time Rademsky, who had so far found nothing of unusual interest apart from the discovery that a piece of moist chewing gum, when pressed against the shinbone of a statue of the Apollo Belvedere, usually stayed put, was getting bored. It was now that the elder Port, the fatter and chubbier and more half-witted of two half-witted brothers, decided that the time had come for him to beguile his classmates with a few conjuring tricks.

The elder Port was an extraordinary specimen whose most distinguished trick was falling asleep in the classroom with his arm looped through the window-cord, so that when he was woken up suddenly, his arm would jerk, the cord would tauten and the window descend with a terrifying crash. The fact that his father was a local glazier may have had something to do with the development of this odd habit, but the sad truth was that the elder Port was a martyr to some form of narcolepsy which caused him to doze off at the most improbable moments.

But on this day he was wide awake, at least comparatively speaking. Blinking sleepily, and stifling a vast yawn with the back of a tired hand, he produced from the recesses of a gargantuan overcoat a large glass marble, which he held up between thumb and forefinger against his closed right eye while he stared at us through his wide-open left eye, announcing in a drowsy voice that the moment Daisy Head's back was turned, he would give us an exhibition of legerdemain so remarkable that the mummies would start calling for fresh bandages. So we gathered round and awaited events, informed by the herd instinct that whenever the elder Port tried to do anything apart from fall asleep, some kind of disaster was sure to follow.

Port announced that the glass marble would be made to disappear before our very eyes, a startling claim which was received with a reverent hush from the entire congregation, including all the Rameses and Pharaohs lurking in the background, who had heard nothing like this for years. Gathering confidence, Port flourished the marble and said, 'You see here an ordinary marble, an Elgin marble, as you might say.' (Five minutes earlier Daisy Head had mentioned Lord Elgin in tones of vitriolic contempt.) Port's intention was to wave the marble, say, 'Now you see it', put the thing in his mouth, and say, 'Now you don't'. It was a very simple plan, which a four-year-old child could have performed without the slightest difficulty. Unfortunately Port was not a four-year-old child, but a ten-year-old child, and having therefore had an extra six years to practise messing things up, now proceeded to perform his trick more efficiently than he could ever have dreamed.

The first part of his performance went smoothly enough. After all, not even Port could find a way of complicating the utterance, 'Now you see it.' It was part two, where he said, 'Now you don't' with the marble in his mouth, that proved too much for him. There was a choking noise, a violent gulp, a brief fit of coughing, and then the slow tide of salt tears trickling down Port's chubby cheeks. And it was at that exact moment, when the glass marble slid down Port's astonished gullet, that our visit to the British Museum ended and Port's visit to the Middlesex Hospital began, leaving us all preoccupied with the problem of whether the surgeons could operate in time to save the marble.

Eventually, the doctors managed to save both Port and the marble … As for Rademsky, having witnessed this amazing attempt by a classmate to digest a lump of solid glass, he had decided that such a gesture came under the heading of an unusual event, and had entered on the first page of an otherwise virgin notebook the words: Prot et Marbel.[8]

As can be inferred from Daisy Head's geographical metaphors and her opinion of Lord Elgin, Miss Head's ambitions did not stop at the mere facts; part of her agenda was to broaden the political and social horizons of her pupils. She was ever alert for reactionary tendencies in Class One:

Appeasement was in the air, and she strongly disapproved of it. As she said to us one frostbound morning in 1937, mystifying us utterly, 'If Neville comes, can war be far behind?' Although according to the rules of the game she was not supposed to pry into the political backgrounds of our homes, she was ingenious enough to find a way round the regulations and get us all roughly docketed along the lines of political demarcation.

It comes back to me that she asked us one day about newspapers, and ended up requesting a show of hands from all those children whose mummies and daddies took *The Daily Express*, for which read Conservative. Immediately, fifteen hands out of thirty-one shot up. She then asked for a similar gesture from those who took *The Daily Herald*, for which read Labour. Again, fifteen hands went up. Clearly, there was an abstainer, which turned out to be me, and when she asked why, I said, 'Please miss, we take *The Racing and Football Outlook* and *The Sporting Life*' …

One day, at the height of the Italo-Abyssinian war, she noticed that Mondelli had come to school wearing a black shirt. Was this a gesture of crypto-fascism? Or merely a bold development in the fashion war which never ceased to rage among those boys desperate to get the girls to look at them? Nobody was sure, least of all Daisy Head, who was eventually unable to control the desire to find out.

So she asked Mondelli what the reasons were for his sudden manifestation as a symbol of the New Italy. Mondelli, who was, as far

83

as I recall, too dim to tell any sort of imaginative lie, smiled engagingly and said that it was all part of his mother's campaign to reduce laundry costs.[9]

By 1938, 'Apart from a few very highly educated and experienced people, such as Cabinet ministers and newspaper proprietors, practically everyone knew that war was coming soon',[10] although even the perspicacious Daisy Head did not realise that it would precipitate the break-up of the British Empire. In the years of Benny's childhood, Victoria's Empire was not only still extant, but had only recently achieved the high-water mark of its expansion (in 1923, with the acquisition of Tanganyika). The legendary pinked-in Mercator Projection map was a fixture on the classroom wall, and Britain's demonstrable supremacy a fact of the curriculum. Daisy Head had her own views on how to demonstrate the global breadth of Class One's dominion. This had produced the class trip to the Pool of London, where the children had marvelled at thousands of craft jamming the world's busiest port, bearing goods from all over the Empire. It also produced another, imaginative tour through Britain's overseas possessions, this time on a culinary theme.

For Christmas 1938, each child was to bring in a cooking ingredient, of any kind, as long as it came from somewhere in the Empire. The result was to be added to the inedible yet edifying British Empire Christmas Cake:

> Of course for pupils like Davis, whose parents had one of those grocery shops with pencils of salami dangling over the doorway, the whole thing was too simple, but looking back on it, and remembering the proximity of so many of us to the breadline, I assume that one or two of our number must have been hard put to muster even the smallest contribution.
>
> In the event, the trouble was not the contributions so much as the form they took. There was, for instance, the curious case of Towbridge, who was so clumsy that when hairs first started to sprout on his legs, he kept falling over. It was the desire of Towbridge's mother to donate towards the cake a bona fide English newly laid egg, but being conversant with her son's wayward ways, she knew perfectly well that there was no way he was going to cover the 200 yards from home to school without spreading the egg all over somebody, probably himself. So she

came up with an infallible antidote to her son's ineptitude. She gave him the egg hard-boiled.

Then there was the even more bizarre case of Ron Lockie, who arrived full of smiles on the Wednesday morning bearing three pieces of lump sugar and a hammer. As for Gardiner, notorious throughout the borough as the only schoolboy extant to have two partings in his hair, and who sometimes turned up for school wearing one of those old-fashioned swimming costumes with the shoulder straps over his shirt and jersey, his offering was an apple he had picked up off Great Titchfield Street market, and which he had magnanimously refrained from eating more than half of.

I see also in my mind's eye the face of a girl, whose name has been erased by the years, her blonde hair ruined by an institutional haircut, her right hand outstretched to reveal a wizened maraschino cherry which, she assured us, must be right for a Christmas cake because it had already been in one the previous year. I remember the great Rademsky, his grasp of geopolitical realities as shaky as his grasp of everything else, going to the trouble of acquiring a fragment of Austrian smoked cheese in the belief that Austria was an abbreviation of Australia. And the idiotic Davis who, having been told by his mother to 'find something in the shop', had finally decided on a pickled cucumber.

Although my own contribution, four ounces of Australian sultanas, was a modest one, particularly as I had eaten half of it by the time I reached school that morning, I took an interest in the making of the cake, the intensity of which far surpasses any later involvement of mine with any of the culinary arts. I think, perhaps, it was a repeat of the business about the leaf of the lime tree. For reasons which perhaps have no logical basis, the scene has stayed with me ever since, of Daisy Head, the aureole of flaxen hair framing her frown of concentration, placing all our offerings on her own large desk, going through the items of this quaint gallimaufry to ensure that no subversives had succeeded in slipping something in from beyond the Empire.

But no, all was as it should be: peel from Cyprus; sugar from Trinidad; flour made from Canadian wheat; nuts from Africa; butter from New Zealand; even a tot of rum from Jamaica, contributed by a girl called Bromley, whose parents had come to an interesting reciprocal arrangement with a public house in Tottenham Court Road, where they agreed to keep it so long as it kept them ... Clearly, it was going to be a glorious, spectacular, unforgettable mess.[11]

Having taken turns at stirring the resultant mixture, the class escorted Miss Head as she bore her mixing bowl to the oven in the first floor Common Room, where it was left overnight. The next morning, the eager chefs arrived at school, looking forward to digesting this culinary impossibility with their mid-morning milk:

> Most memorable of all was the anti-climax of the unveiling, when, after listening to a short address from Miss Head on the theme of the Empire on which the sun never set, we saw with our own eyes that the cake hadn't set either, and that what should have been an altitude at the centre of about ten inches had shrunk in the night to three and a half.
>
> I think I must have eaten my slice with the customary indifference of the normal schoolboy, but I do remember quite distinctly the hapless Winnie having hysterics yet again when her slice was found to include among its African nuts and Jamaican rum one Waterman's pen-nib and a fragment of underdone elastic.
>
> Most vivid of all though, is the morning before; the morning of the gathering-in of our great imperial enterprise. Although it is mid-morning, the lamps have been lit, so that we seem to be safe inside an iridescent bubble of warmth and light floating on the great ocean of soupy gloom gathering outside the windows. Buzzing with expectation we ask excited questions and exchange hysterical jokes, exultant in the knowledge that term is almost over and that once the ceremony of this amazing, phenomenal beautiful cake is complete, days of limitless freedom stretch ahead.
>
> All the pressures and problems have been laid aside against the New Year. Next year. It might as well be next century, next millennium. 1939. It has a surreal, almost Wellsian sound ...
>
> We all watch, contented enough to bake cakes instead of do lessons, blissfully unaware that for this school there will be no next Christmas; that we are its last intellectual heirs, that come next Christmas we will be scattered around the country; that come the one after that the very

room we stand in will be burning in the name of some imbecilic doctrine; that Daisy Head will disappear from our lives as suddenly as she came into them; and that the thirty-two of us, apparently so irrevocably committed to a corporate fate, will soon disperse never to come together again. The baking of a Christmas cake. The end of childhood.[12]

During 1938, Benny had taken his Eleven Plus, and had won a London County Scholarship to nearby Marylebone Grammar. But instead of turning up at his new school, he and Class One were summoned back to Clipstone Street on 1 September in extraordinary circumstances. Their grim-faced headmaster explained that with war and the certain annihilation of London looming, they would be evacuated:

When our teachers foolishly told us of this dark prediction, a few of the boys in the school, sons and heirs of drunken, brutalised fathers, thought this was an excellent arrangement, and began cheering.[13]

A Wartime Adolescence

Country Life 7

Benny's adolescence is bookended by the war. When it began, he was an eleven-year-old about to have his long summer holiday of sport and general miscreance terminated by his 'promotion, if that is the word, to a conspiracy of the higher learning' that was Marylebone Grammar. He spent the morning of September 3rd, 1939 in improbable circumstances, 'a small boy surrounded by strangers in a sunny Hertfordshire garden'.[1] By the time it ended on May 5th, 1945, he was in his eighteenth year, 'a hulking young man surrounded by loyal friends, perched on the window sill of Lyons' Corner House in Coventry Street looking down on scenes of euphoric bacchanalia', and one for whom the intervening years had crystallised his ambitions, and had even seen him begin the long task of their realisation. As markers in Benny's growth, the war's first and last days were for him a strange mixture of the personal, the national and the global:

> Both those moments are etched on the memory, as though for a split second the world stopped turning in deference to the cosmic photographer compiling evidence of a pregnant event. The six years between those two snapshots changed the face of civilisation, recast the map of Europe, wrote some of the most lurid chapters in the long history of the British, saw priceless things go up in smoke, and some others reborn.[2]

As one of those whose experience of the war was comparatively benign, and as it coincided with the bittersweet time of his teenage years, Benny viewed the war period with mixed feelings. On the one hand, his childhood was one of the priceless things that had gone up in smoke, a passage which the Luftwaffe had marked with considerate symbolism by blowing up Clipstone Junior Mixed along with half the other buildings of the district. On the other hand, the war had replaced the narrow world of that childhood, wedged as it was with reassuring closeness into 'a sizeable colony of the poor',[3] with a broader social horizon, even if the means had involved the arbitrary use of high explosives and high snobbery. And at some point in those years, Benny had understood that his potential could only be realised in this new world, and had also consciously decided to set himself apart from his family in the pursuit of artistic success. The shock of the outside world, and the break with the world of childhood that it represented, was felt on the first day of evacuation:

The breaking point duly turned up on Friday, September 1st, when we had no sooner arrived in the playground than we were sent home again for our luggage, and told to return as quickly as possible. We were then marshalled in ranks while the roll-call was taken. A few names went unanswered, this being my first inkling that sometimes the best way to defy authority is simply to ignore it. We were then given identity labels to attach to our coats and marched off to the first way-station en route to Somewhere in England. It was the end of the world as we knew it, and we tried to take it as a bit of a lark, especially when we realised that our destination was the old familiar, the local Underground station at the end of Great Portland Street. Although there were several possible routes to it from our school, there was no way we could have marched there without passing my grandfather's house.

It so happened that the route chosen was due north down Bolsover Street, which meant that we had to pass directly under the windows of my grandfather's first floor workroom. I recall my excitement to find that all along our route, anguished adults lined the pavements, peered from windows, paused in shop doorways clustered in solemn groups, waving or shouting goodbye. There seemed to be hundreds of sobbing women waving handkerchiefs. As we approached the junction of Bolsover and Greenwell Streets, I was uplifted mightily by the sight of my entire family, some standing on the pavement, some clustered at the open windows, gaping aghast at the pathetic crocodile of raga-muffins proceeding down the street and into history. And there, leaning from the window with tears streaming down her face, arms held out, was Ginnie. My mother was there, white-faced but stoic, and my father, trying to put on a cheerful smile to encourage me. What was Ginnie weeping over? Patently not me, to whom she had shown such prolonged indifference for so long. But if not for me, then who? My confusion over this, my desperately hopeful wave to my parents, commingled with my wretchedness at being snatched from the blissful existence I had known, made it impossible for me to gather any coherent impressions at all, but my father's thoughtful smile and Ginnie's hysterical tears have stayed with me.[4]

When the evacuees reached Great Portland Street station, they expected to be taken round the Circle Line to Paddington, 'and from there down to the orchards of the West'.[5] Instead, they were taken to one of the antipodes of the Metropolitan Line, 'a sort of genteel Sleepy Hollow called Moor Park', on the cusp between the outer suburbs and the Hertfordshire countryside.[6] To the inner-city children, it seemed as if they had been decanted into a parallel world of implausible affluence.

We were ordered to alight and stand in a huge nearby tent with field attached, where a group of ladies from assorted voluntary services were waiting to tick off names, many of which must have seemed to them unpronounceable, and bribe us into compliance with bars of chocolate. Two by two, we were driven off in the waiting Wolseleys and Armstrong-Siddeleys to outposts of the Home Counties more opulent than any of us had ever seen outside the cardboard world of Hollywood. I was paired off with a gentle, passive classmate called Max, and taken to a palatial pile a short walk from the station, where, for the next six weeks, we and our billetors co-existed in an atmosphere of mutual loathing. Mr and Mrs D. were a childless couple whose only attempt to fructify a barren alliance was to drink gin and play golf. The size of their house obliged them to take in children, but if they had to do their bit for the war effort, they could at least do it with bad grace.

Much has been made, and I suspect too much, of the sentimental notion that the War brought the classes together. Certainly the evacuation scheme had the effect of flinging disparate sections of society into each other's astonished arms. When Max and I arrived in Moor Park, we were stupefied by the evidence of wealth around us, which seemed so vast as to have nothing to do with us at all. We came from tenements to a detached house with five bedrooms. The drawing room alone was larger than the flat in which I had been living with my parents all my short life. We had been flung out of the crumbling muddle of back streets behind Euston Road, where the appearance of a private car outside a domestic cell was exotic enough an objet d'art to draw a crowd of goggling juveniles, to a home with two cars in the garage. The first intimations of wealth unbounded had come with the presence outside the tent of a few men wearing the livery of chauffeurs, but the final sensation that we were, socially speaking, in over our heads came with the presence in the house of one Kathleen, a bespectacled housemaid crisply starched in the green-and-white uniform of her rank, complete with obligatory crown – the lunatic cap designed for the express purpose of letting the underlings know their place.

Two days after our arrival, on a Sunday morning which proved to be part of an Indian summer, Mr D. gravely requested our presence in the garden at eleven o'clock. The drawing room wireless was clearly audible through the open French windows, and when Mr Chamberlain began to speak we knew that in some mysterious, unspecified way a time of danger was about to begin, but not for us, because we had been secreted away in this suburban bolthole. We listened to the Prime Minister saying that a state of war now existed between Britain and Germany, and then, I think but could not swear, they played the National Anthem. After the broadcast was over, Mr D. began to instruct us in the duties of a patriot, saying that we must conduct ourselves like gentlemen at all times, and that a sure sign of the species were shoes whose undersoles had been polished. He then gravely presented us with an elixir of jingoism – a jigsaw puzzle showing the brave resistance of the Welsh Borderers at Rorke's Drift. A little later we heard for the first time the banshee wail of the air-raid siren, and were led to a cupboard under the stairs, where there were stocked so many cases of tinned food, candles, gin and spare golf balls that there was hardly room for us. Then the 'All-Clear' went, and life reverted to the torpor of an English middle-class Sunday.[7]

A few hours later, relations between unwilling hosts and unwilling evacuees reached a terminal *froideur*. Whatever they may have expected, it appeared that no one had forewarned Mr and Mrs D that apart from being distastefully poor, their charges would compound that offence with their Jewishness:

The discrepancy became especially painful to Mr D. that evening, when his attempt to take us to the local church to pray for victory was undone by the dismaying discovery that he had drawn a brace of infidels in the

evacuation sweepstake. He had conjured a scenario of a benign patri-
arch escorting a pair of chirpy cockneys to the presence of a God whose
mighty power would induce a succession of 'cor-stone-the-crows' and
'cor-strike-a-light-guvnor'. This tableau having been mocked by the facts
almost before we had crossed the threshold of the house, he retired
ruffled, and had no more to do with us during my stay under his roof.[8]

It was Benny's first encounter with class snobbery and genteel anti-Semitism.
He was to have his revenge on the bigots of Moor Park. Forty-four years almost
to the day after his arrival as an evacuee, the adult version of the scorned
evacuee of 1939 accompanied me to a pair of gates that abutted what had once
been Mr and Mrs D.'s garden, for my first day as a public schoolboy. Not that
much had changed in Moor Park in the half-century since his brief residence
there. On my first day, rumours circulated among the predominantly Jewish and
Asian intake that until only a few years before, there had been a 'quota' system
in place to control the number of non-white and non-Christian pupils. Mr and
Mrs D's golf club had still not admitted a single Jewish member, although it has
made a token nod to the modern world by allowing Bruce Forsyth and Jimmy
Tarbuck to trample its hallowed greens during charity matches.

Benny's exile in Moor Park stretched out for six weeks, until his father
ventured out of the West End to bring him the news that his grammar school had
regrouped, and requested his scholarly presence in Redruth, in deepest Cornwall, leaving Max to fend for himself in Moor Park. But this was not the last that
Benny was to see of Max Kaminsky. Several years later, the longeurs of an afternoon in the dark as a film critic were interrupted when Benny, enduring *Ben Hur*,
sat bolt upright with the realisation that one of the galley slaves with whom
Charlton Heston was rowing for his life was none other than Max, now rowing
under the stage name 'Maxwell Shaw'.

Benny travelled down to his Cornish exile by train. It was a long journey, on
which the passengers conducted themselves with suitable seriousness:

The rail journey started from Paddington in the morning, and long before
it ended we were chugging through a Stygian landscape obliterated by
the blackout regulations. Ours was a smoking carriage, and each of the
passengers, when lighting a cigarette, would bend carefully over the
match in an attempt to maintain our cover.[9]

Clearly wishing to preserve its precious crop of human capital, Marylebone Grammar had moved its pupils not to the edge of the city, but to what seemed like the edge of the earth, where the war hardly ever intruded:

> One day at dusk a crippled German bomber dropped a stray incendiary on a pile of rubble at the back of the local railway station, and on an ominous Sunday in the week of Dunkirk we went to Falmouth and saw the troopships unloading their cargoes of fugitive Canadian infantry. Once or twice the warning sirens sounded, but I cannot recall for what reason. The widowed lady and her two children on whom I was foisted was so wild a contrast to Mr and Mrs D. that it seemed I was living in a different war altogether, on a different planet. Mrs Smith, which I think, by the way, was mere euphemism for obscure domestic irregularities, could ill afford to house cuckoos in the nest, but she had taken in a third-former called Drew, and now myself, because she saw in the few shillings per head which the government doled out to evacuees, a chance to show a small profit. Mrs Smith ran the kind of establishment where you had to ask for formal permission before taking a slice of bread and margarine from the plate in the centre of the table. It was the first time I had experienced a poverty more grinding than my own, and I was not altogether grief-stricken when my stay proved to be a brief one.[10]

Mrs Smith's only other source of income was a 90-year-old lodger named Sturt, whose survival, and Mrs Smith's, depended less on his diet of weak tea and junket than on endless amounts of sleep. Deciding that the exuberant Benny represented a threat to Mr Sturt's life and her livelihood, Mrs Smith sent him back to the evacuee pool, from where he was 'promptly rebilletted two roads and a million miles away, in the detached house of a Mr Griffin, a local panjan-drum whose waddling, potbellied eminence was vested in his managership of the local branch of Lloyd's Bank'.

The Griffins lived in Clinton Road, at that time Redruth's smartest address, and although their lives shared the same outward trappings as Mr and Mrs D's (they were childless golfers with a maid), the resemblance stopped there. Mr Griffith 'exuded a comically Dickensian benignity', while his young wife Muriel 'was more like a soft touch of an aunt', and they seem to have treated Benny like their own child, with 'numberless small kindnesses' that allowed him 'to stick it out with them for more than a year'. Meanwhile, the bad news from outside Clifton Road kept coming in:

> The period with them coincided with the worst catastrophes of the war.
> It was in the dining room of the house in Clifton Road that I read of the
> fall of France, of the raging Battle of Britain, of the bewildering twists of
> fortune in the Western Desert ... When Chamberlain was replaced by
> Churchill, I gathered from the general mood of the household that this
> was thought to be a good thing in the muted purlieus of Clifton Road,
> although Mr Griffin retained a few doubts connected with Churchill's old
> reputation as a warmonger. As this seemed the ideal qualification for
> someone leading the nation into a fight for its life, I was amused by old
> Griffin's caution, and thankful for the extent of his patience with a bois-
> terous young stranger. Only once do I recall his tolerance crumbling. I
> had just discovered the delicious joke of 'Three Men in a Boat', and was
> reading the episode of the tin of pineapple in the lounge one tea-time
> when Griffin, intent on the financial pages of The Daily Telegraph, flung
> down the paper and said that if I could not control my laughter I would
> have to continue reading in the kitchen.[11]

More serious news was on Benny 's reading agenda in the flow of letters that his father sent to him from London, describing the nightly bombing of the city, and his brave attempt to keep his regular appointments at its greyhound tracks, bombardment permitting. Hearing of the bombing while being secluded in Redruth must have been intensely upsetting for Benny, particularly when offi- cialdom's own lurid pre-war descriptions of the imminent destruction of entire cities at the hands of the bombers are taken into account. The passage of time had not abated his homesickness, even if his mother had visited occasionally. In the spring of 1941, Benny returned to London for the school holidays, and never went back to Redruth:

> It may strike the modern reader as absurd that a fugitive from air raids
> should return to the centre of the target for something as contradictory
> as a holiday. But this had become common practice among the evacuee
> population, which had quickly realised that the odds against their

destruction were rather longer than those quoted by the politicians of the late 1930s. Certainly the return home was an eye-opener. The Boys' Club I had attended two evenings a week had been blown to pieces and replaced by a huge tank of water for use against incendiary bombs, and one of the little Nash cottages just inside the northern gates of Regent's Park, where once dwelt the uniformed ogre who guarded his conkers from our chair-legs, had vanished into the past, the only evidence that it had ever existed a broad patch of charred grass. Most outrageous of all, some lout had dropped a bomb on Clipstone Junior Mixed, slicing away its top storey and making a mess of the infants' playground.[12]

But despite these cosmetic alterations, 'the district seemed to be bearing up under the strain well enough'.[13] Noticing that enough of his contemporaries had stayed behind or returned to form two full football sides for their daily game in Regent's Park, Benny realised that a modulated version of normal life was still going on in London, and decided 'never to go back to the home of a stranger'. Amid the chaos of a blitzed city and the disorganisation of the school authorities, Benny joined the large population of school-age children whose education had lapsed into anarchy, and he found himself at total liberty, which he busily filled with all the entertainments of his pre-war normality. Inevitably, a central part of that normal life was sporting, and it was to be on the day of one of those memorable outings with his father, so redolent of the long-lost safety of the Thirties, that the war suddenly intruded into that fortress of childhood, his grandfather's house:

I joined a drifting colony of free spirits, and was blissfully happy to realise that in return for bombing and broken nights, it was still possible to enjoy peacetime delights that I had assumed to be locked away for the duration. The reference books tell me that the drawn Wembley Cup Final between Preston North End and my beloved Arsenal which my father and I attended took place on May 10th, 1941, and that in deference to the enemy, attendance was limited to 60,000. The same volumes tell me that my first international match, England v. Scotland at Wembley, was played on October 14th of that year before 65,000, and that the return match on the same ground took place on January 17th, 1942. It was on the night of one of those games that the war, till now a distant impediment to petty pleasures, suddenly became real.

People tended to make their own arrangements for sheltering from the raiders at night. One of my aunts spent the entire war sleeping on the northbound platform of Regent's Park tube station, where she became a citizen of a bizarre nocturnal township with its own conventions. I have a dim recollection of sheltering with my parents once or twice on the lower floors of a large office block facing our block of flats. But on the night when I savoured for the first time the reality of total warfare we were all seated in the cellar of my grandfather's house round the corner. This cellar stretched out under the macadam road surface of Greenwell Street, and may or may not have provided better protection than the cellar under the stairs of the house which I always yearned to explore and never did. The final vote went to the cellar under the road because, in the event of a direct hit on the house, we might survive in the cellar under the stairs but be entombed, whereas if a bomb hit the road then we would all go straight up and come down in the open air.

That night, there was the usual thumping and crumping of the anti-aircraft batteries around the Park. The men sat there engrossed in their game of Solo, arguing bitterly over each other's tactics, when the whistling descent of high-explosive bombs suddenly became close enough to disturb the spindrift of dust and cobwebs on the ceiling. Then there was a much louder screaming sound, followed by the loudest bang I have ever heard. The foundations of the cellar shifted, and the reverberations of the crash were followed by a frightful clatter of broken glass and flying bricks. I can see and hear my father leaping up and shouting to my grandfather, 'They've hit the house, but we're all right.'

Fearful of being buried under the rubble, we poked our heads around the cellar door to find the world had gone to hellfire. The night sky was bruised from the reflection of nearby fires, and pencils of criss-crossing light from the searchlights probed the clouds. We could hear people shouting and the wail of sirens, the clangour of fire-engines. But to our amazement, there the house still was. In the long narrow yard running between the entrance to the cellar and the outer walls of the house were a dozen incendiary bombs sputtering on the damp ground. My father grabbed a broomstick and prodded at one in an attempt to perform some obscure function known only to himself. By this time one of my aunts was standing at his side, complaining bitterly that in saying the house had been hit he was causing unnecessary anguish to the rest of the family, that he had always been a liar and a troublemaker even as a little boy, and that this whole thing was all his fault. At this point, the broomstick burst into flames, and my father offered it to her, saying that she, being an old witch, would know what to do with it. He then began emptying buckets of sand over the bombs, and this is how he was discovered by two ARP men who told us all to run for shelter in the building across the way.

All this time, the guns were banging away to a counterpoint of exploding bombs. We all trooped upstairs in the street, and as we were crossing the road to sanctuary a cluster of incendiaries scattered across our path. It comes back to me that, contrary to my expectations, the fire bombs did not just lie there, but jumped and fizzed like so many spitting cats. We picked our way through them and were soon safe underground. It was then that I noticed my grandfather was still clutching the last hand dealt to him before the interruption to the card game. A week later he was still grumbling that the raid had deprived him of an absolutely certain, cast-iron Abundance.

When we emerged into the still smouldering street next morning, it was to see that a huge explosion had blown away half the block, leaving the northern end flattened except for my grandfather's house, which now stood, like the last decaying tooth in a decrepit head, forlorn in the debris of its old companions. It was a misfortune with consolations, for another of my aunts, the insanely snobbish one, derived much gratification in later years by telling people that her father lived in a detached residence.[14]

The Return of the Native 8

Paradoxically, it was the wartime interruption of normal schooling that was to provide Benny with what he always considered to have been his real education. Set free from the constraints of classroom and syllabus, he was also able to continue his serious investigations into the world of literature that had begun with Daisy Head's parting legacy, a copy of Lewis Carroll's *Alice's Adventures in Wonderland* for the class prize, and had continued in Clifton Road with *Three Men in a Boat*. Furthermore, his temporary liberation from the snobbish mediocrity of Marylebone Grammar by his flight from Redruth gave to Benny's demanding sporting programme the spare time to accommodate a new passion: the saxophone:

> By some obscure process, in the months when I was drifting out of the gravitational pull of the schools, I had experienced what some have defined as the birth of intellectual passion, and was beginning to subject myself to a regimen more rigorous by far than any teacher would have thought practical or even feasible. I had become a passionate music student, to my own astonishment as much as anyone else's, and, by the time of the great raid, was already able to render 'The Bluebells of Scotland' and 'The Sunshine of Your Smile' on the smaller of the two saxophones languishing in my father's wardrobe, dusty symbols of his considerable exploits as a professional musician in the Twenties. To return to school would mean wasting endless hours on Latin and Maths which could more profitably have been spent acquainting myself with the intricacies of improvisation.[1]

Encouraged by his father, with whom he would practise each day on duets, Benny threw himself into regular practice. Often, he played for as long as four hours a day, much to the distress of his neighbours, some of whom worked nights, and all of whom soon tired of endlessly repeated amateurish renditions of 'The Bluebells of Scotland'. But after several months, this epic of truancy had begun to perturb even his father, a man whose own contribution to Benny's education had been disbursed at the White City Stadium, and Dave located a school for him. The large numbers of returned evacuees who were roaming the streets and parks of the city had obliged the government to invert its own policy, and set up schools in the city to continue the education of this new and unruly catchment, where as Benny's form master put it, there coagulated 'the scum of the grammar school system, although the fact that his feat of floating so comfortably on its surface had left him with an oleaginous face seemed never to have struck him':[2]

The William Ellis School, named after a heretic whose persistent handling of the ball when playing football had resulted in the codification of a new game called rugby union, sat upon the southern fringes of Parliament Hill Fields, and had been lying barred and shuttered ever since its pupils had been packed off to the country. At some point after the outbreak of the war but before we heard about it, William Ellis had been selected as the site for a glorious fiasco called the North London Emergency Secondary School, the repository for all the waifs, delinquents, truants, rebels and petty criminals who had used the incident of evacuation as a pretext for a life of reckless hedonism. Because the teaching staff of William Ellis was either serving in the armed forces or teaching down in the country, the instructors at the NLESS were, to use the kindest of euphemisms, the dregs of the profession, or dotards dragged out of retirement, or young ladies with no suspicion of what they were letting themselves in for. I remained in this madhouse for about two years, by far the most memorable of my school career. Not that I didn't learn anything worth knowing there. I greatly improved my technique as a stopper centre-half, was privy to sexual discussions as informative as any I experienced in later life, sharpened my wits in the cause of truancy, was introduced to the unblemished pleasures of running, thanks to the proximity of the Parliament Hill track, and came for the first time to realise that there are clowns in this life whom no restrictive measures can contain, and that when we encounter them we should be thankful.

At the NLESS I encountered at least fifty of the species, among them Woolmer, a goggle-eyed grinning slobberer who spent his lunch breaks wandering around the Heath eating as many insects as he could catch,

102

and innocently terrorising old ladies by standing before them and stuffing mouthfuls of grass down his throat. There was Black, T., who in an attempt to express his idolatry of the then Arsenal forward, inscribed his art exercise book with the name 'Drake, E.', persisting so doggedly with this imposture that when, after a year the art master received the report of Black, T. he complained to the Headmaster that no such boy existed, and furthermore, what had happened to the documents concerning Drake, E.? There was Mr Purdy, a one-armed wreck of a teacher whose disabilities, mental as well as physical, caused him to set fire either to himself or the equipment in the chemistry lab two or three times a month. And there was Morecambe, whose truancy was so persistent that some of the teachers claimed never to have seen him, and whose life was so shrouded in mystery that whenever we happened to bump into him and ask what his game was, he would redden, smirk, and light an evasive De Reszke Minor. All became clear when More-cambe, although no more than a fourth-former, left to get married to the love of his life, a girl at the school next door, who was about to present him with a son and heir ... There was Reece, who openly courted the young Scots lady who arrived one day with the hopeless task of teaching us English Literature. And a very prim-looking bespectacled boy who used plasticine to make a cast of the caretaker's keys and gain access to the school's stationery cupboard.[3]

The only other alumnus of this shambles to achieve public success was the badger-striped sports commentator Dickie Davis, which was rather apt considering that the pupils of the NLESS devoted most of their time to leisure pursuits. For Benny, that meant running rather than the traditional schoolboy activities of smoking and seduction. This was one aspect of our father's early life that his children had trouble digesting. As far as we knew, he was chronically indisposed to any physical activity other than watering the strawberry patch, and target practice with a football, for which pursuit he had trained us in such a way that he could play a full game without ever having to run anywhere. As his first son, Justin became the goalkeeper, who after fending off the half-volleys that rocketed around his ears and over the garden wall, could retrieve the ball and roll it back out to Benny. As second son, I was deputed as right winger, who could scurry up the side of the rose beds and then fire the ball over to Benny, who had ambled up to the six-yard line while I was dribbling around imaginary defenders. Leo, as the third assistant, was prepared for all eventualities, and was able to double as both goalkeeper and winger should either of the first choices be indisposed through homework.

The idea of Benny actually moving at speed without being a passenger in a car driven by a more mechanically minded person was inconceivable. He seemed to think it was a hazardous notion, and when the chance came to prove it, his suspicions were nearly validated. In the early Eighties, as jogging became fashionable, a *Breakfast TV* researcher persuaded Benny, who by now had developed the relaxed figure of the man of leisure, to join in with the show's post-Christmas fitness programme. He was duly weighed on air, an indignity which he took in his leisurely stride, and kitted out with a burgundy tracksuit and a diet plan. We were all following these events with incredulity, particularly my mother, who had spent years trying to lever him into a tracksuit without success.

The next morning, a camera crew turned up, to film him jogging around the village. Kings Langley sits on the side of a steep hill, and so when we turned on the TV that morning we were amazed to see Benny jogging along its crest, looking to the viewing public as if he had just run a brisk half-mile uphill at 8:30am on a January morning. Of course, we didn't realise that he had cadged a lift from the camera crew to the top of the hill, and had then run all of fifty yards. But it was what happened in that short fifty yards that was really worrying. The effort appeared to be impairing his sense of direction, and as he gently trotted on, he was slewing all over the country lane, which was unusually busy at that time of the day, owing to the mothers hurtling their offspring to the school up the road. The morning calm was shattered by screeching brakes, skidding cars and shrieking car horns, in response to which Benny would either furrow his brow still further and stick to his suicidal course, or leap into the bushes at the side of the road. To the *Breakfast TV* audience, it seemed as if the fitness programme was just too demanding for one of their celebrity fellow-dieters, who, exhausted by his uphill sprint, had decided to end the torture by jogging under the wheels of a passing Range Rover. When her mud-spattered husband returned home glowing with athletic pride, he could not understand why my shocked mother banned him from any further excursions of this kind. After the jogging fiasco, Benny never exercised again, although the episode did have one useful function, as he soon developed a taste for tracksuits, which he found very comfortable when lounging in front of the cricket.

But as a teenager, Benny had been an obsessive runner, and to prove it to his doubting offspring could even produce yellowing certificates testifying to his success in middle-distance road racing during the war. With the track on Parliament Hill closed 'on the intrinsically British and fairly imbecilic assumption that nobody would want to train in the winter',[4] he had taken to running regularly around the Outer Circle of Regent's Park. Latterly, when his family drove into London from Kings Langley, Benny would always indicate the spot where he would wash his feet in the Regent's Canal after his exertions. To us children, this seemed faintly comic, an improbably bucolic survival amid the great city of our father's youth, like Evans's Dairy on the corner of Warren Street. We did not realise that he had chosen to wash his feet in the canal because the flat in Howard House had no bath:

> Of course, running was not my life, or even half of it. I considered football and playing the saxophone at least as important, but there was certainly a period when running was on a par with each of those obsessions and might easily have usurped both of them had circumstances and my own temperament been very slightly different. But I never really discovered what you might call the mystical pleasures of running until my first winter. At the beginning of September the track at Parliament Hill was closed, and so I took to the road, running two or three times a week, weather permitting, round the Outer Circle at Regent's Park, a distance of some three and a half miles, trotting back to my base at the youth club as the plane trees of Fitzroy Square flung their long, slanting shadows behind me.
>
> These night runs were lonely – which was their great attraction. I soon found that only in isolation does the runner begin to be hypnotised by the mechanistic activities of his own body.[5]

Perhaps the true attraction that running held is contained in those last sentences. If the only child found friendship with his peers in the park's endless games of football, it was only in the solitude of his wintry jogs that the adolescent Benny could find any privacy. Living in oppressive proximity to his parents, with a chorus of aunts and uncles always ready to offer their pessimistic opinion of his prospects, there was no other way to be alone than to literally run from them at speed. From his evacuee's exposure to the world outside the frustration and poverty of his childhood's tailoring and gambling milieu, Benny had realised because or despite of his father's hopeless example, he would have to choose some kind of profession, and commit himself to it fully. This revelation had coincided with the onset of adolescence, a time rich with dreams. It had been followed by Dave's well-timed gift of the saxophones, which had ignited a passion in Benny. But how to pursue his unlikely ambition to follow in his father's erratic musical footsteps? And how to actually succeed in doing so? In other words, how to become an artist?

A clue can be found in a crumbling diary for 1943, which Benny rediscovered in 1975, although at first he was perplexed by its 'adolescent hieroglyphics':

March 10	3.25
March 11	3.00
March 12	0.10
March 13	Gumboils
March 14	Ditto
March 15	4.10
March 16	4.00

There were enough entries surviving to tell me that in the month of March 1943 I was incapacitated by gumboils four times, a swollen nostril once, a septic thumb once and earache twice, and that if I added up the residue of the figures, they came to 41.30. But the puzzling thing was, 41.30 what? Certainly it wasn't anything to do with earnings, because I never earned anything before 1947. Equally, it was nothing to do with my weight, which, as far as I remember, never fluctuated as wildly as all that, not even when I was afflicted by gumboils.

I then wondered whether the mysterious entries might not be connected with obscure events of the period connected with my attempts to become a great middle-distance runner, but that theory foundered on the rock of the entry for March 12. What distance could I possibly have covered in 0.10? And then just as I was about to give up and throw the scraps of paper away, it all came back to me.

Those seven entries I have quoted, and the ones which followed them, told me that during the month of March 1943 I practised for forty-one and a half hours on the saxophone, that the rigours of my self-imposed responsibilties brought about frequent if minor afflictions connected with the acts of breathing and blowing a metal mouthpiece, and that at 16 I had already learnt enough about myself to realise that unless I kept a statistical record of what I was up to, my innate laziness of disposition allied to my talent for perverse argument would cause me to default on my own ambition even while convincing myself I was doing nothing of the kind.

The rediscovery of those pages from my old diary has tempted me to do a few calculations, and I am now faced with the alarming statistic that between my 14th and 23rd years, I practised one reed instrument or another for roughly 15,000 hours, or roughly 620 days, or nearly two years without stopping to eat or sleep. (At least that is how it must have seemed to the other people in the street.)[6]

Benny had recognised that the answer to his dilemma of realising his aspirations lay in a fanatical devotion to his instrument. In effect, this amounted to a conscious withdrawal from his father's family, and a rejection of the more conventional existence that a grammar school entrant might be expected to follow. To his duets with his father was added a course of lessons from Dave's old bandleader at the Kit Kat Club in Wardour Street,[7] Harry Hayes, the local star of Swing tenor. If anyone deserves the accolade of being the godfather of jazz in Britain, it is Harry, who witnessed the first jazz concert in Britain (the Original Dixieland Jazz Band's 1919 show at the Hammersmith Palais), and who is now in his nineties. Harry recalls Benny as a model pupil. He also recalls Dave as 'a gentleman', notwithstanding a particular taxi journey after one of their gigs during which Dave and one of their female companions had sex in the back of the crowded cab.

But even regular practice was difficult in the unpropitious surroundings of Howard House. He took to using one of the upper rooms of the house in Green-well Street, whose population had started to thin as Benny's aunts and uncles married and moved out. Of course, while this arrangement may have pleased the insomniac night-workers of Howard House, it did not delight Aunt Ginnie, who in the light of the *Alice* books, now seemed to have 'the Red Queen's fury made flesh'.[8] When playing, Benny would beat time with the heel of his right shoe. One day, when negotiating a particularly intricate treatment of 'On The Sunny Side of The Street', he managed to keep time with such enthusiasm that he stuck his foot straight through the floorboard on which he stood. As he noted later, 'in our district, it was not a rare thing for there to be holes in the carpet, but we were the only family with a hole in the floor'.[9]

While Benny persevered with his early efforts on the saxophone, there were other responsibilities to be observed, particularly those that came with the abatement of the Blitz, and the subsequent return of Marylebone Grammar from its Cornish bolthole to its pre-war grounds on the corner of Marylebone Road and Lisson Grove. In 1944, Benny was thus finally obliged to subject himself to the full range of indignities then considered part of a young gentleman's education. His headmaster was a Mr Wayne, known as 'Dickie', a nickname which Benny correctly surmised to be some kind of character reference. The problem lay in the chasm between the traditions of the school as amplified by its headmaster, and the background of its pupils, a chasm into which Benny, with his strong anti-authoritarian bent and class pride, fell headlong. While Marylebone Grammar was outwardly a typical grammar school of the period, it had a special flavour that came from Dickie's determination to foster the 'moth-eaten fiction ... that we were a venerable public school':

> Every aspect of its structure was rigged to that end. The teachers wore black gowns. We were divided into houses even though there were neither boarders nor housemasters. We were awarded colours for games.
>
> The school uniform was compulsory, black jacket and striped trousers in winter, blazers in summer, dark blue with a yellow beehive on the breast pocket to indicate the school motto, 'Industry'. Homework was referred to as 'Prep', the playground as 'The Quad'. We played rugger, not soccer. There was much talk of honour, and precious little of it in relations between teachers and boys.
>
> At the centre of this dotty conspiracy sat Dickie, an unwitting lampoon of a Dickensian tyrant. I came, in time, to despise him for what I can only describe as his moral cruelty, by which I mean his relentless pursuit of certain ideals. We were given to understand that these ideals were vital to our spiritual survival. Whenever we were seen to be faltering, the blood gathered in his cheeks and he thundered with messianic fury ... Evidently believing, like his inspiration Thomas Arnold, that etiquette came before education, he was trying to turn us all into little gentlemen.[10]

The only obstacle to Dickie's dream lay in the vulgar reality of his charges, who were 'the cream of the gutters, so to speak, the back-street academic elite, graduates from the slums of Euston and Paddington and Edgware Road, sons of the working class with a culture inimical to everything that Dickie tried to instil'.[11] Of course, Dickie's assistants in his cultural crusade were the usual collection of pederasts, snobs and philistines that lurk in any Common Room. Benny reserved particular contempt for his English teacher:

> Even the most venerable classics were bowdlerised into respectability, and we were given to understand that Cleopatra had died a virgin, that Dido and Aeneas were just good friends, and that those lines in 'Venus and Adonis' where the goddess instructs, 'Graze on my lips, and if those hills dry, stray lower, where the pleasant fountains lie' were connected in some vague and unspecified way with architecture.[12]

When Benny challenged his teacher's assertion of Cleopatra's virginity, and mentioned Caesarion, her child by Julius Caesar of whose existence Benny had been apprised by his own reading of Bernard Shaw, the teacher was so scandalised that he told Benny to shut up, and that he was fit 'only to be a barrow-boy'. It is not surprising that Benny always had an ambivalent attitude towards education, its sporting component aside. He educated all of his children privately, but did his best to countermand his investment by instructing us to resist all forms of social control. He told us that we should 'ignore all the shit, and take from it what you need'. His face was a strange mixture of horror and amusement when, following his instructions to what I thought was the letter, I presented him with an armful of books, freshly stolen from the school library.

The only time he felt obliged to intervene in my own fraught schooling was when my term report featured my headmaster's laconic complaint, 'His language is occasionally disgusting', and even then Benny objected more on the grounds of limited vocabulary than outraged propriety. When I was sent off in front of him for brawling on the rugby pitch after clear provocation, I walked off towards him, expecting a wrathful reception, to find him smiling proudly. Of course, what aggrieved Benny about almost all educational institutions was not the principle, but the practice. Believing that everyone has a right to a full education, Benny was incensed by his teachers' deliberate mishandling of their responsibility in the name of control, which usually meant invoking social hypocrisies at the price of the quality of teaching. He was a proud autodidact, but only because he had to educate himself in the absence of any professional help, and he knew that he would have relished the intellectual opportunities of a conventional education. In my first term at Oxford, as I showed him around my College's quads, he was awestruck, and kept repeating the same two phrases, 'If your grandfather could see you here, he wouldn't believe it! ... It's a machine for learning!'

As for Marylebone Grammar, Benny eventually achieved every schoolboy's revenge fantasy, and returned to its hallowed portals a few days before its demolition, accompanied by a photographer from the *Mail on Sunday* magazine, before detailing each of the school's stuffy bigotries in print. For a man who was always bemoaning the ugly redevelopment of post-war London, Benny made an honourable exception in the case of his 'alma hitler'. He was delighted that it was about to be destroyed, and even assisted the developer concerned when it came to naming the block that would replace it. Considering the flatulence with which the school vaunted itself, it was surprisingly light on famous alumni. There was the historian Eric Hobsbawm, whom Benny later got to know under his jazz-writing alias of Francis Newton, and there was the England footballer John Barnes. But Benny went for the name that was closest to his heart, and also reflected his own experience of school: Jerome Court, after Jerome K. Jerome, the author of his beloved *Three Men in a Boat*,

who had joined as a ten-year-old in 1870 and left four years later, preferring to complete his education as a ticket clerk at Euston Station for ten shillings a week. Years later, he wrote, 'What a boy learns in six years at school he could, with the aid of an intelligent bookseller, learn at home in six months.'[13]

Fitzroy Square 9

The real focus of Benny's teenage years lay not in the pretensions of Marylebone Grammar, but around the corner from Howard House in Fitzroy Square, whose grand western face runs parallel to Cleveland Street, moments away on foot, but a world away from the slums amid which it sat so aristocratically. Fitzroy Square is the only square in the 'teeming quadrilateral' of Benny's childhood, and after our meander through the back-streets of Marylebone, its high stuccoes and graceful round garden cut an improbably refined and spacious sight after the grimy brickwork and mean proportions of the back-streets. The square is the physical and imaginary focus of that inspired creation of the literary-minded geographer, 'Fitzrovia', a name redolent of the seamier side of high culture in the first half of the century. Yet that name is incompatible with the streets through which we have followed Benny thus far; no one speaks of 'the slums of Fitzrovia' or of Fitzrovian children with rickets, although they do romanticise the poverty of Fitzrovia's struggling Bohemians and artistic dipsomaniacs. Unequivocally, Benny was a child of Marylebone, a far grimmer and less magical place whose quotidian geography happened to overlay the Bohemian streets of Fitzrovia, a distant artistic kingdom whose fortress was Fitzroy Square.

In the centre of the square's south side, there is a pedimented mansion, currently falling from grace as the office of an insurance company. What its refined original owners would have thought of their palace being overrun in the distant future by vulgarian financiers is barely imaginable, although it probably would not occasion as much ghostly surprise as some of its previous tenants. In 1941, after the West Central Jewish Lads Club was bombed out of its premises next door, it moved its operations into this impressive pile. With it arrived its ragged membership, including Benny, who came here on most evenings of an extended adolescence that ran from his return from Redruth in March 1941 to his twentieth birthday in December 1947, when he was too old to be a member of the club. Like most of its membership, he remembered it with unparalleled fondness and gratitude, as it was here that he found fraternal company with like minds of his own generation, and a forum for his burgeoning talents. Of the few bonds that this private man maintained to his last days, most of them were those connecting him to his adolescent confrères at the club, and the names of its members were always familiar to us: Dennis Turim, who made Benny a beautiful overcoat; Sid Eckman, who always ferried bagels out to Kings Langley when he visited; Lennie Pinckus; Sid Spigelman; Lionel Weiser, whose life became a terrible parable of a man eaten alive by marriage; Manny Plotski, whose life became an even more terrible parable of doomed artistry; not forgetting Michael Klinger, who, once he shed the avuncular influence of the club, metamorphosed from conscientious Sports' Secretary to film producer (*Get Carter*, *Zulu*) and porn cinema entrepreneur.

As far as I know, Benny was only ever a member of three clubs. One was Ronnie Scott's, the second was the MCC, and the third was West Central, which, with its beguiling amalgam of English manners and immigrant anarchism, was the closest to his heart. For all his gentle mockery of its institutions, Benny cherished its memory, not only for the friendships he had gained, but also because the club had provided a stage for his first efforts as writer and musician. While his official education at Marylebone Grammar was hurtling towards a confrontational conclusion fuelled by the fires of mutual contempt, Benny underwent an unlikely parallel development at West Central that without exaggeration could be said to have been the making of him:

> In the summer of 1942, by now practising daily on the saxophone, I joined the youth club … It was within the walls of this warren of a Victorian house that, for the next three years, I furthered my genuine, as distinct from my bogus education. Here it was that I acquired the ideals of service, of responsibility, of selflessness. Few of the two or three hundred boys who passed through the club in my time succeeded in living up to all the ideals all the time, but most of us tried, and even in failure were at any rate aware that we had failed. It was here that some forgotten, patient elder made me wise in the ways of committees, taught me to take minutes, encouraged me to speak in public. It was here that I mastered the diabolical machinery of pay-telephones, here that I dared to play the saxophone in public for the first time, here that I edited my first, and as it proved, last magazine.[1]

It was not until after Benny's death, reading the club's magazine *The Fitzroy*, that I realised just how devoted a member he had been, and how crucial the club had been in his growth as musician and writer. This unlikeliest of team players and committee men had not only captained various football and cricket teams, but had at times taken up a position in club affairs which can only be described as responsible, sitting on its committee and editing its magazine. Rather than the alienating snobbery of Marylebone Grammar, the club was an adolescent extension of the familiar Jewish world of his childhood. Encouraged by this approving familiarity, Benny felt able to begin acting out his private ambitions on the public stage. The mildewed copies of *The Fitzroy* that Benny kept with him for the rest of his life trace his rise from the anonymity of junior membership, through sporting success, to verbal outpourings that in the later issues threaten to take over the entire magazine. Equally surprising to me was that until the age of twenty, he used the name 'Bernard' or 'Bernie' Green.

But while we can trace clearly his teenage development as writer through the pages of *The Fitzroy*, Benny's growth as a musician was a much more fraught and obscure process. Although we were always amazed at how casually Benny would wander on to a stage with or without a saxophone and deliver a completely spontaneous lecture or performance with no discernible tension on his part, it seems that his ease in the public gaze was, like many of his talents, the result of hard practice. As the teenage Bernie, he had suffered from extreme self-consciousness, even playing the entirety of an early gig with his back to the audience.

This self-consciousness was twofold. With his innate talent there came a strong critical faculty that was as merciless in its dissection of his own callow efforts as it was the mature phrasing of the great Lester Young. There was also a second, less constructive self-consciousness, a different kind of self-criticism. This was an involuntary self-derogation, as if to pre-empt the hecklers within his family, a family where, with honourable exceptions such as Lily, everyone heckled Dave, and Dave heckled Fanny. As he became increasingly aware of this, Benny realised that he must separate himself from his extended family, in order to find a space in which he could continue the work of creating a new identity, that of artist, by which Bernie would become Benny.

An unpublished piece of early autobiography from the Fifties records Benny's first collaborative efforts on the saxophone, a triumph over his own self-consciousness if not over his audience:

My first real musical activities took place against a communal background, which was true of many tyros of my adolescence. There were several who were, like me, active participants in a youth club, and who found that the familiarity of the surroundings somehow helped to make their early crude efforts less shameful. With me this was not so. Music was only one of my many interests at the time and having distinguished myself in almost every sphere of club activity, I was horrified lest my clumsy attempts to play a saxophone appeared even more inept when contrasted with the comparative brilliance of my extra-musical achievements, of which being very adolescent and rather smug, I was very proud indeed.

By the time I joined the club at fourteen, I already knew of Bix [Beiderbecke] and Eddie Lang, could play the first sixteen bars of Bix's solo in 'Singing The Blues' on an old but still very serviceable soprano saxophone, could distinguish Goodman from Shaw and Joe Sullivan from Jess Stacy. I could play a few scales and knew the names of the notes on the staves. It was an enthusiasm which I kept more or less to myself for the good reason that there seemed to be no one apart from my father with whom I could share it.[2]

While Benny deferred his public debut until the unknown time when he would be 'ready', his friend Sid Spigelman goaded him into taking the plunge. Deciding to test his progress by playing with other would-be musicians, the fifteen-year-old Benny journeyed to distant Hendon for a rehearsal:

I cannot recall the exact details of the expedition, but one night in my sixteenth year I went over to another youth club in the northern purlieus of the city to play with four other young men who were learning to play. One of them, a pianist, was forming a band, and was scouring the youth clubs for recruits. Besides him, there was a trumpeter called Red, a guitarist would could play 'Angry' and 'Chinatown' with very little trouble, and a drummer who had acquired from his doting father a huge and over-elaborate drum kit which filled half the stage we used.

I arranged to go over to their club one Tuesday evening. Spigelman naturally accompanied me. None of us could read music at the time. None of us knew anything about improvising on harmonies and none of us knew very many tunes. Now although I was well aware of my own deficiencies, I was quite unaware of the deficiencies of the other four, with the result that by the time we arrived in Hendon, I had succeeded in inducing upon myself a kind of hypnotic trance of terror at my coming ordeal and shame at my inability. Spigelman kept reassuring me, recounting time and again my assets, the fact that my father had taught me, that I knew a certain amount of jazz history, that I had two saxophones of my own, none of which did much good except to make him stop biting his nails.

When I entered the small theatre of the club with Sid, the four other boys had already begun. For a moment or two, Sid and I stood at the back of the hall listening, hidden by the shadows. What I heard reassured me and discouraged me at the same time. The four of them were all dreadful, certainly no better than I, which meant that we would never succeed in forming any kind of a band, and that none of us would derive much benefit from our association with the other four. It is always the aim of the aspiring artist to work with others who are good enough to teach him, and yet not so much better that they will not tolerate him. On this first attempt to make music communally, there seemed little doubt that I was as good as all of them, except perhaps the trumpeter, who kept playing 'St James Infirmary Blues' with a drinking glass down the bell, which made it sound disturbingly authentic to Spig and me.[3]

What happened next shows just how unconfident Benny must have been in the first two years after Dave had given him the saxophones. Although he had practised assiduously, Benny had not dared to play outside the home. Unwilling to risk public humiliation, his secret 'woodshedding' had made him unexpectedly good by comparison with his less reticent peers:

I discovered as soon as I had taken my instrument out of its case that none of the other four knew any tunes. All of them had their own pet pieces, rather like my 'Singing The Blues' chorus, but none of them knew any actual tunes, an accident which gave me a tremendous ascendancy over all of them, for whatever my shortcomings, I did through my familiarity with the records I possessed know at least a dozen tunes, even to the extent of playing the Middle Eights coherently. The evening evolved into a tune-teaching instructive lecture. I showed them how to play 'I Found A New Baby', a task which took no more than twenty minutes or so, and we began to play. The experience was exhilarating to one who had never played with a live rhythm section before, but the results were too chaotic to give me any real pleasure. I think we arranged to meet once a week, call ourselves The Clubroom Jazzmen, and advertise in the local press, but nothing came of it.[4]

The practising continued for another four years, until one evening in 1946 when Spigelman, who seems to have taken on the duties of Sancho Panza for Benny's quixotic quest, found a group rehearsing in the theatre of a nearby evening institute, and suggested that Benny 'sit in' with them. To Benny's surprise, the group agreed to accommodate this unknown quantity. But he was so unsure of his playing that he felt unable to take up their offer, and had to be persuaded by his friends:

I bashfully declined, while my friends stood around me insisting and urging. Sid was quite violent in his reassurance that I could do myself justice in such company, so at last I agreed, ran all the way home for my instrument and ran all the way back again, arriving back at the hall in morbid fear that they had all gone home and tired of waiting for me, so out of breath that I had to stand outside the building for a full minute or two to regain enough breath to blow my instrument.

Fortified by the partisanship of my four supporters, I joined the trio. It was the first time in my life I had ever played with a rhythm section which knew even remotely what it was about, and at first the experience was too much for me. We played 'Tea For Two', and for the first sixteen bars I floundered all over the instrument, losing my place, to the despair of my friends and the embarrassment of the trio, and feeling all the time an insane desire to burst into shrieking laughter. It was the sheer exuberance of spirit at my release from the solitude of practising all those years in the front room, had I only realised. But soon I gathered myself, remembered all I had done and forgot all I could not do, which was the only thing to do under the circumstances, and settled down to enjoy myself and assert what ability I had.

I suppose 'Tea For Two' lasted no more than five or six minutes, but it seemed at least an hour that night. At the end of it, I had scored a colossal victory over myself. The trio, knowing nothing of my friends and the tenacity of their support, were naturally concerned only with what I could play, and were unanimously enthusiastic. They asked me to play another, which I did, while my friends hugged themselves in delight that one of us had succeeded in impressing anybody with anything.[5]

The group played again together the following night, and over the next six months played several public engagements at the institute's various social functions. Some of them even paid small amounts of money, although in an early taste of the sideman's lot most of it somehow ended up going to the guitarist's girlfriend, who had joined the group as a singer. Despite his chronic lack of confidence, by the time he left the club in 1947, Benny was on his way towards what seemed like the impossibly distant goal of professional musicianship. Ahead lay many more self-imposed trials of this kind, each a struggle between his desire to play and his lack of confidence in his musical powers, beginning that year with the fiasco that was his first professional engagement.

Becoming a jazz musician is a long and solitary process. To begin with, jazz is a minority interest, which means that a prospective musician has little chance of finding like minds if he's not already related to them. This accounts for the preponderance of musical dynasties in the small principality that is British jazz, in which the rudiments are passed down inside families, in the absence of any conventional academic opportunities of the kind standard among classical musicians. Given that Leo and I made our early musical steps in the company of the numerous Dankworths, Parnells, Bushes and Garnetts who were following their own forebears, no one inside jazz seemed to be surprised that a couple of Greens would also be on the scene. This made an amusing contrast to the questions often asked by those in more conventional employment, who construed our career choices less in terms of entering a family concern than in the pathology of the bloodier moments of Greek myth.

Provided the hopeful musician has located a source of records and teaching, then his problems really begin. Ahead of him lies nothing but endless solitary hours of practice, whose monkish style is equal parts Thelonius and Benedictine. For Benny, this was the period in which he eschewed the attractions of the Second World War for 15,000 hours of lonely blowing and heel-tapping. The sheer effort required from even the most naturally gifted student to master not only the baffling mechanics of his instrument and musical theory, but also to develop as an improviser of melodies, while remembering the tunes and changes

117

to dozens of songs, usually dispenses with most prospective players. Those that survive must then face the informal nature of the profession.

As in most freelancing, your employment prospects are dependent upon the contents of your address book. In other, more sheltered musical fields, the necessary contact-making among your peers is provided by the organised world of academic institutions. But not in the case of jazz, where garrulous sociability and a supple liver become crucial assets for the budding player. A problem thus arises: an adolescent who has spent most of his teens in profound and self-absorbed isolation must now seek work by taking often half-hearted part in the sort of aggressive socialising that has been conspicuously absent from his sequestered adolescence. Only then, when a jazz musician can accommodate the schizophrenic mental attitudes required of him by his art and its practice can he be pronounced a full professional, being by now virtually unemployable in any other field.

For Benny, the public self-assertions needed to generate work were difficult steps. Although his membership of the Boys Club may not have provided fellow-musicians of comparable talent or ambition, it did give Benny that network of intimate support that carried him forward when his lack of confidence threatened to publicly derail the talent that he was so earnestly acquiring in private. If it had not been for the Boys Club and his friends, I don't think Benny would have been able to conquer his natural shyness and become a professional saxophonist.

That said, it would be misleading to represent Benny's time at the club as being blighted by his struggle to become an artist. His subsequent success as a musician and writer can distort our perspective on those years, for it seemed that a considerable amount of time was spent in the innocent delinquency that is the natural preserve of teenage boys, even if Green, Bernard was a respectable member of the club committee:

> Mention of such abstractions as committees and minutes of meetings may mislead the reader into thinking that our tiny society was composed of rulers and ruled. Nothing could be further from the truth. Rulers and ruled were one and the same, a claim which requires some elucidation. Every six months, democratic elections were held for committee places. But once you won a seat, this did not mean that your demeanour changed overnight from rapscallion to paragon. In leafing through the

Minute Book, I see my own name leaping up at me like a reproach from the past. On October 24th, 1943 I, a respectable member of the club cabinet, am criticised for 'upsetting the equilibrium of the Discussion Group'; six weeks later I promise to attend compulsory activities more zealously 'once my leg has healed'; on February 10th, 1944 I am banished from the committee weekly meeting for 'behaving badly', and by November I am engaged in such a multitude of petty misdemeanours that my breaches are treated in batches: 'Green was accused of general misbehaviour, irreverence at prayers, creating a disturbance in the street outside the club, and breaking a chair leg in the Senior Billiard Room.'[6]

By the time of the club's reunion dinner in 1974, the minute book's true usefulness had become apparent:

For instance, a portly, balding gentleman insisted on telling me that he was a pillar of the community; all the time he spoke, the words kept floating before my eyes, 'A. was accused of playing dice on the club doorstep for money, and crowing in an offensive manner at passers-by. He was suspended for two weeks and warned that any further exhibitions of this nature would result in immediate expulsion.'

No sooner had this encounter ended than a man slapped me on the shoulders and started talking about his involvement in the higher reaches of local politics. Back came the message from the past: 'B., when accused of swearing, said he had not uttered a sound. Witnesses testified that he had mouthed disgraceful profanities without actually speaking. He was given a severe caution.'

Later, at the bar, two of my friends had a friendly argument about whether smoking causes cancer. The anti-smoking advocate, who reminded me of myself for the way he said that he had not smoked a cigarette for 2,646 and a half days now and never even thought about it anymore, made so passionate a speech about the obscenity of having anything to do with nicotine that he spilt Tia Maria down his trousers. I sat there marvelling at the revenges brought in by the whirligig of time: 'C., when accused of smoking in the junior table tennis room, said he was not smoking at the time. When asked to explain how smoke appeared to be coming out of both his nostrils, he said that it was a very cold night and it must have been condensed air. He asked if he could have his father's lighter back'.[7]

Not the least of the changes that time had made to the members of the club was the story of Benny and the heaviest object he ever lifted, albeit with assistance. I always knew him as a lifelong sufferer of backache, originally caused by the unnatural sitting position in which an orchestra saxophonist held his torso, leaning forward to the left while twisting to the right. This was exacerbated by his fanatical devotion to working while sitting in a comfortable chair. There is the story of how, after several weeks on his back with a slipped disc, Benny wanted to attend Tubby Hayes's funeral:

> My wife managed to lay me flat on my back in the car and drove to the cemetery slowly enough to avoid bumps. We were given special dispensation to drive to the graveside, where a large congregation was already gathered. My wife opened the boot of the car and started to drag me out feet first. Ronnie [Scott] came over while this was going on and, nodding to the shade of the late Bud Flanagan, said, 'Hardly worth going home, is it?'[8]

But there had once been a time when Benny had contributed to lifting a full-sized snooker table. As a member of the club, Benny had assisted several others in moving its heavy, slate-bedded table to a new location downstairs. All was going well until the party came to a switchback in the stairwell. With gravity getting the better of them, all of the porters lost their grip, leaving only the heroic man-child Podemsky between them and disaster. Unable to hold the table's enormous weight, Podemsky was forced aside, and the table shot through a window before impacting on the pavement of Fitzroy Square two storeys below. Fortunately, there were no club members playing dice on its steps at the time. Thus Benny was inducted into the exclusive company of those who can claim to have defenestrated the heaviest item of sporting equipment known to Man.

Apart from providing a ready-made fraternity which could salve the isolation of an only child, the club was also the incarnation of Benny's Jewishness, which he defined as a strong social allegiance uncorrupted by minimal religious content. As the third consecutive generation of Greens not to be barmitzvah,

Benny could claim to be a secular Jew of impeccable pedigree, much to the distress of his mother, who lit the Sabbath candles every Friday, provided Dave hadn't pawned them first. Fanny's ambitions for her son had stretched her meagre earnings to provide him with a short-lived course of Hebrew lessons. Although he had an ear for language, Benny had no taste for it in the service of dogma, and the sum vestige of his childhood brush with Judaism was one word, 'yad' (hand), whose meaning he would demonstrate over lunch by furrowing his brow with Mosaic gravitas and raising an open palm in a manner which was either in impersonation of Charlton Heston in *The Ten Commandments*, or of a Red Indian saying 'How'. In fact, 'swords and sandals' epics were the limit of his truck with religion, which he considered to be a socially manipulative racket, whose practice subverted the very ideals it was supposed to promulgate.

Not that he had no interest in the ancient world or in religious texts. He had a thorough knowledge of the classics in translation, and knew his Aristophanes from his Apuleius, and I was surprised to find amongst his paperbacks a well-thumbed copy of the Koran. But as a youthful Shavian, he was a utopian atheist, and had no time for piety. Indeed, his atheism ran so deep that in later life he was an enthusiastic member of the free-thinking Secular Society, and would regularly harangue back into line any members whose atheism had backslid to agnosticism, deism, pantheism or any other heretical folly. I think the only moment he ever questioned my own often erratic judgement to my face was during one of our nocturnal chats at Langley, after I had begun learning Hebrew. Doing his best to steer daintily around his worst fears, he tried to ascertain whether my interest was philological, or had I undergone some terrible Damascene revelation, and fallen into the ranks of the deluded? His relief when I explained that my interest was merely literary was palpable. Unlike his father, who on his deathbed had ruminated with a straight face, 'You know, I've been thinking. Perhaps there is a God', Benny was a determined atheist to the last, and died as he predicted he would, with a smile. Benny's life was a demonstration of the Jesuitical cliché about religious education, but turned on its head. Given the child of seven, Dave had raised the atheistical man.

Benny was a humanist, and a believer in freedom of conscience and speech. He was not afraid to stick his neck out in print. He once described Mrs Thatcher's government as 'inhuman', and was the only television critic to object when, in the late Sixties the government pressured Thames Television into not screening *Hang Up Your Brightest Colours*, a documentary about the Irish Republican hero

Michael Collins by the Welsh actor and radical film-maker Kenneth Griffith. In his column for the *Jewish Chronicle*, Benny objected not on the grounds of content, but on principle. Shortly afterwards, Griffith made a film about the suppression of his work, and came to see Benny. It was the beginning of a long friendship, based on a mutual fascination with Victoria's Empire, and a mutual sense of being outsiders:

> Benny spoke to me in parables, and they are in the film. He touched fleetingly on the Jewish experience: 'The Jews are the Southern Irish of Russia.' The mutual pogroms, no less. He examined the curious sense of proportion that the British have over censorship. 'Show a tit or arse on television and the Whitehouses are up in outraged arms; remove a historical human fact from the television screens, and ... nothing!'
>
> Benny ... said something to me (yes, it's in the completed film!) which is simple yet profound, I often have cause to pull it out of my memory; Benny said, 'The truth is indispensable.'[9]

For all the youthful loafing that went on, Benny's adolescence was a time of intense work unparalleled in his life before or afterwards. By the time he was throwing snooker tables out of the Boys Club's window, he was well into the foothills of competency on the saxophone, and well into a course of autodidactic reading that would last the rest of his lifetime. These studies were combined with strenuous sporting activities. Apart from endless impromptu games in Regent's Park, he represented the Boys Club as a runner, captained its football and cricket teams, and also played first team rugby and cricket for Marylebone Grammar. Perhaps only the boundless energy of adolescence could make all this activity seem slothful in retrospect.

Salad Days | 10

While the details of Benny's musical development were a secret shared between him and the empty flat in Howard House, his birth as a writer was publicly recorded in the pages of *The Fitzroy*. The club magazine has fixed with eerie precision the fleeting allegiances of adolescence, and the passing fads of language and fashion that are peculiar to each generation. Benny first appears in its pages in December 1943, when after its editor has railed against the release of Oswald Mosley from prison, Michael Klinger recounts the club's latest sporting exploits, and notes that four boys from the club were picked for the Association of Jewish Youth's Junior Cricket XI, 'namely Jack Podemsky [him again!], Allan Tillot, Len Weiser and Bernard Green, who captained the team.'[1] The issue has little else of interest to us, although it did contain the latest instalment of D. J. Simons's series 'Know Your Allies', No. 2: Russia, ('The USSR is the largest compact political unit in the world ...'), and A. Bergman's intriguing rumination on the history of political assassination, from William Rufus (1100AD) to King Boris of Bulgaria (the previous month).

It is in the next issue, for March 1944, that Benny makes his first foray into print, with a report on the junior football team. It shows a firm grasp of sporting journalese, before ending on a note of such resounding leaderly responsibility that I find it hard to believe that this is written by the same B. Green that I knew. 'At the time of going to press', the team was at the top of the second division, even thrashing Cambridge Heath 6–1:

> We were by far the superior team in the first half, leading by 4-0. In the second half, however, our opponents brightened up and scored. They kept on the offensive, but could not decrease our three-goal margin. We made sure of the game by scoring two more goals before the end.
>
> The whole side has improved since the start of the season, and we are now playing as a team. Let's see that this improvement is maintained.[2]

The impression that the club may have contained more than one B. Green is also suggested by one of the letters contained in the magazine from erstwhile club members now in uniform. Private Sid Bernstein, RAMC writes, 'I'm very sorry to hear of Berny Green's accident, and wish him a speedy recovery.' How could Benny have been playing football, and simultaneously recovering from an accident? Then again, he wasn't the only person to be in two places at the same time. Private Bernstein, writing from Somewhere in Yorkshire, seems to have combined his basic training with watching enough indoor games at the club to provide a blow-by-blow report, as he manages to do in this issue. No other clues are given here, although D. J. Simons has now progressed to a third episode – 'Know Your Allies: China', ('No people on earth can surpass them in fortitude under difficulties ...'). And what exactly was Benny's accident?

> One Saturday morning, travelling to Camden Town station to join up with the rest of my school's First XI for an away match, I was knocked down by a Number 24 bus, and spent the next six weeks lying on my back while the ligament in my right knee fell back into place. During that period, which I whiled away by studying the philosophic works of P. G. Wodehouse, a man called from London Transport and offered me the sum of £10 as compensation for having been bashed into by several tons of London bus, a gesture of such reckless generosity that it unhinged the family reason and obliged us to accept.[3]

Compensation aside, being hit by a bus was to have a profound effect on Benny's life. It was while he was convalescing that his interest in literature, which had hitherto been casual and undirected, now came into focus. Apart from delighting in Wodehouse, on whom he later wrote a literary biography, Benny also used his enforced absence from the normal frenzy of adolescent life to discover the writing of H. G. Wells. The fifteen-year-old Benny had found his second vocation, that of writer, an illumination which had been precipitated through the unlikely agency of London Transport. The effects of this revelation are immediately apparent in the next issue of *The Fitzroy*, for April 1944. Under the editor's name are the names of two editorial staff: D. J. Simons, of 'Know Your Allies' fame, and Bernard Green. Inside the magazine, the retiring sports reporter of the previous issue has suddenly turned into its dominant voice. Apart from a football report, there is a short story ('The Eavesdropper') about a maid who believes she has heard her employer committing murder, although the attendant thuds and shrieks turn out only to be the sound effects of a radio play, and a long essay with distinctly Wellsian overtones of Utopian futurism, about 'The Future of Civil Aviation', ('Let us awake to the facts, and welcome Civil Aviation as a thing to benefit humanity; let us not distort it into a weapon of greed'). At the end of the issue is a stop press which marks his sudden literary growth: for this first attempt at a sustained piece of writing, Benny had won a prize:

> We announce with great pleasure that Bernard Green won the London Federation Junior Essay Competition. The examiner commented that Green's Essay was the best entry of both Senior and Junior. Congratulations, Bernie![4]

At this time, Benny's hero H. G. Wells was living only a few minutes' stroll from Cleveland Street, in Hanover Terrace, one of the grand Nash terraces that ring the southern side of Regent's Park. Like Benny, Wells had come from unpropitious circumstances, being the son of a Kentish housemaid. As with his creation Mr Polly, Wells had been apprenticed as a draper, although unlike Polly, Wells had then progressed not towards bucolic obscurity, but towards teaching and chemistry, before finally realising his literary ambitions at the age of 29 with *The Time Machine* (1895). That Wells had achieved so much as a writer despite his modest beginnings was an inspiration to Benny. But, much as he wanted to, Benny could not bring himself to knock at the master's door, and announce himself and his ambitions. A similar shyness was to overcome him when, nearly 30 years old, he was working on the Isle of Wight, and found out that another hero, J. B. Priestley, lived near by. Benny's modesty seemed particularly galling to him when, shortly after Wells's death, he made a surprising discovery:

> I once met a young soldier in my local library, who seeing that I had under my arm a copy of 'An Outline of History', told me that as a civilian he was a slater who often repaired H. G. Wells's roof. It seems that Wells, still as curious as ever about the opinions of the young man (this was 1946), always asked the slater lots of questions and then gave him two shillings for answering them, and enjoyed nothing better than chatting to young people in this casual way. The soldier, having assured me that all I need have done to take part in one of these conversations was to knock on Wells's door, agreed it was a shame the old boy had died, and went on his way, leaving me angry at the flukes of coincidence.[5]

Although his neighbourhood 'was never much of a monument to civic planning, unless you happened to be a mouse or a rat',[6] its modesty did not prevent Benny from constructing a personal Fitzrovia of the imagination as he consumed as much literature as possible. Even his next great discovery, George Bernard Shaw, had Benny's interpretation of his identity anchored in the London of Shaw's time as a young playwright and music critic in the 1880s and '90s living in Fitzroy Square. Benny always cherished his favourite images of the Irish writer, listening to a busker outside a Clipstone Street public house, or pirouetting around Fitzroy Square in the small hours with a policeman. Benny's teenage infatuation with Shaw became a lifelong passion. He wrote a book about Shaw and boxing (*Shaw's Champions*); a musical co-written with John Dankworth about Shaw's affair with the actress Ellen Terry (*Boots With Strawberry Jam*); two musical adaptations of Shaw plays (*The Admirable Bashville* and *Valentine's Day*); and was vice-president of the Shaw Society.

Every July on the weekend closest to Shaw's birthday, the Shaw Society convenes in the garden of Shaw's Hertfordshire house, 'Shaw's Corner' in Ayot St Lawrence for a performance of a Shaw play and a picnic. In the Eighties, Benny, who had now gained a reputation as a Shavian, and Toni, herself a Shavian since her teens, both became involved with the annual production, which was conducted under the stately aegis of one of Shaw's surviving paramours, the actress Ellen Pollock, a woman whose advanced age was no obstacle to her driving a sports car. The evening would begin with a biographical entertainment drawn from Shaw's elaborate personal life, which Benny had painstakingly devised over the previous weeks. As Benny told the torrid story, Ellen and Toni would act out the parts of the protagonists. Then there came the main event, a Shaw play, often produced by Toni's Shavian theatre company, which on one memorable occasion featured my toga-clad brother Leo as a rather unwilling spear carrier in *Androcles and the Lion*. Over several years, audiences grew from several dozen to several hundred, as word spread about the uniquely magical atmosphere of those nights, when Ellen would declaim the roles that Shaw had written for her younger self, with no other sound than the whispering of the wind in the trees of his garden. The enchanting atmosphere of 'Shaw's Corner' was only slightly undermined one year when Benny, awaiting his cue behind a hedge, was horrified to hear the turquoise-clad Ellen's rich tones announcing him with a regal sweep of the arm, 'My lords, ladies and gentlemen, I give you Mr Benny Hill'.

The triumvirate of Benny's youthful literary influences was completed by the quintessential London writer, Charles Dickens, who had himself disparaged the 'wretched houses with broken windows patched with rags and paper' of the back-streets behind Tottenham Court Road in one of his peregrinations in *Sketches By Boz*.[7] Benny's imaginative partiality to Dickens's London acquired an extra piquancy in his twenties, when he gained a musical connection to the house in which Dickens had lived in his prime. When anatomising the destruction of the landmarks of his childhood, the fate of Dickens's house was cited as a high watermark of inspired corporate vandalism:

> Samuel Morse perfected his Code in my street, the Pre-Raphaelites took studios here, James Boswell kept his journal round one corner and Bernard Shaw composed his letters to Ellen Terry round another. Perhaps more real than any of them, Becky Sharp was impelled by Thackeray to visit her dissolute father here.
>
> A commemorative plaque is something, I suppose, but I hope they make a better job of this than they did with Dickens's house in Devonshire Terrace. When they stuck their picks into that one, they put in its place a huge impersonal block inside which I guarantee nobody will ever write anything a tenth as valuable as 'David Copperfield'. Today, the only sign that Boz ever dreamed there is a dubious bas-relief showing a few of the archetypal Dickensian faces.
>
> The Dickens fiasco was the first sign that the foundations were shifting under my feet. When the time came to wipe out the house in Devonshire Terrace, only two groups raised a protest. One was the Dickens Society, wrongly dismissed as a group of old codgers preoccupied with the cut of Pecksniff's waistcoat and Mrs Bardell's vital statistics. Incongruously, the other was the Variety Artists' Federation, involved because the house had been one of the busiest rehearsal rooms in London.
>
> As a young man, I had rehearsed 'Slow Boat To China' and 'The Dicky Bird Song' in rooms festooned with portraits of Little Nell and the rest of the astonishing crew. My performances there were never very good ones, possibly because I was distracted by the ghost of Wilkie Collins whooping it up in amateur theatricals, of Dickens's myriad children dashing about the garden beyond the window, of poor Kate Dickens trying to figure out why hubby was never home.[8]

Although Benny had few allies apart from his father in his quest to become a jazz musician, his ambitions as an author were supported by a true kindred spirit in the form of a fellow Boys Club member, Emmanuel Plotski, aka Manny Page, at that time contributing to *The Fitzroy* under the nom de plume 'Count Plotski'. According to some merciless wag in the magazine, Manny was the shortest boy in the club's history, which means that he and Benny, who was 5'11" and 12 stone 12lb. at the age of eighteen, must have cut a comical sight on their long walks around London, tall and slim with short and fat. Both refused to countenance conventional employment, both were equally fanatical about literature, and both were highly promising as writers.

When I was a boy, we would be joined for several days at a time by a strange house guest. He was short and fat, with a beard like a Greek Orthodox priest, and overgrown greasy hair slick with dirt. He stank of sweat and cigarettes, although the aroma would be less repulsive after a couple of days, when my mother's hygiene regime had chipped a little of the filth from him. At meal times, my father would talk to him with an intensity of concentration which I never saw him use with anyone apart from his wife and children. After a few days, our guest would leave wearing some of my father's old clothes. When he had gone, my mother would have to burn his bedsheets, so ingrained in them was his odour. The guest was Manny Plotski. He had never succeeded as a writer, or as anything else. In his frustration and loneliness, the disturbing eccentricity that I had seen as a child eventually bloomed into schizophrenia. Manny died in a DHSS hostel in the late Eighties, alone apart from the voices in his head, voices from the characters of his unwritten novels. By the end, he had burnt all proof that he had ever existed, and some of the voices were telling him to kill Benny.

Manny's eventual fate haunted Benny, as a paradigm of what might have awaited him if he had failed to succeed as an artist. With each further success that Benny enjoyed, Manny's fate seemed a degree crueller, a parallel progress into obscurity instead of fame, self-destruction instead of creativity. Once, when Manny rented a cottage in rural Ireland to find the isolation necessary for him to write a Tolstoyan novel, he returned saying that on the night he had finished it, a gust of wind had carried the first page of his manuscript up the chimney, and that he had been unable to write it again. There is a grain of truth in this delusion of Manny's. His problem lay less in his inability to finish something, than in his inability to start it at all. Every attempt at adult responsibility ended in disaster. Jobs lasted only a few days. A wife came and went in a matter of weeks.

nny's grandparents,
borah and Joseph
een.

Left: Benny's father David Green (standing) with his cousin Hymie Isaacs, 1916

Below: Saxophonist David Green (front row, right) in the Twenties. On his right is Harry Hayes, later to be Benny's saxophone teacher

Benny's parents, David and Fanny, on their wedding day in December 1926.

Left: His sporting uncle
Henry.

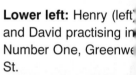

Lower left: Henry (left)
and David practising in
Number One, Greenw[e]
St.

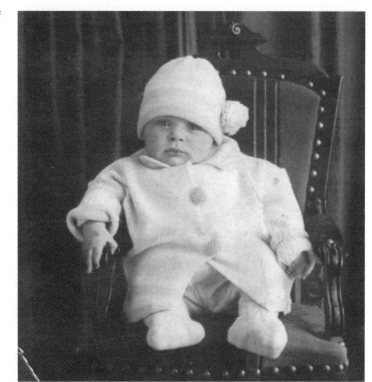

ght: Bernard Green of
eenwell St, 1927.

low: Upper
arylebone Street
hool, May 1934. The
-year-old Benny is in
e back row, third from
t.

Left: His mother's favourite photograph of Benny.

Right: At the seaside with Aunt Rose.

Below: West Central's XI with their trophy, 1945 season. Back row: Michael Unger, Benny, Jack Demsky, Sigmund Weinberg, Alan Tillott, Bobby Matz, Mr Rodbert (coach). Middle row: Harold Blow, Lionel Wiser, Rodbert Junior, Lionel Price, Tubby Lipski. Front row: Lionel Schaffer, Ziggy Bernstein.

Left: A portrait of the artist as a young man in Regent's Park, late Forties

Left: Bernie Stanton in festive mood with Sonny Landau's Orchestra, Golders Green, 1949.

Left: At large in Dundee, 1950, with Leon Campbell (left) and Bernie Stanton.

Right: Roy Fox's Orchestra. Benny and Harry Klein crossing the Firth of Forth en route from Edinburgh to Aberdeen, Amy 1952.

Lower right: New York harbour, 1952. Left to right: unknown drummer, Bernie Stanton, Les Condon, Benny, unknown.

Below: Benny walking the line in Dundee, 1950.

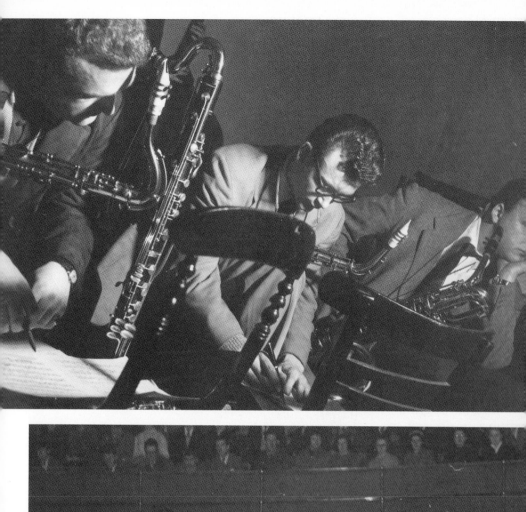

Opposite page, top:
Rehearsals for the Ronnie
Scott Orchestra, early 1953.
Pete King (left) and Derek
Humble (centre) check their
parts.

Above: Archer Street, 1953.
Ronnie's nine-piece
Orchestra about to hit the
road. Looking on (left to
right), Jimmy Deuchar, Derek
Humble, Tony Crombie, Pete
King, Barbara Jay.

Left: The nine-piece with
vocalist Art Baxter at the
Albert Hall, 1954. Front row,
(left to right) Hank Shaw, Ken
Wray, Ronnie Scott, Pete
King, Derek Humble, Benny.
Behind them are Phil Seamen
(left) and Lennie Bush.

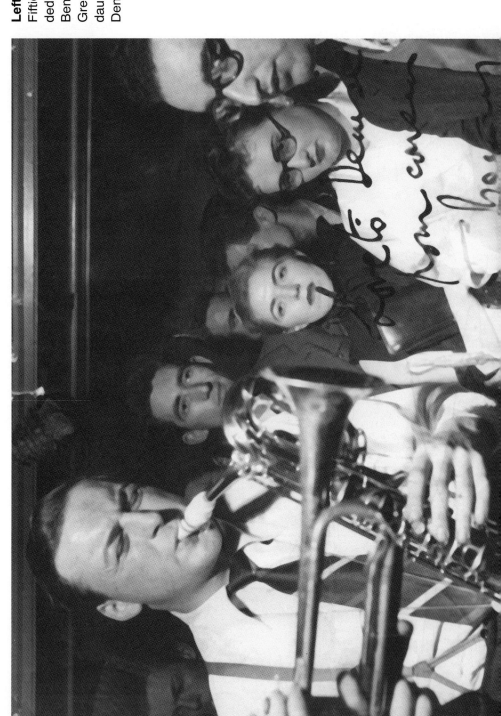

Left: Soho, mid-Fifties. The dedication is to Benny's cousin, Great-Aunt Lily's daughter Denise.

bove: 13 April, 1955. The nine-piece at last recording session. (left to right) nk Shaw (trumpet), Benny (baritone), il Seamen (drums), Victor Feldman ano, vibes), Ronnie Scott (tenor), Lennie ish (bass), Pete King (tenor), Derek imble (alto), Ken Wray (trombone).

Below: The saxophone section of Ronnie's short lived Big Band, 1955. (left to right) Benny (baritone), Joe Harriott (alto), Dougie Robinson (alto), Pete King (tenor), Ronnie (tenor).

Above: With Stan Kenton's Orchestra, February 1958. Maynard Ferguson takes a solo, Lennie Niehaus is on Benny's left.

Below: The Latin-American medley at Brambles Holiday Camp, Freshwater, Isle of Wight, summer 1958.

Taking a solo at Brambles.

Above: With Duke Ellington, 1958.

eft: The Dizzy Reece Quintet, 1958.

Below: Toni Kanal just after leaving RADA.

...ove: 'Oh Boy!'.
...nway Twitty, a
...ay Vernon Girl
...d Marty Wilde
...h the horns from
...rd Rockingham's
December 1959.
...e Blind
...xophonist is on
...e right.

...ft: On the steps
...Howard House
...h Dave and
...nny.

Left: Benny and Toni's wedding January 4th, 1962.

Below: Benny and Toni's wedding: (left to right) George Melly, Manny Plotski, Ronnie Scott, Benny, Harry Klein, Pete King, Bernie Stanton.

Right: *The Observer*'s jazz critic at work, early Sixties.

op left: With Frank Sinatra, London 962.

Above: Benny and Toni, 1963.

eft: Writing in the Sixties.

Above: Playing his Uncle Henry's old soprano at the launch party for 'Swingtime in Tottenham', Soho 1976.

eft: Revisiting Number One, Greenwell
t for the last time before its demolition,
eptember 1971. Count Plotski is holding
the area railings.

Above: My father as I remember him from my childhood.

ft: At Langley House, 1977. Clockwise:
nny, Toni, Natasha, Dominic, Leo and
stin.

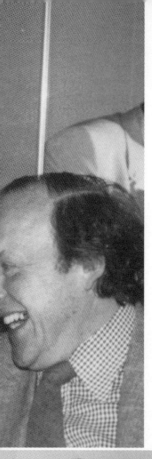

Left: With my father and Oscar Peterson, backstage at the Royal Festival Hall, 1980.

Lower left: The Three Tenors. Leo, Benny and Ray Gelato at Langley House, early Nineties.

Below: Backstage with Ronnie Scott, Scarborough 1993.

Above: Benny closing the show on his 'This Is Your Life', February 1996. (left to right) Robin Aspland (piano), Leo, Benny, Ray Gelato, Dominic. Sitting bottom right and casting a teacherly ear over his promising pupil is Harry Hayes.

Below: Outside Howard House for the unveiling of a memorial plaque to Benny, July 1999. Left to right, Natasha, Toni, Justin, Leo, Dominic.

The dreams and fecklessness which had been Manny's great charm as a young man had been his ruination.

Forty years before Manny abandoned all hope of being a writer and slipped into insanity, he had been Benny's closest friend in the long haul of their twenties. It was a time when neither of them had had the chance to test their literary dreams against reality, and it was a lonely progress, with a small number of would-be artists left penniless in the wake of their more conventional contemporaries, who had headed into the well-paid professional life as soon as their education had ended. In the last eighteen months of Benny's teens, the familiar landscape of the last few years fell away. First, in July 1946 he left the hated Marylebone Grammar, though not before being suspended during his final days. The cause of his headmaster's fury was Benny's performance in his Latin exam, or rather, the lack of it. His entire paper had read:

Latin Examination   *B. Green*

1.(a) Habeo

After which outpouring Benny had decided that being examined in Latin would not substantially affect his prospects as either writer or musician, and had concluded that the rest of the allotted time could be spent more constructively in reading Wells's *Kipps*. It was only after leaving the examination that Benny realised that the correct answer to 1.(a) was not 'Habeo', but 'Habere'. Thus, amid much recrimination ended an academic career that had resulted in little education, but great offence to all parties. His long-awaited liberty was at hand, but there was an official obstacle to be surmounted before he could enjoy it: National Service.

Of all the many mementos I have of my father, none is so supremely improbable as his army pay-book. This innocuous little brown booklet, imbued with Howard House's faint bouquet of cigarettes and damp, is a testimony to the unlikely collision of the world's finest army and one unwilling conscript. Although his fingers were capable of the most delicate manoeuvres on the saxophone, Benny was otherwise notoriously clumsy, and quite bereft of mechanical abilities. In fact, my earliest memory of my father is of him turning round while taking a pint of milk from the fridge door, tripping over our dog Daisy Pooter and dropping the milk, leading to an explosion of milk, glass and wet dog hair,

129

followed by much shouting and an attempt to stop Daisy from drinking shards of glass with the milk that she was licking from the floor. Perhaps that sort of absurd spectacle is inevitable if you name a pet after a character from *The Diary of a Nobody*.

The prospect of 19014367 Bernard Green with a rifle in his hands was one that would have terrified no one but his own side. The prospect of this relaxed and sensible man, a deliberate anti-authoritarian by nature and training, being shouted at for not having polished his buttons or not throwing himself into ditches with sufficient ardour is absurd. In fact, Benny's experience of the army was thoroughly unpleasant. Having left school, he was summoned to an army camp near Maidstone, an irony that he revelled in when we found ourselves playing a concert there. Few of the recruits were happy at having their school holidays interrupted by military training, and many of their trainers were veterans of the war who were delighted at having the chance to work off a few of the tensions they had accumulated under fire on an endless stream of young conscripts.

Away from home and subjected to a regime of aimless brutality, Private Green was miserable. After several weeks of having his sexual orientation queried and his religious orientation derided in the name of character-building for some as-yet unspecified conflict, he hit upon a plan of escape. If the army was going to make life unbearable for him, then he would make himself unbearable to the army. Every day, he reported himself sick, suffering from endless mental and physical ailments, including one memorable headache that just would not go away. Benny suggested that the headache was linked to a bump on his left temple, although he omitted to mention that it had been there since 1927 with no noticeable side-effects. Eventually, the camp doctor, clearly able to discriminate between advanced neurasthenia and advanced shirking, was overcome by either compassion or revulsion, and Benny was given an Honourable Discharge. His Discharge Certificate (Effective: 10 January 1947) notes that he was of 'Good Character', had been involved in 'Nil Campaigns and Service Abroad', and that after 169 days Service with the Colours, this healthy young man who would contract no more serious an ailment than a slipped disc in the next 40 years had been sent home for 'Ceasing to fulfil Army Physical Requirements'.

There were only two consolations for having wasted six months in Maidstone. One was a facility with a compass, as according to his army pay-book Benny had apparently spent 4–6 October 1946 in close company with one, and the other was £20 in army wages, which given the sort of service he had rendered was a generous assessment of his martial talents. As pedestrians in the West End usually used street signs rather than map and compass to find out where they were going, Benny's hard-won orienteering skills were of little subsequent use. The same could not be said of the money. He was nineteen years old, and had no income. Apart from the opportunities offered at the Boys Club, he had no outlet for his talents as a writer, and only blundering amateurs for musical company. He resumed his regular attendance at the club, and kept practising, using some of his army pay to buy a new mouthpiece:

> I was just drifting through the fag-end of my teens, practising the saxophone several hours a day several days a week, but otherwise utterly devoid of any constructive ideas about how to make my way in the world. There I was, standing in our front room day after day, practising scales, learning tunes and trying to control my vibrato, as cut off from the larger artistic life as any monk in his cloister, my only audiences being the occasional incurious pedestrians who would pause in astonished mid-stride at our basement window arrested by the strange noises drifting up into the streets, catch my rolling frenzied eye and pass hastily on, wondering no doubt what the world was coming to.
>
> All the time this was going on, month after month, year after year, the one question which stayed uncomfortably with me like a bone lodged in the windpipe was, 'How do you get started?' Other students in other professions presumably slogged through to the salvation of the requisite diplomas, endured interviews and settled on to the treadmills to which their academic credentials entitled them. But what equivalent was there for the likes of me? Nobody gave you a diploma for rendering 'Body and Soul' without falling over, or advised you to put letters after your name for knowing the difference between Duke Ellington and the Duke of Wellington. And so, in the absence of all hope, I did what was, in the circumstances, the most sensible thing, and stuck grimly to a routine.[9]

Every day, he practised, and every day his practice ended with the same ritual flourish:

> On completing my blowing stint for the day I would dust down the burnished gold lacquer of my instrument and replace it lovingly in its

131

case, having dried my reed and slipped it carefully into its correct slot in its cardboard wallet. Last of all, I would dry the mouthpiece while holding it over my bed, so that if by some catastrophe it should slip from my fingers, it would fall without sustaining any damage.

At that stage of my affairs that mouthpiece was my pride and joy. I had purchased it about two months before the events I am about to describe, and so besotted was I by its combination of decorative perfection and intimations of professional expertise that after cleaning it I would wrap it in a square of white muslin and place the package in my chest of drawers, where it lay in splendid isolation on its bed of freshly laundered shirts and handkerchiefs, safe from any threat of scratches or bumps. Its gleaming, pristine beauty quite overwhelmed me, and although looking back on it across the cruel abyss of time it sounds unlikely, the truth is that I came to believe in the talismanic significance of that mouthpiece, to believe that it was destined to play a decisive role in my affairs – which of course it eventually did.[10]

Nothing happened for months, until, one afternoon in June 1947, his loyal friend Spigelman called round to see him. He hoped that Benny didn't mind, but he had acted on his behalf, and had secured him a gig for the next Saturday, playing as a 'dep' (substitute) in the band hired for a works' dance at the Wilkinson Sword factory in darkest Acton. The fee was to be thirty-two shillings and sixpence. Benny's first professional gig had arrived at last.

Blame it on my Youth 11

The story of Benny's first gig is one that he told regularly. It is at once funny and horrible, where striving youthful artistry is undermined by youthful incompetence. As he relates it, it was an absurd baptism of fire, the perfect initiation into a ridiculous line of work for a young man with not enough self-confidence. If in 1947 one of H. G. Wells's time travellers had taken the trouble of putting the 21-year-old Benny out of his misery, and had informed him that within ten years of his first fumblings in the professional arena, Benny would be a Poll Winner, and a leader in his field with a sideline as a respected critic, he would have not have believed him. If that same Samaritan had added that not only would Benny have succeeded so thoroughly as a musician, but that he would have played so many gigs in so many towns to so many people that he had become heartily sick of the jazz life, he would really have laughed. That kind of total immersion in his art was what he so desperately wanted, even if the challenge to his as yet frail abilities posed by a real gig daunted him:

> I was petrified with terror; my glands suddenly stopped secreting saliva in my mouth; my hands started shaking, and, from that moment to the fateful Saturday night, 72 long hours away, I exchanged the processes of conventional sleep for those of intermittent nightmare punctuated by interludes of hysterical wakefulness in which I imagined all manner of catastrophes, from an invasion by Martians to the occasion of all my hair falling out, preventing me from reaching that first bandstand of my life on the coming Saturday.[1]

Wearing his father's dinner suit, Benny was ferried down to Acton in the van of Aunt Lily's husband David, who dropped him at the Wilkinson Sword factory. Benny found the other musicians, who greeted him with the traditional ferocity reserved for those new to the craft, and began to set up his saxophone:

> The events of the next five minutes, instead of fading with the years, have actually become progressively more vivid, so that every action of

mine, every reaction of theirs, seems as though acted out by giants on a vast stage in a colossal amphitheatre filled by the entire population of the world. I opened my case, put my instrument together, and then opened the small compartment at the front where I kept my mouthpiece. It was empty. I suddenly remembered that I had taken to placing my mouthpiece, my beautiful golden, gleaming mouthpiece, in a muslin cloth in my chest of drawers. It lay there now, four boroughs too far away to be of any immediate practical use. I fished and burrowed in the case, but I knew it was hopeless, and after pulling out an orange, a shoelace and a paperback edition of 'Kipps', rather in the style of a drunken conjuror whose act has gone tragically wrong, I admitted defeat.

At first when I told them I had come without a mouthpiece, they thought I was joking. One of them, the moustachioed guitarist, started laughing and shaking his head in appreciation, as though I had made a fine joke. Then, when I stuck to my story and displayed the empty compartment, they thought I was some kind of lunatic. I told them I was sorry, and they told me they were even sorrier. I then said there was nothing for it but for me to go home and fetch my mouthpiece. Suddenly I thought of my uncle. Perhaps he was still down there, having trouble starting. But when I went to look, the street was empty and the only sign that he had ever passed that way was the thin trickle of oil in the roadway which always followed his van wherever it went.[2]

So Benny had no choice but to race back across London by public transport, retrieve the sacred mouthpiece from its sanctuary in his chest of drawers, and hotfoot it back to Acton. Having left Acton at half-past seven, he reached Cleveland Street at twenty to nine, and was back at the factory by five to ten, only to find that the band had stopped playing for some local bigwig to draw raffle tickets from a barrel:

By the time those formalities were concluded it was ten minutes past ten and time for a Latin American medley, which meant that instead of playing my own instrument, I was required to stand up with the other musicians and display absurd pretensions to bogus Mexican origins by shaking a tambourine. By the time I was finally prepared to dispense my art, it was twenty minutes past ten. In the event, my entire contribution that night consisted of one chorus of 'Pennies From Heaven', and a tentative contribution to the harmonies of the National Anthem.

Later, when we were putting our instruments away – an especially painful ceremony for me, because I had only just got mine out – there was the final ignominy of being paid. The bandleader, a trumpeter called Sid, insisted that I accept my full salary, while I insisted equally emphatically that I hadn't earned it. Sid, however, who, looking back on it, must have been a bit of a psychologist, said that it seemed to him that I had earned it twenty times over, and finally persuaded me to accept thirty-two shillings and sixpence.[3]

Fiasco aside, Benny was now a professional. But how to find work? With the Wilkinson Sword engagement, Benny now began the slow climb through the jobbing ranks of the jazz business that was to culminate on the Sunday afternoon in 1952 when Ronnie Scott braved a tea dance at the Manor House to ask Benny, now doubling on baritone sax, to join his quintet. But in the six years between those two landmarks there lay hundreds of smaller markers, from the leathery chicken dinners of endless Jewish weddings, to the grind of touring with worn-out big bands, and the well-paid mediocrity that was holiday camp work. Every now and then, to make the whole exercise worthwhile, there was a rare opportunity to play some real jazz instead of tired orchestra arrangements, and even more rarely, the chance to lead his own group:

Christmas Eve, 1948: an old, dusty house in Clapham. Our quintet has been hired to provide some music for the family party, but because of the size of the room we are in difficulties. Their piano is a grand, and it fills its room so completely that there is no room left for the rest of us. We adapt by setting up a quartet in the room down the corridor and leave our pianist in glorious isolation, to synchronise his music with ours as best he can.

The system doesn't seem to be working very well. While we play 'Slow Boat To China', our pianist is wrestling with the intricacies of 'El Cumbanchero'. The people who have hired us are starting to get ugly, so I trot along to the grand piano annex and instruct our pianist to play louder, stamp his foot on the floor so we can pick up his tempo, and generally thump as heavily as he can in the hope that twenty feet away, we will be able to pick up his signals.

I return to the quartet room and we begin playing 'Dancing In The Dark'. After sixteen bars, there is a terrible crashing and ripping from the piano annex, followed by muffled screams and showers of dust from our ceiling.

We all stop playing and dash down the corridor. The floor of the piano annex has opened up like the Red Sea for the Israelites, and stuck between it and the room below, like a whale half-submerged in the water and sinking steadily, is the grand piano, with our pianist still sitting at the keys, only now with an even glassier expression than usual on his face. I groan, because I know that in the years to come I will never get anybody to believe that this glorious thing ever really happened.

We return to the other room, and, professional to the last, finish playing 'Dancing In The Dark'.[4]

Benny always referred to the privilege of having had an 'extended adolescence', which only began to end around his thirtieth year. The years of his early musicianship were a bittersweet time. Although he was ambitious and disciplined in his study, he had little organised assistance in his efforts. He took some evening classes in creative writing, which were of little use to his music, and some other, more instructive classes in musical Theory and Harmony at a college in Great Marlborough Street, 'which defended its own musical ideals so zealously that one day its Principal expelled an acquaintance of mine for having polluted one of the Bechstein grands by playing a few choruses of "All The Things You Are" on its keyboard'.[5] Abetted by Plotski, his literary self-education continued, but there was no outlet available for his writing other than *The Fitzroy*, whose pages he continued to pepper with scurrilously humorous letters and Runyonesque stories for two years after he had left the club, by which time the magazine's editors were returning the compliment with their own jokes in a spoof 'Advertisements' column:

Wanted: A reward of one week's subs for any information leading to the capture of Benny Green and his Five, who are now roaming the country disturbing the peace by 'playing' their instruments.[6]

136

The main thrust of his efforts continued to be musical. Meanwhile, the extended band of Boys Club brothers kept on dwindling, as work and marriage thinned the ranks of the previously carefree teenagers that Benny had known. As his chosen path was not a conventional 'career', and as his indulgent parents did not press him to get a job, Benny had trouble understanding why others so willingly threw away their precious liberty. Meanwhile, he kept on practising and reading for the unknown day when all this work would come to fruition. In the absence of any concrete confirmation of his dreams, his passion and his determination to realise it must have been considerable. In photos from this time, none of his clothes fit him properly. In one of them, the flies of his trousers have been replaced by string, and a tie is used as a belt. Every now and then, a few crumbs from the music business's table fell to him, and with them the chance of further improvement and a little money.

Presiding over these years like the twinned Greek masks of tragedy and comedy are the images of two men: Lionel Weiser and Bernie Stanton. They came to represent the polarities of Benny's world view. On one hand lay the high road of artistry, personified in the precocious and confident Stanton, already earning a living as a clarinettist from his adventures in the Jewish orchestras of north London, and leading a Rabelaisian life of artistic libertinism. On the other hand there lay the gaping maw of the conventional world, which Benny derided as the 'Jewsoisie'. Weiser, whom we met two chapters ago in his cricket whites, was a Boys Club confrère on whom the transition from youth to adulthood wrought a particularly dark fate, one which Benny interpreted as the wrecking of a trusting young man's happiness in the name of respectability. He married into a family of women who, though they wore curlers instead of ivy in their hair, seem to Benny to have exhibited all the furious enthusiasm of the Bacchantes as they dismembered Weiser, who eventually died prematurely of cancer brought on, according to Benny, by overwork and the ceaseless pecking of his wife and in-laws. Believing that he faced a choice between conventional work and matrimony, or a life of impecunious artistry, Benny resigned himself to poverty and romantic disaffection.

Stanton was another matter. He had such utter disregard for convention that Benny later accorded him the responsibility of being his firstborn's godfather, in the hope that some of Stanton's brio might rub off on Justin. I shall restrict myself to a single episode drawn from the canon of stories that Benny assembled about his beloved, iconoclastic friend. It was Stanton who, when playing on

137

a cruise ship was caught *in flagrante* with a First Class passenger. This desta-
bilisation of social propriety was compounded by his appearance in the ship's
chapel early one Sunday morning with his clarinet, weaving drunkenly down the
aisle while playing a jazzy rendition of 'Abide With Me'. On his return from
London, Stanton was arraigned before the Musicians' Union star chamber, not
for his contribution to the Sunday service, nor for making love indiscreetly, but
for the more heinous offence of compromising the ship's miniature class system
by talking to a First Class passenger. Stanton denied that he had talked to her.
But, insisted the Union's prosecutor, had he not been caught in the act of making
love to her? That was true, said Stanton with a straight face. Yes, he had been
caught making love, but he never said a word to her.

With Plotski on hand to give moral support, it was Stanton who carried
Benny through the next phase of his bathetic musical odyssey: the passage
through the strange twilight between the worlds of the amateur and professional
musician, in whose dim recesses there dwelt band leaders whose punishment
for unknown musical crimes was the purgatory of the north London Jewish
circuit, weddings, barmitzvahs, and all. This journey through the world of the
jobbing musician was an implausible picaresque through a tawdry landscape of
faded *palais de dance* and suburban synagogue halls. Benny never thought of
Dickens's bizarre gallery of creations as being cartoonish, as he insisted that
'real people really are like that'. They certainly are in jazz, a world which has a
vicious comedy all of its own. Forgetting your mouthpiece is only a minor humiliation compared to being heckled by your own family, and making headway as a
musician is a cinch compared to running a club, a venture in which, as Ronnie
Scott said, the easy way to make a million out of jazz is to start with two.

What crueller disparity with more comic potential in it could there be than
the gulf of intention between the earnest musician and his employer the bandleader, invariably a tone-deaf shyster who runs his petty fiefdom like a tinpot
dictator, and uses this bluster to divert his employees' attention from his real
business of skimming their wages? Or between the pious intentions of the young
tyro set upon the pure goal of musical greatness, and the equally fanatical
demands of the father-of-the-bride, who having cashed in his life insurance to
give his daughter and two hundred close friends a wedding they will be either
unwilling or unable to forget, believes that by engaging a group, he has also
bought the right to decide what songs they will play, while what gentler circumstances would call their audience bury their faces and ears in lukewarm plates

138

of free food? The life of a freelance musician is a glorious shambles, and Benny, with a writer's eye for the marvellous and the pathetic, was perfectly placed to document his voyage through that world.

As he came to realise, parts of his writing now seem like a testimony to a vanished era. It was a time in the shadow of the war that had ended only a few years before, of austerity and rationing, and it was one of dance halls and big bands, where dinner suits were *de rigueur* for musicians. It was also a time when the asinine protectionism of the Musicians' Union effectively banned American musicians from appearing in Britain, and the small world of British jazz was in schism over the new Bebop music that was filtering over from America in the records brought back by 'Geraldo's Navy', the enterprising pioneers of Modern jazz in Britain who funded their journey to the clubs and record shops of New York by playing dance band frivolities in the orchestras of ocean-going liners. But with the honourable exception of London's few jazz clubs, wherever a musician worked, the first criterion for employability was not musical, but sartorial: the dreaded dinner suit. Once again, Dave provided the means of his son's entry into the profession, this time by giving the cash-strapped Benny his own battered suit:

My father has always believed that an infallible sign of a gentleman is the performing of a ceremony known as the shooting of the cuffs, and has therefore tended to design his own jackets accordingly. And as by the time I was coming to the end of my teens my armspan was already in considerable excess of his, it can be appreciated that when in the dying fall of 1947 he made me a gift of his own dinner suit, I presented an eye-catching spectacle the moment I put it on, winning instant renown as the first man in sartorial history to master the art of shooting the elbows. I felt sorely embarrassed by the whole business, and would have done so even had the suit been tailored to fit me with exquisite precision, for I have always found the act of dressing up as fraudulent as it is ridiculous. But it never entered my mind to refuse the gift, recognising it instead for what it was, the key which would open a door I had been trying to force for some years; looking back on it, I see that this willingness of mine to reduce myself to the status of a bow-tied popinjay is the most eloquent proof in the world of the depth of my passion to become a professional musician.

In those days all instrumentalists, whether committing criminal assaults on the classics, or confining themselves to milder acts of aesthetic rapine on popular songs, were expected to report for work dressed like a cross between a fugitive head waiter and the assistant manager of a suburban picture palace, and although a great many of the embryo virtuosi of my saxophone nights were spirits irreverent to the brink of anarchy and very often far beyond it, it never occurred to any of them to question the efficacy of our miserable uniform of servitude. Many of them, evidently as short of ready money as I was, had inherited sets of working clothes even more ancient than mine, and there was one orchestra I sometimes worked in, an organisation of truly stultifying ineptitude which met every Saturday night at Tottenham Municipal Hall with the express intention of ruining the enjoyment of the local dancers, which boasted ten musicians but only nineteen silk lapels, the bassist having lost one of his in a fracas at Tufnell Park Palais and never bothered to repair the damage.[7]

As he recounts in his memoir *Swingtime in Tottenham*, Benny's first employer was Anton Burns, a combined 'conductor, leader, vocalist, publicist and business manager'[8] who was the first man to teach Benny 'life's most important lesson, which is that if you aspire towards a career in music, it is by no means obligatory to possess any ears'.[9] Rather than wasting his efforts on music, Anton had sensibly chosen to concentrate his skills on generating work for his ramshackle ensemble:

As with most bandleaders, the exotic bloom of his musical ignorance was uncorrupted by even a distant whiff of knowledge, but this was more than compensated for by his nose for any special occasion requiring the services of an orchestra. It used to be said of him by frustrated rivals that he could smell an impending festivity at a range of three miles, and I believe the explanation lay in the fact that inside the triangle described by Stoke Newington, Clapton and Manor House, there circulated a vast army of his undercover agents, a teeming clandestine horde of second cousins and old school friends who reported back to him the moment anyone popped the question, and whose valour in slipping inside the defences of unsuspecting families were inspired by thoughts of the five per cent commission which Anton always promised them, and promised them, and promised them.[10]

The only obstacle to Anton's plan for dominating the social functions of north-east London was that most of his prospective customers expected to audition his shambling outfit first, at which point his scheme ran aground on the Scylla of his band's incompetence and the Charybdis of his own bizarre attempts to blind his inquisitors with science, by 'starting an hour late to hint that we had been unavoidably detained by rapturous committees at other auditions, totally ignoring all members of the deputation in order to establish our independence, arranging for bogus telephone calls to come through for engagements which, regrettably, we were too busy to accept, and never finishing one song, a tactic introduced by Anton to frustrate the freeloaders in the audience'.[11] Somehow, and not for musical reasons, Anton's flummery usually didn't work:

> I think myself that the fact that we quoted lower prices than any other orchestra in the district had much to do with the frequency of our rebuffs, for the citizens inside that urban triangle, if they knew less than nothing about how to resolve a discord or sustain a tempo, nevertheless contrived somehow to go one better than Wilde's cynic, and knew the price of everything and the value of everything too, guessing that when five musicians offer themselves for an evening at sixteen pounds, then something called a buyer's market is flourishing to a freakish degree.[12]

Even at sixteen pounds, Anton's orchestra was overpriced:

> Every now and then Anton did manage to clinch a deal, and usually when he did it was by virtue of his arsenal of secret weapons, a battery of begged, borrowed, but mainly stolen Latin American percussion instruments which we all used to scrape and shake in a self-conscious sort of way while Anton contorted his hips with a violence which would have brought tears of joy to the eyes of any mercenary osteopath, and warbled a song of the period called 'Besame Mucho' in what prospective customers took to be Portuguese, but which was in fact a weird doggerel of his own invention. The tactic worked well enough until one night, when we were performing before a bride-to-be who happened to be

141

Sephardic, Anton was vilified by her entire family for having mouthed, to music, the most disgusting obscenities to which the noble Portuguese tongue had ever been harnessed.[13]

And so Benny followed Anton around the weddings of any of the 'Jewsoisie' foolish enough to book him, his father's dinner suit gradually acquiring a patina of dried chicken soup, as he abetted Anton's extravagant solecisms. Although Anton was unburdened by musical talent, that didn't stop him from having a proprietor's inflated regard for his orchestra's worth, especially when it came to that bane of the musical life, Dinner Music. In this exercise, hallowed by harrowing tradition, the musicians are expected to mask the scraping of blunt cutlery on rented plates by providing 'unobtrusive background music, preferably musical comedy medleys played on an out-of-tune violin'[14] while the guests gird themselves for the dancing that will follow after the tables have been cleared and the speeches endured. For Anton, who had the anarchist's keen eye for opportunities where a little 'musical piracy' might be in order, and an even keener one for the petty social humiliations that are invariably part of wedding gigs, the proprieties of Dinner Music were too much to bear:

Anton would have none of this. 'What do they mean, Dinner Music?', he would snarl at us, as though it was his musicians who had established the conventions in the first place. 'You can't have both. It's a contradiction in terms. Either you eat the dinner or you listen to the music. I'm telling you, the minute they start wheeling that soup in, it's them or us, and I say it's us. You think I want to spend the rest of my life playing second fiddle to a plate of lokshen soup?' And so it was that Sunday after Sunday, in the draughty synagogue halls of north London, while innocent young couples embarked on the long matrimonial journey with an innocent smile, two hundred soup spoons would be arrested in mid-flight over two hundred soup plates as two hundred salivating mouths sagged in stupefaction at the spectacle of Burns screaming at the top of his voice the not very edifying message of 'Toot Toot Tootsie Goodbye'.[15]

Although he may have been dismantling most of the accepted principles of music in the process, Anton's erratic style did at least offer proof to Benny that 'it was possible to keep body and soul apart by playing a saxophone in public for money'.[16] The problem lay not in the income generated by Benny's participation in Anton's larcenous recitals, but in the terrible quality of the music they dispensed so mercilessly to the horrified guests who were their captive audiences:

But even as I chuckled at Anton's tactical ploys and marvelled at the uplifting bumptiousness of his alarming vocal style, an instinct informed me that I could hardly go on working for him forever. There was something ineffably parochial about his whole operation, and parochialism was something I was striving to eradicate from my musical nature by practising several hours a day. Although it was noticeable to me that my spirits rose several degrees each time I stepped on to the trolley bus which would, thirty-five minutes later, swish me into the tree-lined road where Anton held court, the still small voice of ambition kept reminding me I was the only member of Anton's band with professional intentions. To the others, music was either a source of pin money or an entrée into the fickle hearts of the girls at weekend dances who gazed rapturously up at us, intimidated into a kind of dispassionate, impersonal idolatry by the elevation of the bandstand, the rake of our bow-ties, and, who knows, perhaps also the eccentric expanse of white shirtsleeves poking through the cuffs of my father's dinner jacket. To me, playing an instrument was a far more serious business than any of this, for it was the only device I could think of for avoiding going to work.[17]

Swingtime in Tottenham 12

From Anton's outfit, Benny moved another step up the ladder of efficiency, if not competence, by joining the orchestra of a certain S., aka Sonny Landau, 'a hirsute little tailor, who, having purchased a trumpet and mastered a series of strangulated gurgles in its middle register, had somehow contrived to reconcile this incriminating talent with the presumption of leadership':[1]

My eventual escape came from the most unlikely quarter of all, for in appearing to take two paces back, I was elated to find myself being shoved three paces forward. One of the several amateur bands with whom I was concurrently associated in the days of my Anton connections was led by a guitarist whose thorough-going grasp of the principles on which human life was ordered had earned for him the title of Mad Harry, any question of my divided loyalties being most conveniently resolved by the fact that nobody could recall the last occasion, or even the first, on which Mad Harry's band had actually performed in public. It was rumoured by those a little too close to him for comfort that never once in his career had he ever managed to play consecutively for thirty-two bars and thus complete a single chorus, a misfortune due to the cruel combination of two factors, the quality of his equipment and the economic exigencies of the period. It was the dearest wish of his life to sing an old jazz standard called 'Angry' while strumming his own accompaniment on the guitar, but what with the dangerous excess of electric current streaming through the frayed wires of his amplifier, and the complete absence of electric current any time Mr Attlee's government decreed it was time for another power cut, the closest Mad Harry ever came to realising his ambition was to sing as far as 'Angry, I'm an ...', followed by a blood-curdling scream as the electricity ran up his arm, and the plunging of the entire street into Stygian darkness.

Like most of the aspiring musicians in the district, Mad Harry appeared to be related to half the people on the electoral register, so when he told me he had a cousin who was a bandleader, it didn't surprise me; on the contrary, it would have surprised me if he hadn't. But one day this cousinly bandleader, finding himself in need of a replacement for an escaped saxophonist, enquired of his mildly demented blood relative of the whereabouts of any likely candidates, and was told of this sensational virtuoso who was actually capable of playing an entire chorus at a time without either falling over or electrocuting himself. So I went for an audition, and, without remotely understanding what I was doing, brought that long, farcical pageant, my apprenticeship, into its final stages.[2]

From its outward appearance, S.'s operation was no different from Anton's. They played the same material, often in the same places and usually for the same money. But S.'s band was entirely different in temperament, as its leader conducted its affairs with 'intense solemnity',[3] despite the presence in its disorderly ranks of Stanton. Benny soon discovered that in this band, 'you were not there to enjoy yourself, a condition of employment which gave us ironic parity with the audiences we played for',[4] although this gravitas was not reflected in the playing, which, though less prone to outbreaks of Anton-style hooliganism, was still without corporate finesse:

Somehow the seven of us managed to combine a relentless professionalism of demeanour towards the music with a rank amateurism in the way we actually played it. The greatest difference of all [from Anton's group] was that with S. you were expected to read music all night, a policy which sounds admirable enough until you realise it was due entirely to S.'s inability to perform his strangulated gurgles unless a sheet of manuscript paper was hiding his shamed face from the customers, and that the moment he was deprived of this shield he was reduced to a mute and comparatively glorious silence. Anton, of course, could not only not read music but, on his own admission, frequently had trouble reading English ...

But with S. it was all very different. His group always worked at least once a week, sometimes twice, and even, in moments of musical dementia in the purlieus of Stoke Newington, three times. What is more, dancers tended to take S. seriously, a mistake no doubt engendered by the anatomical fluke of his facial muscles, which always composed themselves, the instant he contemplated performing one of his strangulated gurgles, into an expression of rigid terror which the customers understandably mistook for solemn proficiency ...

The difference between these two worlds is symbolised by the respective approaches of the two leaders towards sex. When you were working for S., it was understood that while actually on the bandstand in action, you were temporarily castrated, and that any interest you might feel in some transient creature of the night must be ruthlessly repressed in the interests of your status of syncopated eunuch. Even when the interval came and we were permitted to mingle with the aristocrats at the sandwich bar, it was understood that we were to conduct ourselves as though all the girls on the premises were wearing dresses of white samite concealing unbreachable chastity belts, a fiction so palpably idiotic that one of us, my fellow-saxophonist Stanton, having conducted certain surreptitious operations behind that quaint little ballroom near Mile End underground station which proved it to be a fiction, refused to pay it even the scantest regard, and went from synagogue hall to Sunday night social after that like a rampant bullock, acquiring a virtuosity in the priapic arts so impressive that within six months he had outgrown S. forever and become a full professional musician.

In dramatic contrast to all this, Anton actually encouraged Rabelaisian conduct, believing it to be conducive to improved musical standards on the part of those who indulged in it. From time to time he would shout obscure greetings to mysteriously dissipated young girls whose appearance at the dance he had clearly sponsored, and whose sole function, as far as I can make out, was to enliven the proceedings to the point where it would be impossible for any of us to play anything at all. One night I asked Anton about this, after a female welterweight of his acquaintance had vaulted on to the bandstand and tried to sit in our guitarist's lap, and he explained it by saying that he wanted the people who danced to our music to think of us in terms of the good times we had given them. On another occasion, when his ring of espionage agents had informed him, accurately enough as it happened, that I currently coveted a girl at the back of the hall who kept blowing a referee's whistle every time I stood up to play a solo, he countered by asking her, over the public address system, of what, if anything, her sexual morality consisted. After that the whistling stopped, and so did my romance.[5]

As Benny trudged around the circuit, his disillusionment deepened as his technical facility grew. His frustration was twofold. Firstly, there was the numbing mediocrity of those engagements. And then there was the quality of the performers, a group of high-spirited amateurs, presided over by S., whose faux-professional sourness was merely a mask for his incompetence. S. had no intention of risking his well-pressed shirt by turning professional, and was entirely happy with his petty 'campaign of move and counter-move in the papier-mâché jungle of local musical politics'.[6] To him, leading an orchestra was 'simply an elementary game of chess, with the chequerboard extending roughly from the northern end of Seven Sisters Road to the homely water of the River Lea as it bubbled thoughtlessly, like several of S.'s relations, through the eastern approaches of Hackney and finally disappeared in aimless pursuit of Walthamstow'.[7] Benny was beginning to identify one of the strange occupational dangers of being a musician playing too much bad music. With each successive trawl through the same mediocre programme, everything gradually acquires a monotone, soul-destroying flatness. His time with S. soon deteriorated into a dull grind, which in memory seemed to blend into one archetypal night, so undistinguished were the performances and their settings:

It is the winter dance of one of those obscure little social clubs lost in the warrens of north-west London. There is a chalk-sprayed timbered dance floor, a bandstand of perilous rake and unusual elevation, under which the club's tennis equipment lies mouldering, some coloured lights strung around the walls, and, hanging limply from tacks in the wedding-cake ceiling, a few forlorn paper chains. It is a cold night, and the rising heat inside the crowded hall plays all kinds of tricks with our tuning, which is never much good at the best of times. We plod through our repertoire of home-made orchestrations, our 'specials', as Monty, the guitarist who perpetrated them, always describes them; the dancers, the usual crowd, it seems to me, even though I have never set eyes on any of them before, shuffle round and round, too intrigued by the fluctuating fortunes of their curious little caucus race to pay much attention to our music. Perhaps their indifference is just as well, because our drummer, a cock-eyed commercial traveller, is one of those players who believes in varying his tempos to suit the vagaries of his own temperament, which tonight appears to have entered its mercurial phase. As I sit there trying to adjust the rickety metronome inside my head with the bunch of rusty nails inside his, I find myself wondering how long he would retain his position in the band were it not for the possession of the small van which renders him unique in the ranks.

The evening drifts on, the girls swoop and sway past the bandstand, trailing intimations of perfume which rise on the air to pollute the sweat of our comparatively honest labours. Eagerly, I scrutinise their faces while keeping half an eye on the asinine tenor part of a popular hit of the moment called 'The Mad Maharajah Of Mogadore'. But it is clear that there will be no romantic apocalypse tonight. The fine lace filigree of the rime on the ballroom window slowly withers away; tiny puffballs of dust, the residue of last Sunday's social, and the one before that, and the one before that, kick up on the heels of those tango dancers foolhardy enough to try to keep faith with our extraordinary version of 'Tell Me I'm Forgiven'. We then play a printed orchestration, a medley from a film now on release called *Easter Parade*, and follow that by a song by Cole Porter called 'So In Love', which Stanton, rendered knowledgeable despite himself by a childhood shadowed by the lowering skies of compulsory piano lessons, tells me is a bowdlerised version of a popular classic waltz he once rendered in a velveteen suit before the members of the local synagogue Ladies' Guild ... we both miss our entry cue in the last chorus of 'Peg Of My Heart' and get one of those diplomatically dirty looks in which S. specialises.

At Shoreditch Town Hall one lost February night I try to blow a long note, only to be frustrated from beyond the grave by the architect responsible for the building, who has bequeathed to his municipal masters a dome which cleverly continues to sound a note long after the performer has stopped playing it. In a hall in West Hampstead, located up a hill and round a corner and through a lane which serpentines back on itself, a spectral hall hidden by a tuck in the space-time continuum, I am distracted by a glimpse of a dusky female face flecked with the racing dappled shadows of the glitterball spinning overhead. At a youth club dance in Clapton one Sunday, a girl with the face of a madonna and

149

the brain of a small duck watches me in action for several grave minutes and then asks me which hand I play the tune with. She in turn conjures up a misty recollection of yet another club, somewhere in the maze of muted avenues behind Finchley Road, where they used to give the band free cups of scalding coffee in the interval, with one custard cream per musician. Stanton derides me as a clodhopper for dunking my custard cream in my coffee, but pride has a fall when he tries to crunch his biscuit neat and discovers to his horror that a gaping fissure has opened up in the false tooth which his mother gave him on his last birthday. This unexpected amendment to the geological structure of his mouth proves disastrous when it comes to his high-spot of the evening, the performing of the lung-bursting alto solo in 'Harlem Nocturne'. Instead of ending with the last notorious note sustained for fourteen bars, Stanton starts choking after four, and later threatens to sue the biscuit company, the coffee manufacturers, the club secretary, the publishers of the orchestration, his mother, and anyone else remotely involved.

Most nights, Benny returned home on the Central Line, where on the last train dishevelled revellers mingled with musicians returning from engagements in the eastern or western suburbs:

At eleven o'clock, having mangled one of the two obligatory last waltzes, 'I'll See You Again', or 'Who's Taking You Home Tonight', the hired hands would spill out on to the lamplit streets and sprint for the 11:14, perhaps hoping to find themselves sitting facing other musicians across the aisle of that swaying, racketing, somehow festive last train, smiling faintly or nodding to acknowledge mutual membership of a bedraggled freemasonry whose nightly rate of hire was thirty-two shillings. The normal occupants of the carriage, dressed in Saturday night finery which was beginning to wilt around the edges, would gaze with a kind of weary wonder at the instrument cases festooned with colourful, exotic and usually bogus labels, envying us for our sophistication even as we stared at their balloons and sequined handbags and drooping carnations and envied them for their lack of it.

If it was summer and I wore no overcoat, everyone, musicians and laity alike, might goggle in shock at my arm-lengths of resplendent white shirt-sleeve unencumbered by anything so conventional as jacket-arms, which by now were riding triumphantly at my elbow joints. I cared not in the slightest, being so deliriously happy at living the musical life that a carapace of humble professional pride protected me from laughing eyes. I usually passed the journey by reading, glancing up from time to time to check the name of the station, or to run my eye over the piratical girls who boarded us, or to observe at close range my professional rivals, especially the venerable ones, with their cracked patent leather shoes and hair to match, the clip-on bow ties and the fraying braid down the outer leg of the dress trousers. Their facial expressions were blank, representations of a kind of weary satisfaction with their lot. How many of them, I used to wonder, had managed to get through the evening without being plagued by that nightmare saxophone part in 'The Sabre Dance', where you had to play quavers off the beat while everyone else played them on the beat, so that if you weren't half-mad at the start of the performance, you could proceed in the certitude that you would be a gibbering lunatic at the end of it? How many of them had not had to play for the thousandth time 'The Girl That I Marry' or 'I'm In The Mood For Love', or been faced yet again by the tattered music of the Glenn Miller version of 'American Patrol'?[8]

'American Patrol' was a sore point, as many bandleaders, 'having seen "Orchestra Wives" or "Sun Valley Serenade" a few too many times and so vividly conceived of themselves as suburban Glenn Millers that they had purchased rimless spectacles they didn't need',[9] invariably told their musicians to ape Miller's band at the finale of the number by standing up and waving their instruments about:

I had no objection to this kind of tomfoolery, except that every time I became a party to it, the seams of my father's jacket would collapse under the strains of the movements, and I would sit down at the end of it with distinct intimations of a draught hitting the small of my back. Next morning, my mother, noticing the condition of the jacket, would stitch it together again and ask me if 'American Patrol' was the only song I could play.

But the other musicians on all the last trains I ever travelled in always seemed to enjoy playing 'American Patrol', revelling in this short interlude of flamboyance in humdrum lives. They were not really musicians at all, but milkmen and motor mechanics and clerks and counter-hands who once or twice a week put on disguises and joined the ranks of hundreds of suburban cabals and municipal conspiracies called 'modernaires' and 'mellodeons' and 'rhythmettes' and 'swingtettes'.[10]

That the disparity of ambition between Benny and his peers was reflected in the competence of their performances was cruelly apparent once the novelty of regular work had worn off. The final straw came in an East End restaurant, where Benny, a guitarist and a pianist had been engaged to play for a weekday afternoon wedding reception. Having wrestled his shirt-cuffs into position and prepared his saxophone for the trials ahead, Benny suggested that they kick off with 'Lady Be Good', a suggestion which pleased his cohorts, who were 'overjoyed to be asked to play something they knew'.[11] What they didn't know was that over the previous weeks Benny had painstakingly learnt every note of Lester Young's famous solo on his 1936 recording of the song with a Count Basie small group, a solo which marked the beginning of a new era for the saxophone. Taking a deep breath, Benny prepared to unleash his 'secret weapon':[12]

I played the sixty-four bars without a blemish; the aphorisms flowed from the keys and the catacoustic tones echoed powerfully round the hall – at least it did in my own ears. The only trouble was that when I reached the end of the performance it dawned on me that I had executed the entire solo two beats behind the rest of the band.

When the enormity of my crime had sunk in, I stole a shamefaced glance at the pianist, who was tinkling away with the grave absorption of a man perfectly happy in his work; I peeped round at the guitarist; he was contemplating his own fingers with narcissistic awe as they strummed the chords which Gershwin had selected. Then I turned and examined the dancers, awkwardly shuffling their dyspepsia from one side of the narrow room to the other and back again, like mice on a wheel; all of them seemed to be fascinated by the contemplation of their own savoir-faire, and did not so much as glance at the bandstand. I saw that nobody had noticed, that an act of butchery had taken place without a single witness to pay attention. I should have been relieved; instead the albatross of disenchantment settled on my shoulder, and remained there for some time. That the customers should overlook my crime did not trouble me very deeply, for I had already learned, through close observation of certain backward school contemporaries who had rapidly blossomed into fatuous masters of the tango and the samba, that by suggesting the bigger the fool, the better the dancer, Dr Johnson had ranged himself on the side of the angels. But what of my two fellow-workers? Surely they were knowledgeable enough about their craft to know the difference between what I might have played out of my head, what I had tried to play out of Lester Young's, and what I had actually played by scrambling the two? It appeared I was mistaken; the abyss opened up. For I saw that I had been catastrophically wrong to equate ability with recognition, that it was possible to be bad and successful, or good and neglected. In turn, this led to the terrifying truism that a rigorous practice programme might not after all lead to an honourable professional status.[13]

It seems that Benny's accompanists had not had sufficient ears to follow his improvisations, or, as is equally possible, had themselves gained two beats as they ran through the choruses. Either way, he realised that he had to escape the suburban dance scene if he wanted 'an honourable professional status'. Inevitably, help came from that honourable professional, Stanton, although by a typically circuitous route. Tiring of his musical subservience after one audition too many, Stanton reached 'the last extremity of a musical scoundrel',[14] and declared his intention to become his own promoter:

Gathering up his instruments after the audition, he announced certain conclusions, whose gist was that he didn't have to put up with that kind of behaviour from anyone, that he intended raising enough wind to run his own dance, that he would hire his own orchestra, that he was resolved to add to the operation the unheard-of refinement of a girl singer who would possess perfect pitch, faultless intonation, crystalline diction and big tits, and that it was understood that I was to be a fifty per cent shareholder, whether in the tits or the promotion I was not quite clear. He then reached the climax of his peroration, when he said, in a voice quivering with emotion but without so much as a trace of conscious irony, that he was determined to succeed in this enterprise if it took every penny his father possessed. He proved as good as his word, and so it seemed, did his father, for a few days later a truculent Stanton told me he had placed a deposit on a hall called The Refectory, in the north-west suburbs, for a Sunday night in three months' time, and that his research had convinced him that the hall in question boasted so loyal a following that we couldn't fail to make money.[15]

But on the night in question, their services were also required by S., who trusted that they would make the right decision. Which they did, leaving his employ in order to chance their arms as independents. Come the night, the doors opened at eight, although Benny and Stanton had arrived at half-past three, 'to make sure the music stands were in a neat alignment'.[16] Over the next few tortuous hours, they endured the lugubrious agony of watching the door, and counting the thin numbers who dribbled through it. Although eight o'clock had come and gone, there was no sign of any dancers:

At twenty-past eight, unable to endure any longer the ghostly hush echoing soundlessly from the ballroom walls, we mustered a kind of sheepish desperation and began playing a version of 'Slow Boat To China' whose every note reverberated like a shot from a pistol ... By nine o'clock the total attendance had soared to six, which included my parents, who had gallantly insisted on paying for their tickets.

At just after ten, Stanton admitted defeat and called a halt to the private recital which our performance had become. After he had paid everybody off, he and I sat at one of the tables against the ballroom wall silently contemplating our predicament. Somewhere over our heads, the monody of the persistent rain maintained a spasmodic tempo against a skylight. At first we were passionately sorry for ourselves, but gradually, as the sheer enormity of our débâcle came home to us, we became hysterical, just as we had once before in a train travelling in the wrong direction. The whooping and the howling did us good; after Stanton had telephoned home to commiserate with his father on the loss of his investment, we felt even better, and Stanton began discussing ways and means. Clearly, we had no immediate future as impresarios. Even more clearly, we could not crawl back to S. and beg for forgiveness. Which left two possibilities, starvation or a brave crashing of the professional ranks. After due consideration, we decided on the second course. Stanton, a born intriguer, was sure he could find a full-time musical job without too much trouble, and by the evening of the third day had wangled a six-nights-a-week job playing on the Palace Pier at Brighton. To this day, I have no idea how he worked so prodigious a trick, but when I saw him off at Victoria, he took note of my glum face and assured me that if I gave him a week, he could find a job for me, too.

For once, Stanton was wrong. It took him exactly thirty-six hours.'[17]

There was a vacancy in the orchestra playing at Sherry's Ballroom, a faded dance hall on West Street, and somehow Stanton had wangled Benny into it. Facing his first professional engagement, Benny splashed out on a new dinner suit.

On the Road

Fifty-Eight Minutes to London 13

Twenty years after the summer season he spent playing in strict tempo to the shadowy dancers shuffling around the polished floor at Sherry's, Benny wrote a novel about it, *Fifty-Eight Minutes to London*, its title taken from the proud boast that the Southern Railway had hung above the platforms at Brighton station, 'Electric trains to London in 58 minutes'. It is the story of Benny's friendship with Stanton, who, as the philosophically inclined ladykiller and pot-smoking clarinettist 'Landau' is the book's hero and Muse. It is also the story of Benny's coming of age, as experienced by the narrator, Tom. Having been summoned to Brighton by Landau, Tom starts work with Bertie Fields's Noveltones at the Arcadia ('The South Coast's Most Unique Ballroom'), a thinly veiled Sherry's owned not by Mecca, but by Happiness Dancing Ltd:

> The Arcadia at Brighton could have been the Paradise in Manchester, or the Dreamland Gardens in Birmingham or the Romantic at Bristol. Once inside, it was all the same, from the plastic teacups and the gilt-painted wicker chairs to the unperforated paper in the gentlemen's lavatory and the alternating crimson and yellow lights girdling the hall round the lower rim of the balcony. After many years of diligent research, Happiness had succeeded in doing what no architect or regional planner or statesman had ever done. It had contrived to make one town exactly like the next, right down to the musk on the bandroom floor, which no connoisseur of domestic smells could ever have mistaken for anything but authentic Happiness musk.
>
> Every Happiness ballroom housed two bands, and every Happiness band was composed of anything from four to fourteen musicians. How to make this army of sullen discontents as characteristic as the lavatory paper and the teacups? The resource with which Happiness approached this frightful problem was wholly praiseworthy, unless you happened to be part of the army.
>
> The Happiness system is best described as the Iron Fist in the Iron Glove. For one thing, there was no nonsense about the musicians being

treated as creative artists, a decadent view that went out with the Renaissance. Most corporations are in no hurry to reward their employees. Not so Happiness. Instead of being presented with a watch at the end of his time, the musician was presented with a book of rules at the beginning of it, and was well advised to cherish it, partly because it was the only thing Happiness was ever likely to give him for nothing, but mainly because of its elaborate system of fines for serious offences such as talking to customers, failing to address the ballroom manager as 'Sir', and arriving on the bandstand with untied shoelaces.[1]

Twice daily, the orchestra staggers through its repertoire, from tea dance nostalgia pieces to the frenzy of the Latin medley. Not that the audience were impressed, or the band that impressive. From reading *Brighton Rock*, Benny had been led to believe that Sherry's was 'a steaming den of iniquity', but it seemed that Graham Greene was either exaggerating, or too easily scandalised:

Sure enough, after playing at Sherry's for only a few days, I saw that Mr Greene was quite wrong, if only because in order to get a bit of original sin going, you need people, and of all the things Sherry's in my time didn't have (and indeed didn't deserve to have) people was what it didn't have the most. Average attendance at afternoon tea dances was eight, including the members of our quintet, one of whom, the drummer, had been reduced by economic pressures to the desperate extremity of augmenting his princely salary by doing a milk-round, which meant that by nine-thirty every evening, when it was time for the general-excuse-me-Latin-American-medley, he was fast asleep over his sets of maracas, conga drums and assorted ironmongery.[2]

In *Fifty-Eight Minutes to London*, Landau educates Tom in the ways of musicianship, leading him through a succession of bawdy parties and faded boarding-houses in the company of a similarly marginal cast of seaside figures, such as Vivienne, the tarot card reader, and Maxine, the prostitute who lives upstairs from Tom and occasionally bestows her favours on him when she isn't working. Landau is a hedonist, whose diary contains the entry, 'I must practice more and chase girls more', while Tom is shyer and more diligent, nursing a private dream of being a writer:

160

On the wet mornings, while Landau slept alone in the empty ramshackle house in Kemptown, I pottered in the high-domed reading-room of the Public Library, composing ribald limericks and even on rare occasions scribbling a few pages of prose in a six-penny notebook.[3]

After Tom and Landau are fired from their respective jobs for writing to a musical paper criticising their employers' musical policy, and for playing too jazzy a version of 'After You've Gone', necessity forces Landau to address the perennially delicate balance between commerce and art. Landau wonders how to get rich despite his calling as a musician, while Tom is coming to realise that if you are going to sacrifice stability for the pleasures of artistry, then you can't expect the best of both worlds, an apothegm that Benny often offered to Leo and me as generous compensation for the often meagre financial pickings of the jazz life.

By now, the two refugees from responsible life have been joined by two other defaulters. There is Victor, a tissue salesman with 'a droopy unbuttoned look', who loves jazz and F. Scott Fitzgerald and has absconded from his job, but is unable to resist the lure of responsibility. (This character was Benny's only legacy from Marylebone Grammar, being a fair rendering of his friend Vic Bayliss.) The quartet of work-shy dreamers is completed by Blitski, an unemployed political activist and would-be playwright who stands 61 inches tall when not on his soap-box, and who is a precise rendering of that troubled spirit Manny Plotski.

One afternoon, Victor returns to the boarding-house ashen-faced. He was passing the afternoon in a dance hall, when who should appear on the dance-floor but his boss, down in Brighton on business, and who has promptly fired Victor on sight. But what was the boss's business in Brighton? It turns out that the boss was a regular of Maxine's, and that his pillow talk had mentioned that he was in Brighton to assess a rival for a takeover bid. Victor guesses that the company concerned is a local one, Marine Filox. This sets Landau thinking. The group changes its allegiance from Syncopation to Speculation, as Landau returns to London, borrows three thousand pounds from his long-suffering parents, and puts the lot into Marine Filox shares. After several days, the share price rockets from eleven and threepence to fifty-one and sixpence. It looks like the four speculators will get rich. That is, until Happiness Dancing sue Tom and Landau for their scurrilous letter, and the consequent legal action swallows most of the proceeds. Tom leaves Brighton at the end of the season, hung-over, broke and chastened by his adventures in commerce, but now sure of his artistic purpose.

That first season in Brighton was a profound liberation for Benny. Away from home for the first time on his own terms in a town with a reputation for seaside high-jinks, playing daily and with the money to buy as many books as he wanted, it was a golden time. If the doors of the Boys Club in Fitzroy Square were the portals through which he passed on leaving adolescence, then the doors of Sherry's Ballroom were the portals through which he entered his early manhood. As he acknowledged in the novel based on that summer of 1949, the hours spent playing the sax in the perpetual midnight of Sherry's at last gave Benny an inkling of confirmation that his strange desire to be a musician was not wholly insane, and that other, even more ambitious dreams might yet be possible:

> He [Landau] hopped back into the pit, opened the piano lid and ran through the small repertoire of songs he knew really well. These were mostly the old Broadway standards. Without realising it, he and I were becoming connoisseurs of the popular song through our incessant burrowings through the files of the bands whose ranks we passed through. I sat there in the darkened theatre listening to Gershwin and Rodgers and Romberg and Kern floating up from the pit while through my mind's eye drifted absurd phantasms of the dramas that had inspired them, the mysterious strangers, the mistaken identities, the anonymous legacies, identical twins, rich heroes and poor heroines, poor heroes and rich heroines, impoverished dukes and bogus duchesses, butlers posing as socialites and socialites as butlers, lawyers and chorus girls, comic cops and escaped cons. The weak rays from the fan-light played around Landau's head, forming a butter-coloured shifting aureole about him. The music wafted me away on a tide of old associations, and before long I was telling myself that in a few years' time, after the jazz world had been conquered, it might be enjoyable to write a few musical comedies. Between novels, of course.[4]

Back in London, Benny 'returned to the ranks of the unemployed with a confidence born of long practice'.[5] A little dizzied by his successful entry into the ranks of the profession and his undignified departure from Sherry's, and still unimpressed by his own playing, he had expected his life in London to return to his pre-Brighton routine of solitary practice leavened with the occasional tea-dance or wedding gig. This repose was quickly interrupted by an offer of further employment, this time from a holiday camp orchestra immured in glamorous Selsey Bill, on the Sussex coast. Not the least surprising aspect of this second engagement was that until then Benny had been under the impression that Selsey Bill was not a place but a person:

> There thrived there at that time a small privately owned holiday camp, which employed an orchestra of five musicians. One of these musicians, having embroiled himself in the private affairs of ten or fifteen of the lady campers, had suddenly found himself obliged to fulfil a pressing engagement in Inverness, and I, who had just been fired for competence from my first job at a Mecca ballroom in Brighton, was the replacement.[6]

With every gig, Benny's skill on the saxophone increased, even if it was at the price of having to wade nightly through 'some of the great masterpieces of the Western tradition (for instance, 'The Hokey Cokey', 'Underneath The Spreading Chestnut Tree', 'Somebody Stole My Gal', 'Mairzy Doats' and various other arguments for blood-letting in Tin Pan Alley)'.[7] The progress that Benny was making in these early years of his career was not through the most glamorous echelons of the business, but through its commercial underbelly, a hidden world whose denizens became the more bizarre the lower he delved. But his ambitions were greatly at odds with this commercial world. While Benny was trawling the murky depths of the seaside orchestras and wedding dance bands, somewhere in the light and airy regions above him, where they played only the ambrosia of pure, uncompromising jazz, there floated a small elite of his contemporaries, their evident talents garnished with bounteous confidence. How was he to join that company, at whose head stood the precocious Ronnie Scott, already the featured soloist with Ted Heath's Orchestra, and only twenty-one?

Benny had first become aware of Ronnie Scott one afternoon in 1945, when his daily casual game of football in Regent's Park was interrupted by a well-meaning acquaintance who, as he passed, called out to Benny, 'Have you heard about this Ronnie Scott? They're saying he's the English Coleman Hawkins!' This was deeply distressing to Benny, not least because of his private dream that if anyone was going to be the English Coleman Hawkins, it was going to be him.

Events had proved otherwise, however, as by the time Benny was floundering through his early gigs, Ronnie was already a star player. Ronnie was a true virtuoso, whose own rapid ascent through the profession had been an inspiration to Benny as he slowly levered himself first into some kind of regular work, and then the right kind of regular work.

Years later, when Benny and I were peregrinating around the West End on one our customary Friday afternoon historical tours around the sites of his old life, we were chewing over how to negotiate painlessly the 'diminished' passing chords which act as bridges between the main chords, and do so much to give jazz its harmonic seamlessness. Unfortunately with such complex analyses, if there are no instruments to hand, there is no other way to elucidate your suggestions than to sing it to your fellow musicologist in a stream of ba-ba-doo, dee-ba-doos while calling out the chord changes in between the phrases. As neither of us could sing in tune, we both understood each other perfectly, although I did notice that other pedestrians tended to give us a wide berth. We were ambling along, taking turns to howl short bursts of tuneless gibberish at each other and then analysing the result, when I asked Benny when he had first grasped the slippery nature of a diminished chord, a beast which is so hard to pin down in theory, and yet utterly essential to the practice of jazz. He said that it was in 1946, when he was eighteen years old. Despite all his earnest wrestling with musical theory, the penny had not dropped until one night at the London Swing Club in Oxford Street, when he had heard Ronnie Scott negotiate the diminished chords of a sequence with an easy grace that belied his callow years. Passing on a priceless gem of jazz technique, Benny then sang the phrase to me. It goes: 'Ba-ba-di-di, Ber-ba-di-di'.[8]

During Benny's engagement at Sherry's Ballroom, he had been blowing through the usual desultory tea-dance repertoire one afternoon when word filtered through to the bandstand that in the balcony was none other than the great Scott, down for the day with his girlfriend and sports car. By 1949, Ronnie was the leading tenorist in Britain, and the radical Bebop-inspired Club Eleven group he and John Dankworth had put together was causing a considerable stir. Benny was overcome by the mere idea of his hero being present, albeit invisibly, in the ballroom:

> The moment I heard this, the saliva in my mouth mysteriously disappeared and I was unable to produce a note. Being a lover of good music,

he didn't stay long; after he left, my saliva returned and I was able to function again.[9]

Only occasionally able to enjoy the rare luxury of playing real jazz, it seemed to Benny that he would never make it to the first rank of jazz players, and that a future of underpaid mediocrity loomed in the dance bands of north London. But in 1950, his perseverance paid off, when his graduation from the Jewish social circuit to the heights of Sherry's led to the next rung of the profession: the professional orchestra musician, a harried figure whose working life was spent trapped for week- or two-week-long periods in any town worth building a ball-room in, or haring up and down the country's badly lit, single-lane A-roads on a gruelling succession of one-night stands. For the next decade, this was to be Benny's life.

The existence of a touring musician is a strange one. The normal rules of social life are inverted, as you work when others are relaxing, sleep when others are working, eat whenever you can, and are in a permanent state of motion without ever arriving anywhere. Each destination becomes not the terminus of your travels, but the stepping stone to the next stop, and the next, and the next, until you are long past caring where exactly you are, but under a compulsion born of habit to get to the next town, even if you don't care where that is. You are suspended in a state of inspired tedium, living in a bubble with a bunch of charming degenerates, as if in a fog from which you can only occasionally make out the vague outline of the life enjoyed by the rest of the world:

For several years, I was transported around Britain, free of charge, by a succession of agents and bandleaders who asked nothing of me in return except my undivided attention twenty-four hours a day. To all of us involved in this comically squalid contract, the towns of the four kingdoms took on an appearance unknown to the compilers of the guide books. Cambridge to us was not an ancient seat of learning, but the place where large quantities of American cigarettes were mysteri-ously circulated among the patrons of the local dance hall by the band-leader, a drummer whose awareness of his own professional shortcomings had at least been acute enough to stimulate him into working up this little sideline. When we entered Edinburgh, it was not to gawp at the Castle and buy butterscotch at exorbitant rates, but merely to hope that the bouncers in the ballroom up at Leith were in good condition. As a matter of fact, we could never be said to have visited these places at all, not in the ordinary, everyday sense that people mean when they say they were once in this or that town. Travel, somebody once suggested, broadens the mind; so far as my experience goes, it only flattened ours.[10]

In the first week of a tour, the transition from your familiar normal surroundings to the alien and many-faceted ugliness of motorways, travellers' hotels and transport cafés, is quite painful, so vicious is the contrast. But gradually, fond memory is annihilated by an accumulating layer of your new regime, which settles on the old life like dust until by the fourth week, you are as dependent upon the little comforts of this new half-life (your regular seat on the bus, the precise arrangement of your potted life when your repack your bag each morning) as you used to be on the old. Having achieved a state of perfect equilibrium with the ridiculous demands of touring, it is inevitable that the bus that has been your cocoon and only retreat from insanity for the last weeks then deposits you on your own doorstep at six o'clock on a freezing Monday morning, leaving you to relearn how to live normally, a painful process seeing as you have only just succeeded in training yourself to live abnormally. Equally inevitably, once you have readjusted to adult life, you can be sure that within several days of your return to normal consciousness, the same bus will take you away again, to repeat the whole debilitating cycle.

This pattern is repeated until the subject is mentally and physically ruined, after which he comes to a fork in the road. He can recognise his existence as a nightmarish kidnapping episode that followed on inexplicably from a perfectly reasonable adolescent desire to play music for a living, and do his best to escape from the road life with as much of his sanity as his wrecked physique can carry. Or, now thoroughly habituated into this madness, he can plunge still further into it, and eventually become one of those rococo figures who have become so damaged by incessant touring that their malformed personalities make them legends of the sort who, though the muscles of their lips may have acquired the same elasticity as those of their gut due to their epic medicinal consumption of drugs and alcohol, can always be relied on to fall on to the stage at the appointed time, with their flies undone and their left eyebrow neatly shaved off. Whole bands can disappear in this way, especially on the endless roads of America, where a touring musician hears stories of ghostly tour buses still plying the high-ways and road houses like motorised *Marie Celestes.*

The years of hard labour that Benny spent on the road break into three neat sections. The first three years were spent with what turned out to be the last of the big bands, tottering dinosaurs from the Thirties whose faded leaders were obliged to restock their ranks with young or second-rate players. The middle three years were those with Ronnie Scott, which were the apogee of his playing career. The last three years were a hard time, when Benny was forced by habitual and economic imperatives to return to touring with commercial big bands, even though he was by then heartily sick of life on the road, and was trying to escape music for writing. In short, he spent most of his twenties on the road, and given the length and variety of that experience, it is not surprising that his odyssey around the ballrooms, by-ways and boarding houses of the British Isles was an experience which set him apart from other people. Along with the manifold discomforts of touring there are precious consolations, ones that Benny would miss long after he stopped touring. There is the satisfaction of being totally immersed in your creative passion. And there is also the intense emotional life that comes with touring, where deep friendships are formed through shared hardships and the unrelenting intimacy of days spent travelling and playing with the same group of people.

After he left the jazz world for full-time writing, Benny never formed any other friendships as deep as those from his playing days. As with his extended family, perhaps he had dispensed with the need for them in the long struggle for creative satisfaction that dominated his twenties and early thirties. But I think there is another reason. Almost all of the friendships he found after the late Fifties came from the theatre, a world whose intimacy and vagabondage is a refined version of that of the touring jazz musician. I think he sought the company of those who had been through the same formative experiences, so unusual by any of the standards of normal life. Benny always warned Leo and me about the fundamental unpleasantness of the touring life. Allied to his horror stories of the exhausting lifestyle were the equally corrosive circumstances of his employment, where the musicians worked for tyrannous and usually ignorant bandleaders, played a diet of music where often ludicrous material rubbed against the odd gem, and spent longer engagements under the roofs of equally dictatorial landladies. If you weren't a cynic before joining such a circus, you very quickly became one.

167

But oddly enough, he was also pleased when Leo and I went touring, and would swap stories with us about life on the road. I don't think it was mere nostalgia for his youth, and the passionate friendships that youth forges. It was because he knew that through touring, Leo and I would be better able to understand him, as we would have our own knowledge of the backstage world of music, so much of which is incommunicable. Although Leo was prolific and precocious enough to be on the road at seventeen, I was as slow out of the traps as one of my grandfather's greyhounds, and much of my early experience of being on the road was with Benny. For our part, one of the reasons that Leo and I were so drawn to music was because we had somehow intuited that while the clues to who our father had been lay in the back-streets of Marylebone, somewhere in the chaos of the jazz life we would find the clues to who our father had become. And, having spent my own twenties as a musician, I think that this elaborate strategy worked. I suppose it is in the nature of things that when Leo and I were at our most immersed in touring, he was at his most ill, and that no sooner had we begun to understand his life, than he died.

For Benny, his decade as a working musician was the backdrop to his growth to maturity, from the callow 20-year-old who got off the train at Brighton with his new dinner suit, to the exhausted 29-year-old who one day sat down on the pavement in Dundee and announced that he simply couldn't go on living like this. As Benny used to joke on our gigs, an old, withered musician with a croaking voice and collapsed shoulders is usually at least 30 years old. What surprises me is that he stood it for that long.

Archer Street 14

With Benny's entry into the world of professional musicianship, our wanderings around the West End now take us into Soho. At the foot of Great Titchfield Street, we cross Oxford Street just below the 100 Club, a London institution that sits like a gatehouse on Soho's northern frontier. Once we have crossed Oxford Street, with Benny stepping eyes-front into the traffic, wandering across the torrent without the slightest glance to his left or right, we appear to be heading for the doors of the Marks & Spencer store built in the old Pantheon building, but instead descend a short flight of stairs almost hidden at its side, into the silence of Ramilles Place, a dead-end lagoon shaded by high office-blocks.

We are in Soho now, a different kind of 'teeming quadrilateral', where there coexists a world's worth of pleasures licit and illicit. Poised on the imaginative cusp between the two sits jazz, a music born in hedonism and matured by intellect, and buried somewhere in the maze of streets to our left is the spiritual centre of British jazz, Ronnie Scott's Club, whose red neon sign promises, against all commercial odds and considered advice, 'Jazz Nightly'. This Friday afternoon, we are not heading for Ronnie's, where Benny will drop in for no particular purpose other than to catch up with Ronnie and his barrel-chested, imposing partner Pete King, another veteran of the famous nine-piece, while Leo and I sit on the leather sofa in front of the giant picture of Charlie Parker trying not to make squeaking noises as we crane our heads to see into the reddish gloom of the club, recognising the faces on the walls from concerts or the record sleeves we have seen at home.

Instead, we head southwards almost as far as Shaftesbury Avenue, to Archer Street, a short, quiet street behind the Lyric Theatre whose western end peters out into an NCP, and whose only feature of note is the offices of Soho's largest landlord, Paul Raymond. Benny would often steer us past Archer Street, but the visit that sticks in the memory is from the summer of 1992. With half an hour to go before the Lyric's curtain went up on the first night of his musical *Valentine's Day*, Benny suggested a stroll, and we slipped from the stage door of the Lyric into the steamy air of a July evening in Archer Street. After the tumult of the theatre, it seemed unnaturally still, but then for Benny it must always have seemed unnaturally still on our visits, as he had known it in its prime, when Archer Street was so paramount in the musical life of the city that it was known simply as 'The Street'.

In order to find casual work, a musician of the Forties and Fifties would go to Archer Street, 'which in those days used to be the musicians' al fresco employment exchange, for no better reason than I could ever think of than that the stage door of the Windmill Theatre was located there'.[1] It was the musical equivalent of a Roman slave market, where the suitability of a prospective employee was assessed not from the strength of his teeth or muscles, but from the shape of the instrument case he carried, and whether he possessed a dinner suit with both arms attached. With a little luck, a player might find work for that night, and if not there was always the chance to mingle with his peers in 'The Street's' café, The Harmony Inn, which was the preserve of a long-suffering Hungarian called George Siptak, a name which Benny realised in a moment of unemployed inspiration was 'katpis' backwards. All musical roads led to Archer Street, and from 'The Street', they went anywhere:

> We would usually arrive at dusk, which meant that if it was any time
> between September and April, which it always seemed to be, the town
> or the city (we were never sure which) would be doing its best to
> conform to Whistler's famous description when 'the poor buildings lose
> themselves in the dim sky'. This meant that the rows of houses in the
> rows of streets were always disguised by the uniformity of half-light. We
> would spill into some country hotel, gaze at the venerable, fly-blown
> portraits on the walls of cows glaring balefully at a bunch of sheep –
> sometimes it was refreshingly different, and in the portrait the sheep
> gazed sheepishly at a bunch of cows – and then retire to our rooms, two
> by two, in strict if unconscious observance of biblical precedent. Then
> we would change into the crumpled finery of the evening, depart in our
> coach for the wrong end of town (the ballroom always turned out to be
> at the wrong end of town), perform for three or four hours, then come
> back to a late supper of cold meat and pickles presided over by some
> dropsical night porter who hated us with a fierce and consuming passion
> for having obliged him to do his job, sleep till seven the next morning,
> when spindly legged chambermaids would pleasantly wake us by
> flinging all the dirty dishes in the municipality at all the walls in the

building, fall into our clothes, fall into our coach, where we would resume our slumbers, and wake hours later dull-witted and blinking through the coach windows at another dusk in another town whose brilliant shop windows and flashing traffic lights made a silent clangour to play on our much-exercised nerves.[2]

British hotels are still notorious among musicians as the most over-priced and the least hospitable in the world. The sort of accommodation that has to be endured during extended touring in the British Isles is, like a spell at Eton, the ideal preparation for a long prison sentence. I can only imagine how spectacularly unpleasant British hotels must have been 40 years ago, and how much the miserly Fawlties who ran them must have detested the jazz musicians who returned noisily in the small hours, hungry, but with nothing to eat apart from what the proprietors euphemised as a 'cold collation', which meant 'six ham sandwiches among twelve of us, and a pot of lukewarm coffee':[3]

> Once I started touring as a musician I quickly became a connoisseur of hotels, learning to tell from a single sniff of the smell in the foyer what the service was likely to be like, able to assess in two minutes the subtle differentiations in cutlery, in linen, in the proportion of bathrooms to bedrooms, in the elaboration of the embossed notepaper, which distinguished a three-star from a four-star and a two-star from a no-star.[4]

When he took his family on holiday, Benny always sat in the shade with a book on his lap, occasionally wandering back to his room to write an article. We could never understand why he hated to leave home so much, but it seems that his tolerance had been so aggrieved over several years of third-rate accommodation that he had taken a vow never to sleep in a strange bed again if it could be at all avoided, with the sole exception of The Ritz, where he and my mother would decamp for their wedding anniversary. In my childhood, I remember the front door banging in the small hours of the night. It was Benny, who, rather than spend a sleepless night in an alien hotel, had preferred to spend one on the motorway, driving home from some unknown speaking engagement. Although he'd hardly slept, he would stagger into the kitchen in time to see us off to school, sitting hunched at the breakfast table in his dressing gown while we bellowed our childish preoccupations into his ears.

171

Sometimes, it must have seemed to him that he had spent most of his adult life having his sleep interrupted:

> When the housemaids started smashing all the crockery at six o'clock the next morning, we would stagger out of bed and call down the corridors, asking them what they thought they were doing making such an unholy racket at such an unholy hour of darkness.
>
> Sometimes the ensuing debate would cause us to be barred from that establishment for life, which meant that the next time we were due to perform in that town, we had to write our booking reservations under bogus identities, passing ourselves off as a party of Polish students, or a group of neo-medieval mummers, or a visiting delegation from the Antipodean Glassblowers' Society. British hotels are really exceedingly trusting organisations, and we found that, no matter how outlandish our assumed identity, it was always accepted in good faith. But as we always paid our bills and almost never misbehaved, everybody was reasonably satisfied in the end. I say 'almost never' because there was one orchestra I was in where half the brass section was adept at making gas meters spring open almost without physical contact. And once we had a girl singer who tried to escape from a hotel in Grimsby with the bedroom eiderdown hidden under her coat.[5]

The big bands in which Benny worked in the early Fifties were mainly antique leftovers from a golden age that had departed, but not taken its environment with it on its journey to oblivion. The provincial dance halls and ballrooms still stood, as, occasionally, did Benny's employers, 'several of the once-famous lions of the movement, running around rather like chickens who hadn't realised their heads had been chopped off'.[6]

> As late as 1952 I went on the road with Roy Fox's orchestra, although by then Roy, the sweetest of men, had long since lost his pre-war eminence. One day, when we stopped for lunch somewhere up in Scotland ... Roy told me that at one time he had been so famous that he had had to hire a double in order to escape the attentions of the fans.
>
> What happened was that the double would dress up in a top hat and opera cloak identical to Roy's, and then run from the stage door

while Roy made his escape by a side entrance. While he was telling me this, we were sitting in a crowded lunchtime cafeteria, and not a soul recognised him.

At one time, Roy had been the centre of a famous controversy concerning the big bands. Around 1934, at the height of his fame as the leader of the band at the Monseigneur Restaurant in the West End of London, he had been taken ill and had to go away to Switzerland to convalesce. When he came back, it was to find that his pianist, Lew Stone, had taken over his band.

The argument was over whether or not Stone had behaved like a gentleman. Frankly, it was all so long ago that I didn't care one way or the other when Roy told me about it. In any case, you could have put Roy's band and Stone's band together and multiplied them by two or three million and the end result still wouldn't have been worth the musical value of Duke Ellington's laundry bill.

But by a colossal coincidence, six months after leaving Roy Fox, I joined Lew Stone's band. He was leading a group at the Pigalle in Piccadilly, and I never liked it much because you had to go through the kitchens to get to the bandstand, and I was worried about catching the Black Death.

Each night during our break, we would get a free supper from the management – spaghetti and baked potatoes – and as we munched on this disastrous diet, Stone would hold court, modestly telling us all the things he was wonderful at. I soon decided that, no matter what the evidence was, I sided with Fox in the ancient controversy. But what puzzled me about both of them was how they had ever managed to survive. Musically speaking, their talents seemed to me to be minimal. At least you could say that Roy cut an imposing figure on the bandstand, pretending to conduct the orchestra (in dance music there really is no such thing as a conductor; the baton is a bluff), but Stone was a tiny man of unprepossessing appearance with a head shaped like a triangle. I used to wonder sometimes if he ever realised how lucky he had been.[7]

Like his friend from his big band days, the altoist Harry Klein, in 1951 Benny had broadened out from the popular tenor saxophone to the baritone, a heavier, deeper instrument which, though unsuited to soloing, gave vital ballast to the

173

brassy orchestral palette. Although his 'apprentice efforts on the new instrument were blood-curdling enough to put a music lover off for life',[8] he had 'hardly possessed the instrument long enough to default on the first hire-purchase payment'[9] before a prestigious bandleader offered him a job. It was the pianist Ralph Sharon, now Tony Bennett's accompanist:

> I was mystified by his generosity which, I soon discovered, was qualified. After some weeks of existing on tour on a miserable pittance, a deputation consisting of the band in toto went to Sharon and demanded a rise of ten shillings a night. He then told us an admirably constructed and meticulously rehearsed cock-and-bull story about how all the contracts for the rest of the year were already signed and the monies allocated, but that come January 1st, we would all get our rise. Sharon sacked the lot of us on New Year's Eve.
>
> A fellow of such infinite jest might reasonably be relied upon to divert the course of artistic history down some unsuspected byways; and sure enough, when, a long time after, Sharon and I met on Broadway and I asked him why, all those years ago, he had given a job to a saxophonist so intent on playing out of tune, he gave me the most old-fashioned of looks and said he thought I knew the way things were. It appeared that in booking his string of one-nighters, Sharon had been obliged to accept the less desirable dates on the touring circuit, at venues where the musical appreciation of the inmates was generally rated somewhat lower than their tendencies to demolition. He had therefore decided to engage not the best musicians he could find, but the largest, hoping that when trouble reached the bandstand he could hide behind his phalanx of hired muscle. I was astonished by this explanation; but when I began to think about it, everything fell into place. I was a large young man in excellent physical condition. Perry, our alto player, was an ex-Petty Officer, and the second tenor was an ex-policeman called Allard, who had just completed a year of point duty in the stimulating environment of Millwall.
>
> But Sharon needn't have bothered, because apart from the fact that there wasn't a man in that orchestra who wouldn't gleefully have thrown him to the wolves in a crisis, no crisis ever developed, or was likely to. Even the audience of miners in a Nottinghamshire village who smashed

up the joint one night in tempo to our rendition of 'Tell Me I'm Forgiven' never came within a yard of the poverty-stricken minstrels puffing and sucking away on the bandstand.[10]

Benny moved from orchestra to orchestra, inching up the ladder of prestige and competence. The names of their leaders are a mixture of obscurities from faded posters, and legends of the day: Bertie King, Kenny Baker, Tito Burns and Geoff Love. With the honourable exception of the trumpeter Kenny Baker, who encouraged Benny to make his own way, Benny bristled against their authority. None of his engagements lasted very long, usually ending in what musicians euphemise as 'musical differences', which are nothing of the kind. Benny left Lew Stone's band after making some saucy remark to the bandleader, at which the great Stone bridled, 'You shouldn't talk to me like that. I'm old enough to be your father.'

'No, you're not,' Benny rejoined, 'you're old enough to be my grandfather.'

To which Stone rejoined with rapier wit, 'You're fired.'

With Roy Fox, the normal pattern took a strange inversion. After a romantic imbroglio lasting for most of the tour, Benny left the band, sneaking out of their hotel while his fellow musicians kept watch. It seems that Roy had decided to break up the long haul to Green's Playhouse in Glasgow by stopping over in Manchester. This reminded Benny of an unfinished affair of the heart that he had begun on a previous visit to that city, and so as soon as they arrived in Manchester, he and Harry Klein went to visit her. No sooner had they knocked at the door than it was flung open, revealing the imminent arrival of 'a white lace cannonball which crashed into me, wrapped itself around me, and generally behaved as though it were Mafeking and I the relieving force':[11]

I now fell wildly, utterly in love. By the time I had extricated myself from the cannonball, I had already reached the conclusion that the path of my life had now been fully charted. The next twelve hours were blissful but unreal, and I will pass over them because there are some human moods and experiences which are beyond words. Troths were plighted, promises made, and I remember an attempt to consummate the affair in the stockroom of the shop, on a bed of beetroot sacks, flanked by hillocks of cabbages. By the time I walked drunkenly along the road looking for a taxi or a late night bus, it was past five in the morning. In a few hours

175

we were due to move on to points north and an assignation with a dance hall in Sunderland. When Klein asked me how I had got on, I told him that if he wished, he could be my best man, at which he burst into hysterical laughter, and informed the rest of the band that I was ill.

It turned out to be one of those curiously ill-fated tours. At Hawick, Roy Fox put his foot into a cow-pat and sprained his ankle. In Leith, our Canadian second trombonist became so terrified by the air of violence in the town, imagined or not, that he went out shopping and returned with a sword-stick. This gesture of unilateral rearmament brought about a visit from the local constabulary, who were only partly convinced when Roy told them that in deference to local customs, the band was rehearsing a sword-dance routine. And at the Beach Ballroom in Aberdeen the local grass widow, an eccentric lady called Olive, suggested I decamp from the band that night and come and live with her, and in return for any light duties I might perform I would receive a salary of ten pounds a week. At first, I thought she was a farceur, but when she handed me her gold wrist watch as a surety of her good intentions, I realised that I had a genuine offer on my hands. During the band's break, she and I sat on wooden chairs arguing the issue, and I became so involved in the struggle between lust and duty that I never noticed the band was back on the stand. Thirteen of them were sitting in their places, headed by Roy, and they were all following the debate with fascination. I rejoined the ranks with the issue still unsettled, but when at the end of the night Olive came to collect me, I submitted willingly enough.

Three hours later, I was once again wandering drunkenly along a strange street looking for a taxi to take me back to our hotel. Olive, who was not an ungenerous girl, had given me a pound for my fare, but I ended up thumbing a lift from a lorry. Klein was waiting up to see how I fared. When I told him about the offer, and how I had decided not to accept it, he told me I was mad, turned over and instantly began to snore, leaving me lying there in a whirl of romantic confusion.[12]

Olive's last words to Benny had been that she would meet him in Glasgow. As she was 'rather a demanding lady', Benny decided to get some exercise, under the supervision of the band's singer, who had once been on Sheffield

Wednesday's books. Unfortunately, 'while executing a delicate shimmy with the ball',[13] Benny sprained his ribs, and had to spend the next week 'with a repugnant green oilskin across my chest. What would Olive say when she saw it?'[14] But she didn't turn up, causing a threefold reaction in Benny. Firstly, he disposed of the oilskin. Then he treated himself to a consolatory paperback edition of the *Journals of Arnold Bennett*. The third was to remind himself that he was in love with someone two hundred miles away. Meanwhile, 'industrial relations inside the band were sinking fast. Roy's policy of paying us once a week for only five or six nights work meant that we were all now so deep in that none of us could see how we would ever escape':[15]

> The crunch came at the end of the first week at the Playhouse. Roy, who now owed me the huge sum of £33, surreptitiously slipped me six fivers during the Latin-American medley. The thought instantly occurred to me that this was as good as it was ever going to get, and that if I allowed matters to drift on, the debt would quickly grow to unmanageable proportions. There was only one course of action left to me. I would have to leave the band, here and now. During the band break, I told Roy that my grandmother had died, and that I would have to return to London instantly. Strictly speaking, this was quite true; my grandmother had turned over in bed one night in 1936 and handed in her dinner pail. But Roy would not hear of my leaving.[16]

Benny conferred with Klein. There were two offers on the table, true love in Manchester, or a tenner a week in Aberdeen. Klein advised Aberdeen, as Benny would have no means of support if he left Fox's band. But Benny chose Manchester, trusting to his instinct, which 'in those days was always infallible. Infallibly wrong … '[17] Staggered that Benny was not only leaving a £3 a week job, but turning down a £10 a week contract for a strictly amateur engagement, Klein nevertheless arranged for a local player to fill Benny's seat in the band:

> One afternoon, while Roy was asleep in his room down the corridor, I sneaked off to the railway station, carrying one saxophone, one type-writer and a carrier bag crammed with dirty washing. I wired the girl my time of arrival, and when the train pulled in, there she was waiting, Mother Courage in high heels. I felt greatly elated by my act of reckless-

ness, and it was several days before I began to admit that the course of true love never runs smooth. I took a train home with the dirty washing untouched.

I still see Klein from time to time. He says he knows of cases where a man has spurned an income for the sake of romance, but that I remain the only fool he has ever heard of who turned down two incomes for it. If anyone reading this account of youthful indiscretion happens to know where Olive is, perhaps they could get in touch. I figure she still owes me £1.43 for one seventh of a week's work, less a pound for the taxi.[18]

Back in London the situation looked bleak, apart from the six fivers, some of which went towards a new Remington typewriter. Unable to find any other orchestra work, Benny opted for the last resort. He took to the high seas.

Geraldo's Navy 15

An idiosyncrasy of those years was the musical rite of passage that was a stint before the mast of 'Geraldo's Navy', the orchestras which that famous band-leader would despatch on transatlantic cruise ships. For the younger musicians who did not view such engagements as a kind of maritime semi-retirement, there was a simple exchange involved in accepting his shilling. In return for their labours in the ballrooms of the pitching liners, they would receive in addition to their wages two precious days of shore leave in New York, while their ship was readied for its return leg. For Benny, the absence of any paid work on dry land, and the opportunity to visit the jazz world's Mecca, were a potent combination. First, though, there was the traditional pitfall, an audition. It was invigilated by Geraldo himself, although his whispered comments were relayed to the band by a functionary who seemed to be employed for no other end than to relieve his master from the onerous business of talking to supplicant musicians. Given the purgatorial quality of the music on cruise liners, the orchestra, which had been assembled hastily for the occasion, easily passed the audition and soon after-wards sailed from Southampton.

Surprisingly for a man who detested travel, Benny had a pronounced fond-ness for ocean cruises. I didn't understand why until my mid-twenties, when I crossed the Atlantic with him on the *QE2*. To stop the passengers getting so relaxed that they fell overboard, Cunard devised themed entertainment programmes, and on this occasion had decided on a Gershwin cruise. In return for a free passage to New York and air flights home, Benny had to provide a show one afternoon on the life of George Gershwin. He duly concocted a production similar to his Shaw's Corner presentations, hiring Toni as his fellow-reader and Annie Ross as his singer. I was engaged as his Musical Director, which gives an indication of the generous extent of his nepotism. The entertainment was a great success, although as it took place in a Force Eight gale, the audience looked even more nauseous than usual by the end of the show. Their duties dispensed with, Benny and Toni spent the rest of the cruise in amiable companionship with two friends, Jack Rosenthal and Maureen Lipman, who were also working their passage. After a few days, I realised why he enjoyed cruising so much.

Almost as soon as we had left the Solent behind us, the passengers had fallen into the relaxed rhythm of cruising life. After breakfast, why not recline with the ship's newspaper, before taking a short turn round the deck before lunch, which itself would run inexorably towards afternoon tea? Read a book for a while, and it was time to dress for dinner. People wandered around the decks with beatific expressions on their faces, telling complete strangers how happy they were to lead a life of such deep relaxation. It was then that it dawned on me just why Benny enjoyed this mode of travel. For once, everyone else had slowed down to his own calm pace of living. As the storm cleared and the sea became as smooth as green glass, New York got nearer. Taking a constitutional before lunch in the Queen's Grill, Benny primed me about New York, and reminisced about his own first visit.

Coming from a Britain still in the shadow of war and rationing, America had seemed impossibly fecund and affluent. Benny and Stanton had spent their shore leave racing from club to club in the famous 52nd Street, hearing Dizzy Gillespie at first hand, buying modernist ties that could be profitably resold in Archer Street, and even meeting some of the names on the spinning labels of their much-played records. As a memento of his visit, Benny bought a new mouthpiece, a white one in the style of Charlie Parker, which he used to the end of his life. As much of a totem as the prized original that had been left in his chest of drawers on the night of his first gig, this new mouthpiece marked him as a player of the new, Modern jazz, which smooth though the passage of time may make it seem to our ears, was raucously controversial at the time. But, as he found out on his return to London, he was still a modernist in search of other modernists.

As suggested by the new typewriter that had been financed by the Roy Fox débâcle, Benny was still as fanatically committed to writing as ever. It was in 1952 that, in an effort to supplement his meagre earnings from the big bands, he began to send material to the 'flyblown Aristotles'[1] who ran the music papers, at first with little luck. The lightning stroke that transformed Benny's life for ever came a few weeks later, on a Sunday afternoon when, as if by magic, his hero interceded in his life and changed the path of a career which was fast becoming a disappointment. In the autumn of 1952, Benny was working at a jazz gig at the Manor House jazz club, a gig best described as 'an island in a sea of alcohol':

> I was playing in a big band which had been cobbled together for the
> occasion, and sounded like it. For what seemed to me to be half a life-

time, but which couldn't have been more than three years, I had scraped
a living by working in dance halls. I was sick of tango dancers and smelly
boarding houses and lonely days in strange provincial towns. At twenty-
three, I was thinking of trying to make a living by writing. Only the fact
that I was starting to get bits and pieces of specialised work in the jazz
clubs kept me going.

The music went well that night. I blew several solos, there were no
critics in the house, several friends in the band, and it was too early for
the star guest, Ronnie Scott, to have arrived. I knew that when he did, I
would clam up. I had known him socially for about a year, but I hero-
worshipped him so desperately that to attempt anything while he was
on the premises was a physical impossibility.

That night at Manor House, he arrived much earlier than I realised,
and was sitting out of sight at the bar listening to the music for at least
half an hour before I spotted him. Once again I clammed up, but later
that night, he asked if I would like to join his quartet. I felt like a substitute for Accrington Stanley reserves who had been asked to play for
England. The upshot was that I worked alongside him for the next three
years, enjoying a vicarious celebrity. Goodbye landladies, goodbye
'Lavender Blue, Dilly Dilly', goodbye ten quid a week.[2]

For the next few weeks, Benny played baritone with Ronnie's quintet. Always
modest, he later insisted that the main reason for his elevation as the rising star
of the baritone was that while there were many tenorists around who imitated
Lester Young, no one else apart from Harry Klein was playing good jazz on the
baritone, and Harry, exhausted by the road, was resting. Benny's first gig with
Ronnie was a revelation:

Among the other musicians, he was a natural leader. In the quintet on
the night of my baptism, nobody questioned any of his decisions, which
he dispensed with a minimum of fuss, a nod here, a pointed finger there.
His mood was dramatically altered. The puns and the persiflage, the lust
for a good taste, the relish for a comic anecdote, all this was so much
fluff dispersed on the wind the moment he went to work. He was an
intense performer, preoccupied with the conundrums of improvisation
to the exclusion of all else. He played with his eyes closed. The intensity

of his concentration was not something I had encountered before; when he finished a solo and stopped playing, for the briefest moment his eyes were still clouded with the rhythm of invention. I knew within a few moments that he was one of those musicians, both cursed and blessed, who pursue the ultimate performance night after night, hoping for that Platonic ideal of an improvisation which only the very great ever approach. It was all a matter of surprising oneself, of suddenly producing a fragment of invention which delighted you with its freshness. But how could it be fresh and how could it surprise you when your own brain had conceived it? That was the ultimate dilemma faced by every jazz musician, accepted with more aplomb by some than by others. It was clear that Ronnie was still Hunting the Snark, and was fated to do so for the rest of his days.

That first gig was in a Gillingham dance hall, and so euphoric was my condition that I have retained no image of its contours and no idea of its whereabouts. The local panjandrum announced us, and we emerged from our tiny bandroom into cheering and lots of flashing lights. We threaded our way painfully through the crowd, holding our instruments aloft to keep them from any damaging contact with the hoi polloi, and at last mounted the band stand. The audience pressed as close to us as it could, and I noticed that nobody was dancing. All the men gazed at us with a mixture of awe and envy, as though we were exotic creatures from another planetary system. I had never been the object of such idolatry before, and its effect was to induce a sort of creative vertigo which made it impossible for me to keep anything in focus.

But there was another part of my brain, the dominant part, which was in a state of uncontrollable panic. I knew I was about to be flung into one of the most terrifying ordeals of my life. In the event, it turned out to be much worse than that. I was hopelessly unprepared for the furious pace of the night, thrown utterly out of my stride by the drummer's bewildering cannonades, reduced to embarrassment each time it was my turn to take a solo. To be honest, I was closer in spirit to the massed ranks of the fans than to the group of which I was a part. To me, the other members of the quintet were mythical beings whose doings I read of in the weekly musical comics, and the obligation to sustain the pretext that I belonged with them induced something close to cerebral paralysis. Years later, I asked one or two of the musicians who played with me that night if they had sensed my predicament, but they hardly seemed to grasp what I was talking about.

When the gig was over, we decamped for London, where we were booked to appear at an all-night club in Soho. I sat alone in the bus, gazing at the houses as they fell away behind us, and wishing that I was in one of them and fast asleep. I hoped we might never arrive, because the thought of undergoing the ordeal again was too much to bear. I could never convey in words the depth of my despair during that journey. I had just been on trial for my musical life, and had been found wanting. Perhaps there was still time to try writing for a living, and give up this chaotic business.

I was still considering the possibility when we arrived at our destination and began preparing to take the stand for the second time that night. The same deafening noise, the same lights, the same bombardment from the drums. I did what I could, but when the time came to pack away our instruments, I was convinced that Ronnie would have no choice but to dispense with my services, apologise for his error of judgement and find a replacement. Instead, he paid me one or two light compliments, and handed me eight £1 notes splayed out like a deck of cards. He gave me the details of the next gig, and then drifted over to one of the tables; within a few seconds he was laughing. I decided to walk home.

It was a crisp, clear night, and I needed to distance myself from the evening's events. The only person I talked to apart from myself was the policeman who asked me if I'd had a good night. He knew what I did for a living, and no longer wished to know what a young man was doing walking through the small hours humping a large case. By now I was part of the nocturnal furniture and troubled him not at all. The crowning irony of a night of raging incongruities was that I felt very well.[3]

Within a few weeks, there occurred a turn of events that turned what could have been a passing association into a long-term one. Ructions in the ranks of Jack Parnell's big band had led to a mass walk-out of the best of his young players, who were some of the best young musicians in the country. Suddenly, the human material was available for Ronnie to realise his ambition to escape from the tiny treadmill of fly-by-night jazz clubs, not through playing in somebody else's conservative big band, but with his own small orchestra, just as his contemporary John Dankworth had done with his Seven. His quintet already used the pianist Norman Stenfalt, bassist Lennie Bush, drummer Tony Crombie, and Benny's baritone. By adding the refugees from the Parnell band to this quintet (altoist Derek Humble, trombonist Ken Wray, trumpeter Jimmy Deuchar and fellow tenorist Pete King), Ronnie formed the famous 'nine-piece'. Over the next two years, this group became legendary, as one of the high-water marks of British jazz.

Forty years later, it is often difficult to imagine why the nine-piece was so controversial, both professionally and critically. Much of the controversy can be traced to the peculiarly straitened musical atmosphere of the times. In 1953, London had no jazz club that hosted exclusively Modern jazz, and indeed would have to wait until 1959 before it did, when Scott launched his shoestring operation in Gerrard Street. Meanwhile, the commercial orchestra market was clogged with superannuated, genteel Swing orchestras. In combining the aesthetics of Modern jazz with the orchestral format, Scott hit upon a magic formula for commercial success, hip enough for the cognoscenti, but formal enough for dancers in the ballrooms where the big audiences lay, and for the radio broadcasts that were the only route to the big world outside the jazz clubs. This alone inspired a certain amount of critical jealousy. To this was added the opprobrium of the band leaders of the day. As there was no money to start up the group, and as all concerned were sick of the prevailing orchestral mores of the time, it was to be a co-operative venture, a notion that to the old-style band leaders 'smacked strongly of syncopated Marxism'[4] that could incite similar radical demands from their own dissatisfied ranks.

To generate some free publicity from the music press, rehearsals for the band were held in public. Among the proud parents offering their assessment of the band's chances was Benny's father Dave, who was snapped by the *New Musical Express* wearing his characteristic expression of furtive surprise, as he opined, 'I taught my son, Benny, to play the tenor sax, so I'm biased. The band is West End material already.' After several weeks' rehearsal, on March 7th, 1953 the band went to Manchester's exotically titled High Street Baths Ballroom for a low-key debut performance, taking Manny Plotski with them as bandboy and factotum. When they arrived, Benny was astonished to find suspended over the stage a large banner that read 'These Men Are Heroes', with their names following. It was a heady notice that his engagement by Ronnie had catapulted Benny from obscurity to limelight. Once again, the gig was received with the same fanatical reception and the same thunderous noise, but this time amplified by the addition of a full horn section. To complete Benny's weekend, the band had to be back in London the next day for another watershed in the modest history of British jazz.

At this time, the Musicians' Union still persisted with its idiotic policy of only granting work permits to American musicians if a reciprocal number of British jazz musicians were to be employed in America. However well meant, this rule was in principle, its practice amounting to a virtual embargo on all live performances in Britain by the American jazz players who were the originators and masters of the idiom. The embargo deprived British players of first-hand education from their idols, which in turn reduced their chances of being employed in America to nil. Britain's pristine isolation came to an end the day after the nine-piece had debuted in Manchester, through the twinned agencies of the elements and Norman Granz, an American promoter who was himself a natural force to be reckoned with. The winter of 1952–3 had seen catastrophic floods in Britain, and Granz offered his barnstorming 'Jazz At The Philharmonic' package tour for a fund-raising concert, with all objections from the Union to be waived in view of the charitable nature of the concert. The Gaumont in Kilburn was hired for two sell-out shows, and after many years of waiting, British musicians at last had the chance to hear their idols.

The first half of the concert featured the local talent, while the second half was given over to Granz's heavyweights: Oscar Peterson, Ella Fitzgerald, and the languid hero of Benny's teens, Lester Young. In a life which covered so much ground in such different disciplines, the night of March 8th, 1953 is an identifiable turning point for Benny. Those twinned tracks of music and writing that ran through the day he was born, and which he was to spend so long trying to reconcile, came together on that Sunday evening, which became in retrospect the pivot between his old life and new life. It was the night of a musical coming of age for which he had been striving for a decade since his first fumblings on Dave's soprano, and it was the night that engendered his first significant piece of writing. Assembled in the Gaumont that night were all the important figures of Benny's musical life.

With Dave watching in the audience, the evening began with Harry Hayes's group, with his erstwhile pupil Benny on baritone, followed by two other local groups, and then Benny's new employer Ronnie Scott and a sextet, all of whom acquitted themselves with vigour. But their enthusiasm was revealed in all its callowness by the opening salvoes of 'C Jam Blues', as Oscar Peterson opened the second half with a dazzling display of just what the British players had been missing. Now sitting in the audience in his secondary capacity as budding critic, Benny was as stunned as the rest of the audience. When Lester played, Benny listened from the side of the stage, as his idol produced his enormous sound from a borrowed mouthpiece and a plastic reed, a sound that never left his head for the rest of his life.

With Harry Hayes, Ronnie and Lester on the same bill, the night was a summation of Benny's playing life to date. But also present that night were three others with whose names he would become associated in the future: Norman Granz, and his Verve recording artists Oscar Peterson and Ella Fitzgerald, each arguably the leading exponent of their respective fields. While Ella's personality may have been curiously shallow considering the skill with which she delivered often complex lyrics, Benny was to become good friends with both Norman and Oscar, with Norman giving him extensive work as a writer of sleeve notes for many of the classic albums that Verve issued over the next three decades. That night, reviewing Norman's show for the *New Musical Express*, marked the beginning of those associations, and of Benny's real writing career.

But all of that was still in the future. As the lights came up at the end of the night, Benny was thrilled at having encountered his heroes, if chastened by the evident superiority of the Americans even over the great Scott. There was only one problem that night: Plotski. Part of a bandboy's job was to scale a wobbly ladder to the gods, in order to give instructions to the resident lighting engineer. Unfortunately, Plotski's limited professional qualifications for his post did not include a head for heights. Having previously tackled nothing more dizzying than the odd flight of stairs, it was not until Plotski was in his perch in the Gaumont's rafters that he realised he suffered from chronic vertigo. He clung to the ladder, refusing to move. At the end of the night, there occurred a protracted and traumatic (for Plotski, anyway) stand-off between Plotski and the dots on the ground far below him. Eventually, he was carried back down, and the Scott band could begin work.

After spending a month's voluntary exile in Manchester, the band made its London debut playing opposite Ted Heath's Orchestra at the Palladium. An anonymous reporter from the *NME*, which was sponsoring the band, was on hand:

Last Sunday at the Palladium, [the Scott band] approached its most difficult hurdle to date, a concert appearance in the West End on the same
bill as the finest large band in the country. Presumably, it approached
that hurdle with some nervous tension, but it proceeded to clear it in a
manner which delighted the three thousand fans who filled the Palladium to capacity that night.

In twenty brief minutes the new Ronnie Scott Orchestra established
itself beyond any doubt as the one of the most formidable and impressive combinations anywhere in Europe today.'[5]

It is hard to be sure, but it seems as if the above eulogy was written by Benny.
Preceded as it is by details of the band's domestic life during their Manchester
exile, it is followed by what is surely the *NME*'s first and last reference to the
relationship of Greek mathematics to girl singers:

After the inspired buffoonery of Dickie Valentine, the Scott band could
easily have been an anti-climax. And presuming that half the audience
were males, then at the time the Scott Orchestra made its appearance, there were fifteen hundred people in the crowd preoccupied
with the thought that when Euclid said that the shortest distance
between two points is a straight line, he had evidently never seen Lita
Roza.[6]

In December 1952, the *NME* had printed Benny's first article outside the
pages of *The Fitzroy*, billed as 'An impossible but seasonal story by a sax-
player with a sense of humour', involving Harry Klein, Vic Ash, Stan Tracey
and a boarding-house run by a medium. It was the first of a torrent of
humorous pieces by 'the musician with a sense of humour' about dance band
life, most of them heavily indebted to Damon Runyon and S. J. Perelman. An
unforeseen benefit of being hired by Ronnie was the paper's willingness to
give Benny more work, as an inside contact with the hot band of the moment
who could also write was rare in musical circles, and virtually unprecedented
in the musical journalism of the time. This led to Benny's first piece of jazz
writing about the JATP concert in March, which in its turn led to a mixture of
writing. The *NME* wanted humour, billing his efforts for the edition of 8 May
1953 as:

> It's the Damon of Dance again (or, the Runyon of Rhythm, if you prefer it!) In between playing baritone-sax with Ronnie Scott, he has still found time to double typewriter and tell us about 'The Most Beautiful Girl In Manchester'.[7]

Within a year, Benny had a weekly column, leaving the *NME*'s editors with the challenging task of devising ever more fatuous descriptions of the strange new species the paper had discovered, which could not only operate the keys of a typewriter with more aplomb than its regular staff, but could also perform even more arcane manoeuvres on the saxophone. He was 'The music business' wittiest writer', 'The musical profession's foremost literary humorist', and 'The saxophonist with a twinkle in his typewriter'. Oddly enough, while they trumpeted what they quaintly referred to as Benny's 'potentialities', the *NME*'s editors seem not to have hit on the brilliant notion of sending him to review another concert until June 1955, when he was despatched to the Finsbury Park Empire to review one of the music hall's dying gasps, Sid Seymour's Jazz Mad Hatters.

Not that he wasn't busy in the meantime. With Benny taking his typewriter, the Scott band went back on the road, and were to spend most of the next 26 months on a musical odyssey along Britain's A-roads that was to become a legend, one of the founding myths of Modern jazz in Britain. For Benny, this exhausting round was as incredible as it was unforeseen. Emerging from his long apprenticeship thanks to Ronnie, he had become one of the best-known jazz musicians in Britain, playing with the cream of his contemporaries in a band that stormed all before it. To top it all, he had made it into print after a seemingly endless adolescent obscurity. Having begun 1953 a recently returned sea-dog with no work in the book other than the odd quintet date with Ronnie and a four-night stint playing Irish dance tunes at Kilburn's Galtymore Ballroom, he ended it as a Poll-Winner in the *New Musical Express*'s annual awards. Not the least surprising aspect of this sudden acclaim was that Benny, who had been discreetly but diligently plying his saxophone around Britain for the last three years, had won the vote for 'Most Promising Newcomer'.

Ronnie 16

After its debut in March 1953, the Ronnie Scott Orchestra quickly became a hit. They appealed both to specialist jazz fans who recognised their Boppish influences, and also to the broader public, whose anxieties about jazz were ameliorated by the group's matching suits and music stands, which in true Fifties style were curved plexiglass affairs with the musicians' names on the front. Those trappings alone are enough to notify us that we are considering a lost epoch of high musical standards and Swing-era conventions. Indeed, the Scott orchestra was one of the last musical phenomena to occupy popular music's centre stage before rock'n'roll appeared and changed the business forever by unleashing the teenage spending power that was a by-product of post-war affluence, and washing away the certainties of Archer Street almost overnight. From our jaded vantage point, looking back across a landscape littered over forty-three-years'-worth of rock-'n'roll's bastard progeny, the notion that an orchestra playing predominantly instrumental music of high rhythmic and harmonic complexity from a sitting position might possess anything other than novelty appeal for a mainstream audience seems almost comically unlikely, a snapshot from an earlier, more innocent age.

The story of that band, like so much of the pre-rock'n'roll music business, is a strange blend of harshness and quaintness. They spent much of their 26 months together rattling around Britain in an ex-British European Airways coach with no heating and no radio, on a diet of fried food from the transport cafés 'that dotted the country's highways like a run of acne'.[1] Yet they remained deeply committed to their ground-breaking music and to each other, taking Modern jazz to Britain's unlikeliest backwaters. Conventional in their appearance, and with more than a nod to the traditional proprieties of onstage deportment, they nevertheless managed to antagonise the critics, and to attract young fans. Disillusioned as he was by the incompetent, corrupt bandleaders and mechanistic, dull repertoires of the dance bands, Benny found playing with the nine-piece a liberating experience:

> Sometimes a musician gets in a band whose musical policy he believes
> in. But you never get a *whole* band who believe in it. You often get a

189

whole band which pretends to believe in it, for politic reasons – but that is a different thing. In the Scott band there was a fervid delight in the music we played. We were inordinately proud of what we played, and hated anybody who said things about us that were untrue.

We used to get bitter about critics who reviewed us, because we did not consider that they were qualified to criticise us. I think we were right about that. I also think we were underrated by many reviewers who kept writing how loud we were without ever stopping to hear how soft we could be, or how large a percentage of originals comprised our library, or how much less mercenary we were towards our music than were those selfsame critics who used to accuse us of trying to attract attention to ourselves.

We encountered in our two years of life much petty jealousy from bandleaders and none at all from musicians. The inference is obvious. A thriving co-op band is a dangerous thing so far as many bandleaders are concerned. They see Communism round the corner and start worrying about how far they may go on exploiting their own musicians.[2]

Freed from the usual treadmill, and with several talented writers and arrangers in the band, the Scott Orchestra had the rare blend of youth, common goals and good timing that marks the best and most successful bands. For all concerned, it was a golden time. Even obstacles turned out to be blessings. When Crombie and Stenfalt left to form their own groups, they were replaced by Phil Seamen and Victor Feldman, who doubled on piano and drums, leading to a battle-of-the-drums between the two that became the high point of the show. But when he recalled the band, Benny was often ambiguous. There was a worm in the apple. Beneath the band's crust of well-tailored respectability, there lay a taste for anarchy and indulgence that would have shamed many of the rock bands whose depravities are the stuff of self-publicised legend. Incongruous amid the devastation is Benny, ever his mother's serious son.

An almost logical extension of the Beboppers' passion for all things, Charlie Parker was to imitate the trappings of his genius. This could take the harmless form of buying the same mouthpieces and shirts as the master had sported, or the wholly admirable form of dissecting the curlicues of his recorded solos phrase by phrase, as Benny had done with his and Parker's hero, Lester Young. But in this period, a third form of imitation became common, first in America, and then in Britain: heroin. Jazz had always had a self-destructive streak, born of equal parts hedonism and alienation. No sooner had the music been born than one of its earliest masters, Buddy Bolden, drank himself to death. The great Lester had compounded the injuries of societal racism and the US Army's electro-shock treatment with prodigious drinking and marijuana smoking, which by the time of his 1953 visit to London had reduced him to a tired shade of his former glory. Like the music itself, the heroin epidemic of the Forties and Fifties that accompanied the rise and fall of Bebop was a raising of the traditional stakes, but with more serious effects.

A list of musicians in that period whose careers were derailed by heroin reads like a Who's Who of Modern Jazz, from Miles Davis and John Coltrane, to Phil Seamen and Tubby Hayes. As with the last two, who were among Britain's best musicians, the long-term effects could be fatal. In Britain, to the youthful enthusiasm of Parker's admirers was added a dangerous dash of naïvety. In these strangely different times, widespread drug use and drug education were both inconceivable. When Ronnie Scott had been caught in possession of cocaine at Club Eleven in 1950, the judge had not only been unaware of what Bebop was ('A queer form of modern dancing, a Negro jive' was the police's estimate), but had even believed Ronnie's excuse that the cocaine was for a toothache. A lack of awareness as to the depth of the waters into which they were swimming meant that many of the addicts of Benny's generation had begun using hard drugs without being aware of their addictive potential.

At first, taking heroin was primarily an affirmation of allegiance to Modern jazz, the ultimate secret code of membership of a small musical elite alienated but not insulated from the repressive, rationed world of post-war Britain. In this self-mythologising understanding of the uncaring 'straight' world, heroin was only one of the totems to hand. There were its philosophical fellow-travellers, existentialism and nihilism, and their own vulgates: the deliberate rejection of the conventional in all its forms, and the anarchic, humorous language of 'hip', part jazz argot, part Marx Brothers, and part Goons. Of course, the enthusiasm for everything American, from music to clothes to humour to language, now seems to us not the indicator of a refined sensibility, as it was in the Fifties, but an index of the cultural isolation and naïvety of the time. Once again, we return to a jarring image, one that reveals Fifties Britain in all its contradiction, a bizarre blend of Cold War conformism and pre-rock'n'roll rebellion. Benny, who at this time had not smoked so much as a cigarette, found himself surrounded by improbable debauchery, rooming with a heroin addict, and regularly witnessing scenes of *outré* sexual indulgence.

But he himself didn't indulge. Later, he told me that it was more because his younger self had been 'squeamish'. I think there was a second element to the reason why. Perhaps because he had been an indulged only child, and perhaps because he had realised at an early age that his were not ordinary abilities, he had a great awareness of the responsibility that comes with a talent. And with that awareness comes self-consciousness and self-criticism. While his playing may have been inhibited by his inability to 'forget himself', this same inability may have been his salvation when faced with the manifold temptations of the travelling musician. Even at this stage in his playing career, a Poll Winner in the public eye, he was still planning his escape from music and his maturation as a writer. Instead of plunging in to the shenanigans, he observed them as a good writer should, and filled the longeurs of travelling with reading, which gave rise to the running joke that was still circulating among musicians when Leo and I joined the profession, that while the rest of the Scott band went to bed with whoever they could find, Benny went to bed with a crossword.

An unlikely testimony to Benny's moderation is from Michael Parkinson, who in 1953 was working as an occasional barman in a club in his native Barnsley. Taking a tray of drinks to the dressing room during the interval, Parkinson encountered the usual heady backstage atmosphere as he entered the room, the shouting and laughter, the clinking of glasses and the whiff of unconventional cigarettes. The only non-participant in the revels was Benny. He was sitting in the corner, reading a Russian novel. In the end, Benny cracked, although his sole concession to the depravity around him was a typically moderate one. In an uncharacteristic loss of control, he started smoking:

> The first cigarette I ever smoked was a Markevitch Red & White. I was in my twenty-seventh year and the misdemeanour took place outside a transport café somewhere north of Towcester ... I gather from contemporaries that my complete abstinence until the age of twenty-six was so rare as to be almost unique among my generation. Most of my friends had already smoked their fifty-thousandth cigarette before I had even started, and why I should have succumbed I am unable to say, unless it was the sheer boredom of sitting in a touring band's coach day after day, mile after mile, or staring out of boarding house windows at the slanting

rain. One thing I am certain of. It was nothing to do with wanting to belong. I have never been a joiner, always a cat that walked by itself.

It should be remembered that in those days there was no such thing as a guilt complex about smoking. Nobody seriously believed that smoking caused cancer, or indeed anything, except possibly smoke. On the contrary, there were plenty of fifty-a-day men who contended that smoking was good for you because it choked all the germs to death. Admittedly, children were warned that smoking would stunt their growth, but as these warnings came from giant adults who had been puffing away practically from the cradle, we could hardly be blamed for refusing to take the warnings seriously. (My father once told me he had smoked his first cigar at eleven.)

But my reasons for abstaining were not that I respected the unwritten law, or that I was worried about being a midget, but simply that smoke smells unpleasant, that nicotine stains look ugly, and that cigarettes would undoubtedly cramp my style as a saxophonist-footballer. And so I went through schooldays as unsullied as a boy scout. I even navigated that time of the septic ego, the Teens, without weakening … Then there came that black night outside Towcester.[3]

It was to be seventeen years before Benny was able to stop smoking. He never stopped berating himself for that momentary lapse north of Towcester, especially after he developed a cancer whose origins could be traced to that night and which would eventually kill him. As he always enjoyed a joke, the irony of being killed not by one of his occasional acts of principled foolishness, such as when he showed his contempt for the internal combustion engine by stepping into a busy road, but by one of his rare acts of weakness, was not lost on him. Nor on us. As he had lived on little else but fried eggs and sweet tea for the first half of his life, and had spent much of its second half constructing sandwiches composed of equal-sized slabs of bread, butter and cheese, our money was on a heart attack.

Glamour and delinquency aside, the Scott band's life on the road was the familiar grind. They would congregate in Archer Street in the early hours of a mid-week morning, before heading off for a string of one-nighters, from which they would return after the weekend. The long tedium of the road journeys was the ideal breeding ground for the bonding of idiosyncratic quipping and silly pranks that occupies much of a band's leisure time. Perhaps the main difference was that as well as being musicians of a superior quality to the average group, their misdemeanours were similarly elevated. Hence the famous testimony to the abilities of the band's trumpeter and arranger, Jimmy Deuchar, who, while chaos raged all around, could write out note-perfect charts for a new tune en route to the gig. Hence also the equally notorious testimony to the pugilistic talents of the band's driver, an ex-boxer called Les Bristow. One day, tiring of his charges' endless fooling around after the altoist Derek Humble had thrown his jacket over Bristow's head while he piloted the bus down a country lane, Bristow screeched to a halt, and then chinned Humble.

One afternoon, killing time before a gig at a US Army base, Benny noticed that the band's dressing room was the office of the base commander. He and Ronnie made use of the office's typewriter and headed stationery to write an outraged letter of complaint from the base commander to the band's agent, Harold Davison. Apart from listing imaginative combinations of unprofessional and downright hooligan behaviour, and the making of improper suggestions to an officer's wife which were not likely to advance the cause of Anglo-American friendship, the letter complained that the band 'had turned out to be specialists in fraud and larceny, as well as the dance band repertoire of 1953'.[4] A few days later, Pete King was summoned to his office by a horrified Davison, and had to break the news that the letter he was waving around was a spoof.

As with all touring, farce was never far away:

> We did a one-night stand in a southern Irish country town where the crowd was so sprightly that the bandstand was halfway up the wall of the building, with two layers of chicken wire between Us and Them, so that the customers could keep themselves happy chucking chairs and bottles at us without interrupting the flow of the music.
>
> In 1954, when we appeared at the old Gaumont State, Kilburn, for a big charity show, they put us on the small rising stage. After we had done our strictly rationed thirteen minutes, down went the stage, but only halfway, leaving us stuck there, visible from the waist.[5]

The band had a rare camaraderie that spilled from the stage to the other 22 hours of the day. When they passed bucolic Blackheath, they would stop off for an impromptu game of cricket. Otherwise, gambling was another shared

194

passion. Ronnie even went to the extent of buying six small cars and a pack of playing cards for races conducted on a length of green baize cloth purloined from a hotel store cupboard. The object was to bet on a car, whose progress was dependent upon the value of the card turned over. Over the winter of 1953, the Green Baize Cloth became a corporate obsession, with a nightly race meet that ran from after the gig until dawn:

> Until that fatal winter, I had never allowed the touring life to get a grip on me. I still managed to live a kind of Jekyll and Hyde existence, wallowing in bacon rinds and old saxophone reeds on the road, and behaving decorously at home … The last grains of conventionality got crushed out of me over those two years. My system became attuned to a different routine. F. Scott Fitzgerald's dictum, that somewhere inside a man there is a place where it is always three o'clock in the morning, became sheer nonsense. Within the partnership, three o'clock was the peak hour of the day. At first, it was strange to me, but I soon came to realise there was a certain insane logic to this calculated inversion of day and night … After several weeks of this I began to show signs of strain. I found myself falling asleep in the street, and once I suddenly collapsed while sneaking out of a hotel.

To get some rest, Benny threw in his share in the racing cars, but such was the general dismay at his un-teamlike behaviour that Derek Humble came up with a compromise. It seemed there was no escape from the family destiny:

> And so, for the first and only time in my life, I found myself working as a bookie's clerk at a shilling a race. I sat in hotel lounges all over Britain, staring glassy-eyed at the six little cars while I clutched a pencil and paper in nerveless and often trembling fingers, recording the debts and counterdebts of my partners as they speculated on the green baize cloth. The fantasies woven by the fortunes of war on that small stretch of green baize were often so ridiculous that they kept me awake till seven or eight each morning.
>
> Several times, somebody won everything there was to win, including the wives, chattels and worldly goods of the other players. There was one period over three races, lasting five terrifying minutes

when Ken Wray, through the eccentricities of the cars, owned five of the nine shares which comprised the company. For five ghastly minutes he consisted of his own majority and could have called off the game, summoned a shareholder's meeting and voted us into some foul act, like signing over to him the assets of the company.

This he never did, no doubt because at the time the assets of the company consisted of £345's worth of debts, a set of magenta plush velvet ties nobody ever succeeded in tying into a civilised knot, a bandboy called Emmanuel Plotski for whom Ronnie Scott and not I was entirely responsible, and the goodwill of a nymph called Jean who lived in Yorkshire and loved everybody in our band and everyone else's band in equal proportions.[6]

Marathon poker schools were also popular, and there was always the horses, especially when Ronnie noticed that the coach was passing a racecourse. On one occasion at Doncaster, their leader bet the entire co-operative's savings on a horse, and lost. There can be no better testimony to the respect that the band had for Ronnie than that there was no lasting consequence of Scott's carelessness other than amusement. For Benny, it was enough to be working with his hero. The nine-piece's gigs left Benny with a particular satisfaction that was apparent even when he talked about them four decades later. Although he always felt that his playing was hampered by his own embarrassment at being in such exalted musical company, the elation that comes from playing with great musicians is a rare elixir. He was unashamedly nostalgic for those two years, yet was relieved to see them gone, as there was an undertow of recklessness to them which he found disturbing. For every harmless anecdote, such as the prospect of their eccentric vocalist Art Baxter shouting curses as he ran naked into the winter sea at Ramsgate for a bet, there was another, uglier one, as when the bus had to pull up in a lay-by for an abscess to be cut from drummer Phil Seamen's leg as he lay over the bonnet. Balanced against the innocent pleasure of a group of like-minded young men finding happiness in their shared love was the looming shadow of hard drugs. Meanwhile, the exhausting grind of the road wore on:

My diaries tell me that in the period 1954–55 I slept in no fewer than 314 [beds] apart from my own. You are not to deduce from that alarming statistic that I was some kind of latterday Casanova, but only that I was a touring dance band musician whose professional itinerary used to average out at about twelve hotels per month.

As I look back on it all, those 314 beds magically merge into one symbolic bed which followed me around unmade, like an unkempt sheepdog, as I wandered the highways and byways of Britain, a bed which never seemed to behave the same way twice or even, on those occasions when no accommodation was to be had at all, once.

In Crewe, it tilted up from the foot to the head, in Nelson from the head to the foot; in Swanage it listed dramatically to starboard and tipped me out twice before dawn; in Dublin it had no legs and smelt faintly of coal-dust, and in Nottingham its over-oiled castors whisked you around the room like a motor-cycle whenever you took a deep breath. Of course, I can laugh about it now, but at the time, it was both horrific and permanently debilitating.[7]

This is as close as Benny got to writing about the Scott band. It was simply too personal, not least because Benny was emotionally close to its members long after he had left London and music for the country and writing. He was always very aware of the journalistic tendency towards sensationalism when it came to jazz, and knew that any accurate account of his time with the band would include a large slice of unsavoury detail that would quickly become salacious when separated from his musical recollections. And so he wrote very little about the high point of his playing life.

The two years in the Scott co-operative band were more than I could ever have dared hope for. Most jazz musicians in this country are lucky if they get two days of that kind of set-up, let alone two years. As a matter of fact, being in the band was such a personal thing that I am not comfortable any more talking about it. There was a time when I did nothing else, but today it seems too much like stalking a ghost. It was just an episode that happened to happen, that was unexpectedly rich in its musical and social relationships. It possibly coloured the lives of all involved in it, but such is the world we live in, it no longer has a scrap of significance. Only the scattered gramophone recordings prove that it took place at all.[8]

What the band did leave behind was those recordings, mainly made for the Esquire label. The men of taste at the BBC had caused a storm in the musical press by turning down the band soon after its formation, but fortunately private enterprise showed more initiative, with the result that this crucial moment in the growth of jazz in Britain was recorded. As with the blue gaberdine suits, the plexiglass music stands, and the arguments over whether the foxtrot was being executed at the right tempo, they sound like they are findings from a time capsule that has been unearthed in Old Compton Street. When Leo and I sat down to listen through the Scott Orchestra records, two things struck us immediately. Firstly, there was the high standard of playing and composition, both of which were unusual for the time, and still are. Secondly, the performances themselves, which appeared to belie the controversy the band caused. Much of the repertoire was what we would consider the meat and potatoes of the Modern style, standards taken at audacious tempo with long solos. After all, this was a band whose last recordings flirted with the Cool style of Miles Davis's current group, and even involved a harpist, hired from one of the respectable orchestras for the day. Undoubtedly, it is good music, but why did it cause such a fuss? The answer may well bear out the suspicions that Benny and the rest of the group had entertained at the time about the music press, with its willingness to generate controversy, and the music business, which preferred to view musicians as a form of indentured labourer.

The bandwagon rolled to a halt on Easter Monday, 1955. For Benny, when he got off the bus at dawn after that last date in Nottingham, there was a certain familiarity to his position. It was back to Archer Street and the Harmony Inn. But otherwise, his professional situation had changed irreversibly. From Mecca ballrooms and suburban dance bands, he had ascended the dizzy heights of the stage at the Albert Hall, and played opposite Woody Herman, Illinois Jacquet and Coleman Hawkins. And it wasn't over yet. Not wanting to rest on his nine-piece laurels, Ronnie was forming a big band. Benny, now enjoying as mercurial a rise as a jazz pundit as he had as a baritonist, was an obvious choice.

Kenton 17

When I asked him about Ronnie's big band, Benny replied that the only person who had got any real pleasure out of that ill-fated union was generous Jean from Yorkshire. In theory, doubling the size of the band from nine to eighteen was straightforward, but its practice quickly deteriorated into a logistical ordeal for Pete King, while the conflicting egos of so many talented players never gelled into the band of brothers that the nine-piece had been. As Benny put it to Ronnie's biographer John Fordham, 'Its most intense and creative activity was its poker school, famed for the unblinkingly dispassionate physiognomy of [Joe] Harriott, and trumpeter Hank Shaw's touchingly prudent habit of instantly posting whatever winnings he would make to his wife.'[1] At least Benny could get more sleep this time, as he was rooming with Harriott, who was out all night after their gigs.

Joe Harriott was the first of two Jamaican musicians with whom Benny would become close in the late Fifties. A passionate, Protean player, he later became one of the pioneers of the British avant garde in the Sixties, his recordings sometimes using none other than the pencil-playing drummer of Benny's return to the stand, Bobby Orr. As if pioneering a difficult, unapproachable music weren't enough, the adversities of being black in Fifties' and Sixties' Britain were also to trouble Harriott, who was to acquire a reputation for irascibility. But Benny found him to be a relaxed, charming companion. One night in Manchester, Benny was lugging his baritone out of the stage door when he found his path blocked by two women, fighting on the floor, in front of Harriott, who was leaning on a lamp-post smoking a cigarette. Benny asked Harriott what was happening. 'Nothing, man,' he said coolly. 'They're just fighting over me.' In the following months, both musicians became fascinated with the changes of 'Deep Purple', and would crawl the after-hours clubs of Soho, playing the song with each group they sat in with.

That the big band was not going according to plan became brutally apparent on the last night of 1955. As Fordham notes in its obituary:

Musically, it was living proof that an assembly of diverse talents doesn't always make a living band, and it might have been the insecurity of the outfit's musical perspective that sowed the seeds for the unrest that was frequently under its surface. Harriott was unhappy with being second alto to Dougie Robinson. Trumpeter Dave Usden and Phil Seamen even fought publicly on the bandstand in Morecambe on New Year's Eve 1955, and accompanied the ensemble's final rendition of 'Should Auld Acquaintance Be Forgot' with a three-act opera of shouting, deprecations, abuse and all-round indifference to the perplexed revellers. It was not a happy ship, and the most surprising feature of its voyage was that it took so long to go down.[2]

In the early months of 1956, Benny, by now writing a weekly column for the *NME* which was adorned with a cartoon sketch of its author, felt able to make the decision that had been looming for the last three years, and which his unexpected success with Ronnie Scott had deferred. In his spare time, he had begun to mine the memories of his childhood, the Boys Club and early touring days for the anecdotage that was to be the mainstay of his writing style. But he was dissatisfied with the results, and judging from the response of the newspaper editors to whom he sent this material, his critical faculties were at this stage more advanced than his creative ones. He decided that if he was to make real progress as a writer, then he had to undergo the same process of 'woodshedding' as an aspirant musician. He broadened his reading to include authors who he may not have enjoyed reading, but who were great stylists, and he tried to write every day.

As for music, he felt equivocal. He began to feel that he had played his best, and that he had reached the limit of his abilities on the saxophone. Certainly, by 1956 he had been chasing Lester's train for fifteen years, but for all his protestations he was not a man without talent or diligence, and the mathematical ramifications of jazz's chordal web are endless, if you can maintain the enthusiasm for hunting your personal Snark. And that was the root of the problem: his motivation. Disillusioned by a deep ennui with touring by the time he had joined Ronnie, he now found himself on a plateau. He had played in the country's best band with its most able musicians. If he hadn't said everything that he had to say, he had certainly said enough to feel that the numbing repetition of his dance band days was about to return, albeit in more elevated form. And even its most elevated echelons were beginning to lose their appeal. At 28, Benny was at the top of his profession. But he was still living with his parents, and the dream of being a full-time writer still tempted him like a mirage.

He made a drastic decision. At the apogee of an ascent through the jazz world that had seen him become respected as both musician and humorist, he chose to disappear, to absent himself from the scene for twenty weeks, and write. He took a summer-long engagement at Brambles, a holiday camp on the Isle of Wight. When Leo and I were starting out as musicians, we could never understand why, just as his career as a musician reached its peak, Benny had turned his back on music. After five years in the profession, we understood perfectly. The music business is a business built around music, and it often consumes its own. Furthermore, ambition must always find new ground. Tired of the jazz life, and still burning to write, Benny had made the right decision, a crucial turning point in his life. But before he could make his escape, there occurred an event even unlikelier than his engagement by Ronnie, a true stroke of fortune, helped in part by 'the digestive peculiarities of Harry Klein's innards'.[3]

That April, the Stan Kenton Orchestra, which was the most contentious and exciting orchestra of the day, were touring Europe. Apart from the totemic significance of his orchestra for the Modernists, Kenton's arrival had extra impact, due to the long-overdue lifting of the Musicians' Union ban, making his 1956 tour the first visit of an American bandleader since 1937. Midway through the British leg of the tour, Kenton caught two of his band smoking marijuana:

> Kenton – who tended to think of himself as a father-figure to the younger
> musicians in the band, suddenly discovered that one or two of them had
> a very eccentric idea of how English law required them to behave. And,
> being a stickler for respectability, Kenton had no hesitation in shipping
> them home.[4]

As with the similar indisposition of Paul Gonsalves during Duke Ellington's tour of 1963, where the errant tenorist had been replaced with Tubby Hayes, Kenton now had to find himself a 'dep' from among the local players. Don Rendell was hired to fill in for Kenton's disgraced tenorist for the last two British dates. For the baritonist, the first choice was Harry Klein, but due to the above-mentioned digestive discomforts, he was unavailable. The second choice was Benny:

> Which explains how it came to be that one day in April 1956 I took a
> train to Bolton, went along to the local theatre, dressed up in the hand-

me-down band uniform I was given, and became, for a brief hour of glory, a member of the Stan Kenton Orchestra and hit the high notes in 'Peanut Vendor' and the like.

I should explain that, in those far-off times, a great many sensible people and also a lot of jazz critics regarded Kenton as the most advanced, the most original, the most exciting band in the world. That verdict I imagine must have caused Duke Ellington to fall out of bed from laughing. As professional musicians were well aware, the band's inflated reputation owed much to clever publicity, and I always had a shrewd suspicion that Kenton himself knew that perfectly well.

Whatever he may or may not have been, he was no fool and if his band wasn't as phenomenal as people said, it was at least as spectacular, highly musical and technically demanding. That was why I so desperately hoped I would not commit any disastrous errors that night. In the event, I made just one, of what you might call a non-musical nature.

Things seemed to go very smoothly. Before the concerts began Kenton gave me a few guidelines about when to stand up and when to sit down, introduced me to the other musicians and then asked me if I had brought my wife along. I said no, that I was a bachelor and had always walked like that. He grinned politely and left me to settle in.

We played two houses that night, both packed to the rafters and both received with hysterical cheering. Kenton would rush over to the piano and play a bit of some imaginary concerto, but for the most part he stood in front of us doing those curious arm-stretching exercises for which he was famous.[5]

The 'imaginary concertos' to which Benny refers were Kenton's ambitious attempts to blend big band jazz with classical orchestral music; the concerts were topped and tailed by Kenton's treatment of Ravel's, 'Artistry In Rhythm'. The programme for that concert gives the orchestra's set list. For Benny, it must have seemed strangely familiar. Here at the dizzy heights of the profession, the orchestra musician of 1956 was asked to play on the off-beat all the way through the 'Sabre Dance', just as he had done in the draughty social clubs of north London in 1949. The hurried circumstances of Benny's engagement produced another scene that wouldn't have been out of place in his semi-professional days. As often happens with a band's most popular pieces, the baritone part for

Kenton's 'Peanut Vendor' was missing from the folder on Benny's music stand. Aghast, Benny turned to the altoist Lennie Niehaus, who was sitting next to him, and asked him what he should do. Unperturbed, Niehaus replied, 'Just keep playing a low B^b, and when I nudge you, go up to B.'

Among the orchestra's original material ('Intermission Riff', 'Concerto To End All Concertos'), there was a selection of standards that evoked a life accompanied by popular song, and also the musical growth that had taken Benny to that stage in Bolton. There were Swing Era numbers like 'Stompin' At The Savoy' and 'Out Of Nowhere', Boppers' favourites 'Cherokee' and 'Stella By Starlight', and classic songs of the times, such as 'Love For Sale' and 'Yesterdays'. Kenton's band may have been marketed cannily, but his musicians were among the best. Although the repertoire may have evoked some wry memories, Benny knew he had, as he said of his ex-employer Bertie King after King had played with Coleman Hawkins, 'touched the hem of greatness'. Kenton may have gone in for a familiar brand of arm-waving, but that was where the resemblance to the 'popinjay' bandleaders of Benny's youth ended. As Benny observed in the *NME* the following week, ('Our columnist plays with Kenton'), it was a world away from the internecine pettiness and parochial amateurishness that have always dogged British jazz:

> He has left us with a memory of tremendous technical ability, great enthusiasm and genuine sincerity in presenting the music, without, I remind you, the aid of a variety act, a compère or a vocalist.
>
> The heartwarming personal consideration shown by the entire Kenton band, from the leader to the second horn player, towards the British musicians who took places in the band, cannot be too highly assessed.
>
> It forces me to the conclusion that we have been visited by a band of grown men, from whom our own groups of squabbling schoolboys can do well to take example.[6]

It was not until he came off stage that Benny realised the reason for Kenton's odd question about Benny's wife, and why he hadn't got the joke that Benny had offered by way of reply:

> At the end of the night, [Kenton] said that the agent would reimburse me for my train fare, which surprisingly turned out to be true, and handed me a tenner for my labours, in those days a princely sum for a night's work.

Then came the worst part of any one-night stand, the getting home. It was now midnight, and I knew I could count myself lucky to get home much before six in the morning. If only I could sleep the journey away. And I now made the discovery about Kenton which marked him as a *genuine* original.

The gear was being loaded into two coaches. I had never seen this before. I had often worked for leaders who travelled in private cars, so that we would not pick up any contagious diseases from them, but I had never seen two coaches before. There were twenty in the party, so why the duplication?

I soon found out. One bus was for marrieds, the other for the fancy-free. As a confessed bachelor, I was ushered into the second coach, and spent the next six hours deafened by shouting, screaming and ribald songs. If only I had told a lie and brought along an imaginary wife, I might have got some sleep. As it was, I arrived home feeling like last week's dirty washing.

So Kenton was a true original after all, the only American band-leader to put up with me, and the first to have one bus for the sober, and another for the hooligans.[7]

Then, in one of those bizarre juxtapositions so common in jazz, Benny made his way to his self-imposed exile in Freshwater, Isle of Wight, 'not so very far from where Lord Tennyson perpetrated 'The Charge of The Light Brigade'.[8] Brambles had decided to make the most of its unlikely catch, billing Benny as 'Straight From The Stan Kenton Orchestra!' His duties were minimal, playing every night from seven till eleven in the camp orchestra, which left plenty of time to 'pace the floor of the tiny concrete box laughingly described to me before I arrived as a chalet, or to wander around the island looking for convenient spots to write something, or to mix with the customers and find out in which way, if any, they resembled myself'.[9] After the road-running and nightlife of the last eight years, it was a strangely calm and sunlit interlude, one so abstracted from the nocturnal tread-mill of the jazz life that it might never have existed. Years later, intrigued as to why the pursuit of his art had led to him passing a whole summer in voluntary sequestration on the Isle of Wight, Benny dug out the evidence:

I went to a large cardboard box, ferreted around and came up with a bizarre photograph of myself standing on a holiday camp bandstand in the

Isle of Wight, apparently in the act of hitting an unseen opponent over the head with a tambourine. Behind me on a chair lies my saxophone, and around my neck covering my Adam's apple at an angle of about fifty degrees is a black bow-tie. On the back of the picture is written the name of a certain holiday-camp, followed by the date: June 10th, 1956. The next snap shows four young ladies in shorts smiling out of the sunshine at the camera. I have no idea who they are. The four exclamation marks on the back could mean, I suppose, anything you want them to. In a third photograph I am in the bar surrounded by musicians and assorted young ladies. Behind us, standing on the bar, is a man in a false beard eating a handful of empty crisp packets. On the back is written, 'The food is terrible'.

The photos bring it all back to me, and how marooned we all seemed to be (we worked seven nights a week, and the season lasted twenty weeks). It was the summer of Suez, the summer of Jim Laker's nineteen wickets, the summer of Bernard Shaw's centenary, the summer when every Sunday evening, at what was laughingly called the camp concert, I played 'When I Fall In Love'. For this I was paid an extra £1 a week. In readies.

Every other Saturday a fresh supply of young ladies was most considerately delivered to the camp by the management. Our trumpet player had a special mohair suit made, which he wore only on Saturday mornings, plus an American tie. He dabbed his face with aftershave, which in those days was available only from America, and strolled up and down the camp forecourt until the coaches arrived with fresh consignments. He hoped to meet an heiress. He never did, of course. I don't know what happened to him, or to our bandleader, who used repeatedly to disappear in mid-song to go to the fruit-machine room. He had keys to all the machines, which may have had something to do with him paying me my £1 bonus in small change.

While we were not supposed to mix too freely with the campers, we ate in the same hall, and our table was always served last and was never provided with a second helping of chips. Eventually, we staged a workers' uprising and won the right to be fed with more grease and chips. I put on half a stone that summer.

One night soon after I arrived I was awoken in the night by a noise halfway between a factory whistle and a trombone. I slipped on some trousers and set off around the camp to locate the noise. I made two circuits of the premises before realising that the noise, which always seemed to be coming from just round the next corner, was the fog warning from the mainland.

One Sunday evening, after the overture for the camp concert I had about an hour free while the conjurors and acrobats did their stuff. I decided to take a bath, and accidentally locked myself into the wash house. The laundry girls battered the door down, and gave three cheers when I stepped out of the bath. I played 'When I Fall In Love' that night in a dressing gown; when I took my bow, there was a pool of water at my feet.

That little camp disappeared. But it still exists in my mind's eye, right down to the greasy chips, the owner's enormous stomach, and the way I used to hang my overcoat over my chalet window in a pathetic attempt to keep out the morning sunlight. If it wasn't for those photographs, I wouldn't be at all sure it ever happened.[10]

At the end of the season, there was little other option than to get back on the touring treadmill, which by now was eroding Benny's very spirit:

And so it went on, a town a night, week after week, month after month, year after itinerant year, until at last, incredibly, a whole decade had drifted away under the wheels of coaches and charabancs and converted buses, and the names of the towns held so little meaning that we no longer bothered to enter them in our diaries, but simply stepped into the coach and submitted to be driven wherever the driver had been instructed to take us. The upshot was that there were often days when it never quite registered in our minds precisely where we were. Sometimes in the middle of the night the regularity of the bumps in the road half-woke you to tell you that the coach was passing over that stretch of new road at Towcester, or the glimpse of sulphurous street lamps glistening on wet pavements hinted that it was raining in Newcastle again and that we were, mercifully, just passing through. But such clues were sparse and seldom looked-for. Many creative artists in history are said never to have known where they were going, but we were different; we never even knew where we had been. Ironically, the only time any of us made a genuine effort to see the sights, it was all a terrible misunderstanding. We were touring the Scottish Highlands when one afternoon, en route from Aberdeen to Inverness, one of our trombonists, who had been slightly tipsy ever since crossing the border, suggested we go and see the Elgin Marbles ...

One or two of my friends from this footloose period claim to have still in their possession letters they received from me postmarked Winchester, or Cirencester, or Matlock, or Tintagel, so I suppose I must have visited these places, or at least passed through them and stopped for long enough to lob a bulky envelope through the mouth of the local pillar-box. Every now and again, although with less and less frequency as the years go by, the fog which envelops my travels lifts for a moment; the mists disperse and I catch a brief glimpse of myself which astonishes me, against a backdrop I could have sworn had never framed me.

I have been led to believe that in old age recollections of youth become suddenly clear once more, so perhaps when I am a nonagenarian, smugly anticipating the receipt of a congratulatory telegram from the Queen, the recollection of my past life will suddenly flash before my inward eye and I will sit there and be as paralysingly bored as I was the first time round. But I really do hope not.[11]

Exhausted and demoralised by years of touring, and perhaps inspired by the literary horizons that had been glimpsed from his island retreat, Benny was walking along the street in Dundee with Harry Klein one autumn afternoon when he found himself involuntarily slowing to a halt. He sat down on the pavement, and told Harry he couldn't go on living like this. He felt so desperately depressed that he would rather have no money than continue on the road. He was burnt out. He was not yet thirty.

Lord Rockingham 18

When he got back to Cleveland Street, Benny lay in bed for two weeks, sleeping most of the time, and wondering what to do. As this type of behaviour was not unusual in her household, his mother did not realise until thirty years later that he had undergone some kind of nervous collapse, instead attributing his lassitude to heavy flu. His life now enters an interstice, between full-time playing and full-time writing, a difficult transition given the practical dilemma of finding sufficient work as a journalist, and the emotional wrench of leaving the small and familiar circle of the working jazz elite. His thirtieth year was one of emotional disappointment and professional discontent. For the first time, the enormous sense of purpose that had driven him this far began to falter with the onset of maturity. He knew that he had tired of his 'extended adolescence', but his painful awareness of dissatisfaction did not offer any solutions as to how to proceed. He was as bored with the fleeting dalliances and protracted melodramas of adolescent romance as he was with playing court jester to the *NME*, but where were the wife and work that would bring him fulfilment?

With nothing better to do, and taking the opportunity to spice up his *NME* column, he took a busman's holiday. In February 1957, Ronnie Scott took a sextet to America, and Benny and Jack Sharpe sailed with them. After having to leave drummer Phil Seamen in Southampton when drugs were discovered hidden in his drumkit, they sailed for New York on the *Queen Elizabeth*. Now that he was a paying passenger rather than an employee, Benny discovered the joys of being perpetually waited on, and passed a relaxing trip, writing in his cabin and strolling on the deck. That is, until the fourth day:

> The luxury of shipboard life in the company of six beloved scallywags was the perfect curative for the ennui of the London musical life. The first three days afloat passed in a haze of five-course meals and banana splits at four a.m. On the fourth day, there was an announcement that, owing to the outbreak of a dock strike in New York, we would be delivered

instead at Halifax, Nova Scotia, from which outpost of Empire we would be flown into New York, with Cunard footing the bill for the air fares. There were groans all round, but no real concern. A glance at the map told us that the air flight wouldn't take much time.

It was when we docked at Halifax that the bits began falling off the machine. What none of us had considered was the disparity between shipboard and air light baggage. On an ocean liner nobody cares about how much luggage you bring aboard. We all knew, even in those innocent days, how rigorously airlines limit the poundage you can carry aboard. In Halifax, it was explained to us that we would leave our surplus baggage at the airport. The following day, it would be flown down into New York on a freight plane, and we would be able to collect it without any difficulty.

I did not like the look of all this. Leaving a load of socks and cardigans in the hands of strange colonials struck me as a recipe for disaster. But what could I do? I did consider posting the surplus baggage home, but our plane left in half an hour, and there was too little time. I sat in the tiny airport lounge feeling thoroughly sorry for myself, and wondering if the whole thing wasn't a scam designed to deprive me of my surplus underpants and my pristine new single-breasted blue overcoat.

The Lounge was empty apart from me. Everyone else was rioting in the cafeteria, buying up stocks of food and drink, but I was too sick at heart to think of my stomach. And yet nobody else seem bothered by the crisis. A fat man in the Eugene Pallette class waddled across the Lounge into the Men's Room. He was whistling, and didn't seem to have a care in the world. Funny how the air companies ration your luggage, yet they don't ration you. That fat man, I idly told myself, must weigh more than me and my baggage put together, yet he was not being penalised. The injustice of this anomaly grew in my mind until at last it exploded in a wild burst of creative energy. A broad smile lit my face as I picked up my three cases and followed the fat man into the Men's Room.

Fifteen minutes later, a young man bearing no more than a superficial resemblance to me waddled out again, carrying one full suitcase and two empties. I made my way to the plane in extreme physical discomfort, but happy in the knowledge that my wits had enabled me to avert a major disaster. My one full suitcase was safely aboard, and so was I. I was home and dry. Or rather, home and distinctly damp. We had hardly left the ground before the sweat began to trickle down my face. This did not surprise me, for I was sitting in my seat wearing three vests, three pairs of underpants, three pairs of trousers, two pairs of pyjamas, three shirts, two pullovers, two jackets, three pairs of socks and a pair of gloves. None of the stewardesses noticed anything, or if they did, they said nothing. The only people in on the joke were my travelling companions, who laughed at me all the way to New York, through Customs and into our hotel. My reputation as an eccentric was really flowering now.[1]

The laughter stopped abruptly after breakfast the next morning. Due to adverse weather over Nova Scotia, the freight plane was delayed. Ronnie's sextet went off on their tour without a change of clothes. Benny and Jack Sharpe hung out in New York, touring the clubs, and gaining an audience with the legendary Baroness Pannonica de Koenigswater, the aristocratic patron of New York's jazz musicians who had gained brief notoriety in 1955 after Charlie Parker had expired in her suite at the Hotel Stanhope. The most memorable night of that trip was after the sextet had returned from their travels, when Ronnie dragged Benny from his room at the President Hotel and across the New Jersey Turnpike to hear his latest discovery, Sonny Stitt, Parker's heir on the alto, who doubled up on tenor and baritone for good measure. Three years later, Stitt's session with Oscar Peterson was to be the subject of Benny's first sleevenote for Norman Granz.

In 1957 I watched the Sonny Stitt Quartet working in Newark, New Jersey. I was impelled to go by the words of Ronnie Scott, who had already paid Stitt's group a visit. 'I don't care how tired you are,' said Scott. 'Come and see the world's greatest saxophone player.' And so I did. Stitt played alto and tenor on alternate numbers, picking up one saxophone and laying down the other with that swift resolution which is so dominant a feature of his actions and conversation. He played superbly well on both horns, well enough in fact to bear out Scott's description of him. It was perhaps the most memorable jazz I have ever heard in the flesh.[2]

Back in London, the months passed. Benny formed a quintet with Dizzy Reece, the second Jamaican collaborator of these years, a fine Boppish trumpeter who was to leave Britain in the late Fifties for New York, where he would record for Blue Note. Playing with a musician of Reece's calibre reminded Benny of how much he loved playing the saxophone, and why he had started in the first place:

> The experience of working next to him ... has revived for me the rare sensation of true musical exultation which one may experience when playing next to somebody whose trains of musical thought are fresh and exciting. I cannot remember having enjoyed this uplift very many times in my entire career as a musician, but it is a sensation always well worth the waiting.

> I felt it the first time I played with Ronnie Scott, with Joe Harriott, with Tony Crombie, with Victor Feldman, and at the present moment I am feeling it with Dizzy Reece ... his improvising exhibits most of the qualities of greatness in jazz, from the ear of the natural musician to the fire and panache of an original and resolute mind. Several times over the last three or four weeks I have looked around at the rest of the quintet while Dizzy has been playing, and caught on their faces that expression of amused enlightenment which may only be impelled by the quality of wit.[3]

Working with Dizzy Reece was to be something of a final flourish for Benny as a jazz musician. Coupled with his disillusionment with the lot of the working player were the first intimations that the ground was shifting under his generation's feet. Although two years had passed since its noisy arrival, rock'n'roll showed no sign of abating its rise to power over the youth of the Western world. The summer of 1957 was not a bad time for a 30-year-old Modern jazzer to be thinking of getting out of the profession. With painful slowness, the diligence and quality of his jazz writing began to lift him out of the 'comics'. In October 1957, he left the *NME* for its rival, *Record Mirror*. This time, he had half a page, 'Heard and Seen By Benny Green', with a large picture at its head showing Benny with his eyes shut in concentration as his body twisted in the act of negotiating a particularly Modern phrase. Just in case any free-thinkers among the readership were confused, the blurb ran, 'Modernists! Benny Green is the man for you!'

212

Benny disparaged his *Record Mirror* pieces both at the time and after-wards, but he must have been aware that the change was a step up. Certainly the *Record Mirror* realised after a few weeks that it had got more than it had bargained for; within three months, it appended to his page a banner reading, 'The Most Critically Constructive Reviews On Modern Jazz Ever Published'. And they were right. As Benny suggested with the title of his first book, *The Reluctant Art*, jazz, America's only indigenous art form and perhaps the quin-tessential twentieth-century music, had not been taken seriously as an art form by the 'respectable' musical establishment, and had consequently been disinclined to take itself seriously. This snobbery had extended to the small literature that had accumulated around the music, which at that time was divided into three types.

There were the extended fantasies that were the 'rare but undistinguished species' known as 'jazz novels',[4] which were usually badly plotted and always badly written, with cynical use of music, black men and nightclubs to add spice to their mediocrity, such as Dorothy Baker's risibly-titled *Young Man with a Horn*, or the college-boy Beatnik fantasies of John Clellon Holmes's *The Horn*. There were similarly sensationalistic autohagiographies by old musicians looking to supplant the earnings of their dotage with a publisher's advance, as in stride pianist Willie 'The Lion' Smith's *Music Was Not Enough*, or Swing Era pothead Mezz Mezzrow's *Really the Blues*. Although a useful source of anec-dote and atmosphere, these were of primarily documentary use, and minimal literary value; in the case of the elderly 'Lion', writing clearly wasn't enough, either. Coming a poor third in this shambolic collection was a thin trickle of criticism, none of it written by anyone with any practical experience, most of it written by men who wouldn't have known which end of the saxophone to blow into, and all of it having a strong whiff of fraudulent self-publicity, as in the ridiculous witterings of Philip Larkin, whose efforts mark a pan-global nadir in jazz writing.

In America, a school of writers had developed who could at least string a sentence together, even if it relied on hip argot of the 'These cats can really blow!' variety to bolster its credibility. Willing as the Hentoffs, Feathers and Gitlers were to consider jazz as an art form deserving serious discussion, their sleevenotes didn't really say much that any fan wouldn't know just by listening to the record itself, and in the absence of technical knowledge their journalism amounted to little more than puff pieces. The problem was that no jazz writer

213

worth his typewriter ribbon had any musical experience of value, which was the essential prerequisite of writing about a musician's music. Even the great Leonard Feather, doyen of the American writers, fell on his face with alarming adroitness when it came to the technical aspects of his subject. When discussing a solo by Philly Joe Jones, one of the greatest of drummers, Feather was capable of solecisms such as 'Philly has a solo for sticks in which you may notice that everything, even the high-hat, achieves rhythmic variety',[5] an observation which with marvellous economy simultaneously suborns the honour of a great drummer by implying that his high-hat might be subject to either monotony or arrhythmia; patronises the listener by assuming that he might not notice a good solo when he hears one; and suggests a woeful lack of elementary technical understanding on the part of the author for being surprised that Philly Joe knew his way around his high-hat, as it is just that part of the kit which carries the beat in Modern jazz.

With his blend of musical experience and literary talent, Benny was uniquely placed to be the first, and quite possibly the last, comprehensively authoritative writer on jazz. Having played the music, he could see through commercial flummery. Unconcerned by fashion, he considered the focus of his job as jazz critic to be 'how to codify the harmonic life of such musicians [as Charlie Parker] without reducing the actual writing, at least so far as the layman was concerned, to technical gibberish'.[6] Like Norman Granz, who ignored the controversy of the day by pairing supposedly antithetical Swing and Modern players on his barnstorming JATP tours, Benny could hear in the newer music a consanguinity of tradition which overrode mere fashion, realising years before any other jazz writer that 'Modernism in jazz, and indeed in everything else, was not a style, but an attitude'.[7]

As he had served his time in the galleys of the commercial orchestras, and was utterly sure of jazz's status as art, he saw no reason to moderate his comments when integrity or quality were at stake. In time, he would acquire a reputation as an uncompromising controversialist, as with his onslaught against the self-absorbed 'chamber jazz' of the Modern Jazz Quartet and Dave Brubeck, which in their efforts to make jazz seem dignified had taken most of the fun out of it. But even with the posturing Brubeck, Benny's criticism was leavened by an ear acute enought to pick out the undeniable quality of Paul Desmond's alto playing when he dissected a Brubeck release on behalf of *Record Mirror*'s readers:

214

Most people have already made up their minds what they think of Brubeck by now, so there is little hope of any critic influencing opinion, one way or the other. For my part, the outstanding playing of individual members of the group, particularly Paul Desmond, was quite eclipsed by the use of the most outrageous device any musical group has ever employed since the first jazz record was ever made.

Please note that this recording includes two versions of 'The Trolley Song'. One of these tracks is a rehearsal for the later version on the record. We are all treated to the edifying sound of Brubeck instructing his three companions how he desires them to play. I can see no possible excuse for this kind of drivelling device to fill up the tracks on a recording. The rehearsal track is of not of the slightest musical significance. It adds not a jot of enlightenment to the appreciation of the proceedings of the later 'Trolley Song' track, and could have been omitted from the record without the slightest loss of any musical value. Brubeck has been guilty of some lapses of musical taste in his time, but this is the best yet. It will be interesting to see how far the record-buying public can be induced to go in the search for pointless novelty. Anybody who appreciates the finer points of saxophone playing is advised to get this release for Paul Desmond, and to skip the unfortunate rehearsal gimmick.[8]

Meanwhile, the 'Most Popular and most widely followed Modern Jazz Writer of Today' found himself to be an accomplice to the undermining of jazz in the affections of the nation's youth, with the final, farcical act of his professional playing career. When not castigating Dave Brubeck, Benny had developed a secret life as a rock'n'roller. Since 1956, the musical terrain had been changing quite alarmingly. Every now and then, Benny, Ronnie, Harry Klein and other sessioneers would journey to the Decca studios in West Hampstead, honk out a few old blues riffs over a crude twelve-bar, collect their fee and leave. The resultant singles would then become massive hits, leaving thousands of teenagers demanding more of the same, while even the hardened jazzers wondered what was happening. Still, at least it was work, and the money was good enough to persuade many jazz players to jump on the bandwagon. In 1957, Tony Crombie had launched his Rockets, who soon acquired such a reputation for on-the-road misdemeanours that they were obliged to check into hotels as 'Professor

Cromberg and a party of students'.[9] Benny told the story of a drunken saxophonist named Wally Bishop, who when auditioning for a rock'n'roll band was asked if he could play on his back. 'Sure he could', replied Bishop, 'but who'd pick him up?'

As for the music, the most challenging aspect of it for a hired jazz hand was coarsening his playing to the required degree of roughness. Benny once found himself at a recording session starring one of rock'n'roll's primeval forebears, the Country Blues singer Josh White. There was considerable trouble in getting the band and White to synchronise, as with a performer of White's style and vintage, a twelve-bar blues had the habit of being eleven bars long in one chorus and thirteen bars in the next.

To capitalise on the rock'n'roll fad, an eccentric producer named Jack Good had persuaded Anglia Television to air a weekly rock'n'roll show, the first of its kind: 'Oh Boy'. A house band was needed, and a cricket team's-worth of mercenary jazz players were duly roped together under the name 'Lord Rockingham's Eleven'. Featuring the early efforts of such talents as Cliff Richard, Marty Wilde, Joe Brown and the Vernon Girls, and the first indigenous manifestations of teen mania, 'Oh Boy' quickly became a massive hit. Benny, now draped in the band's regulation pink or green suits, realised to his shame that he was in danger of being recognised:

No fiasco I ever lived through came within a million miles of the calamities of 1958, when, against my better judgement I joined an orchestra called Lord Rockingham's Eleven, scheduled to appear on prime-time television each Saturday evening playing a sort of blend of primitive rock'n'roll and sheer chaos. The reason I allowed myself to become involved was to do with money. I didn't have any, and they were offering £30 for each Saturday's show. At our first rehearsal, the show's producer, a Mr Good, listened to a few bars and stopped us, saying, 'It doesn't sound fascist enough.' We had no idea what he meant, and neither did he. Eventually, he worked it out. He said we were playing in tune, and he wanted us to play out of tune. So we began to play hideously out of tune, and an angelic smile lit Mr Good's face. We were now ready to be presented to the public.

I expected brickbats and a cancelled contract. Instead, within three weeks, we were the new sensation. My own position was awkward. By this time I was a respected musician and critic, and here I was involved in this appalling travesty of a band. At the rehearsals for the first show, the national press turned up in force, so I donned a pair of sunglasses in the hope of not being recognised. This plan went terribly wrong. Mr Good spotted the dark glasses and said, 'Terrific! You look like a dope fiend. Keep them on for transmission!' This seemed better than I had hoped. Now perhaps none of the viewers would recognise me, either. However, within a month I was receiving a large weekly fan-mail, addressed 'To the Blind Saxophone Player'.

The TV shows were such a riotous success that we were signed up to make recordings. The leader of the band was a Scot, and he had the bright idea of taking a folk song from his native land and orchestrating it as a rock'n'roll number. So he selected 'A Hundred Pipers', rechristened it 'Hoots Mon', and much to my astonishment we zoomed to the top of the charts, where we remained for three weeks, with total record sales of just under 700,000. To this day, people say to me, 'You must have made a tidy sum out of that', to which my stock answer is the true one: 'Yes I did, but nothing lasts forever, not even three quid.'

It was while I was in the Rockingham conspiracy that I first realised that the times were leaving me behind, and that I ought to start thinking about making way for a younger man, say, somebody aged six. This wisdom came to me one evening in our break before live transmission. I went out of the stage door of the Hackney Empire, which had just been converted into a TV studio, to find hundreds of fans waiting there. What alarmed me was that their average age was somewhere between ten and twelve. They were waiting for Cliff Richard, who was about to make his first TV appearance on that evening's show. As I threaded my way through, it occurred to me that the time had come to find a different way of avoiding going to work.[10]

Help was at hand. Out of tune saxophones may have come in, but it was not all for the worst. At *The Observer*, the iconoclastic drama critic Kenneth Tynan was leading a personal crusade for fresh and candid arts reviewing. Benny had met Tynan on a Saturday night in 1956 at an all-night jazz club in Lisle Street, when Tynan's debut as *The Observer*'s drama critic was only hours away. It is not known what Tynan thought of the Blind Saxophonist, but as a jazz fan he had enjoyed Benny's early critical writing, and as a critic he recognised a pungent phrase. In the summer of 1958, he telephoned Benny out of the blue to tell him that *The Observer* was looking for a jazz critic.

Jazz Writer 19

In the transition from obscurity to celebrity that he made in the Fifties, Benny had three patrons: Ronnie Scott, Kenneth Tynan and Norman Granz. That fateful phone call from Tynan marks the point at which the balance of Benny's creativity finally swung in favour of writing. When Benny published the collected fruits of fifteen years of *Observer* jazz reviews in the 1973 collection *Drums in My Ears*, it was to Tynan that he dedicated the book as a gesture of gratitude. In one bound, Benny had left the 'comics' of the music press for a respected Sunday broadsheet, where he was at last at liberty to write with due seriousness about the music he loved. After receiving Tynan's tip-off, all he had to do was disentangle himself from his musical commitments which, with the exception of working with Dizzy Reece, had arisen from the aimlessness and frustration of the previous two years. This was not going to be easy, not least because the Queen had requested a privy audience with her Lord Rockingham and his Eleven:

> By 1959 everything and everybody connected with ['Oh Boy'] was a household name, like 'drat' and 'disgusting' so it was no surprise when we were selected for the Royal Command Performance. In the normal way this would have been a day's engagement only. But this time the show was to be staged in Manchester, which meant three days in the provinces.
>
> Now it is a recognised tradition that nobody gets paid for appearing in a Command Performance, which is never much of a problem because usually the stars appearing in it are successful enough not to think of such petty matters. But our case was peculiar to us. We were all fly-by-night unemployed musicians who had happened to stumble into this rich and successful world without being in any position to capitalise on either the riches or the success. We were, it is true, to be paid our bed and board for our provincial trip, but it did mean that any work we might otherwise have been offered for those two nights would have to be sacrificed.

Rebellion smouldered in the ranks and some of my colleagues actually announced their intention of not turning up. This threat affected the executive producer and the bandleader not at all, for they had realised by now that when you are swathed in apple green serge, one musician looks much like another. So when a few of the musicians dropped out, they were quickly replaced by new musicians who fitted the suits.

We then arrived in Manchester to find that there were further impediments to our happiness; the star of the show was to be Liberace. When I began writing this reminiscence, I looked up the occasion and was surprised to discover that although I can recall little of the actual entertainment, included on the bill were Benny Hill, Al Read, Jimmy Clitheroe, Jewell and Warris, Roy Castle, Arthur Askey, Tommy Trinder, 'The Army Game', Dickie Henderson and the Hallé Orchestra. This last group caused Rockingham's lot immense amusement, because for the climax of the proceedings we all had to play 'God Save The Queen' in unison. The sight and sound of the Hallé and Rockingham coming together was one which I will almost never cherish, but it did give me the right to claim with perfect truthfulness that I have played under Sir John Barbirolli.[1]

No less bizarre a feature of the disorder of Benny's life was a short-lived incarnation as jazz club entrepreneur:

At that time, although still a working jazz musician, with the Dizzy Reece Quintet, I happened to be involved in a very brief but very exotic episode as the figurehead of an enterprise called 'Jazz City', an institution which must surely have established some kind of record for the amazing rapidity of its decline from opulence to utter pauperdom, there being 1,050 paying customers at our opening Saturday night, and twelve at our closing one six weeks later. (On our second night, having booked John Dankworth's Orchestra, we found ourselves so flooded with customers that at one point, while helping a relative of mine to sneak in for nothing through the back entrance, I was locked out of the building, and had the piquant experience of bunking into my own club.)

Tynan agreed to come down to 'Jazz City' one Saturday night to collect my literary samples, and although I have no idea what it was I gave him to read, I do recall quite distinctly that in spite of the strict orders to my partners in the box office that Tynan, being on an errand of mercy so to speak, should be allowed in free, he and his friends were obliged to pay 8/6 a head for the privilege of collecting a few of my press cuttings. Nevertheless some months later I joined The Observer.

I am unable to account for any of the incidents in this odd tale, least of all why Tynan, who hardly knew me, and had almost certainly never read me, should have taken so much trouble to have altered the course of my life, which he did beyond any question, in the most benign sense.[2]

His first review was of the Beaulieu Jazz Festival, on the August Bank Holiday of 1958. Jazz had changed almost beyond recognition since Louis Armstrong recorded 'Struttin' With Some Barbecue' on the day of Benny's birth, and in the 40 years since 1958 it has undergone an even greater transformation, obituarised and yet palpably influential across most of pop's genres. In the late Fifties, it was poised between its rise and decline, between innocent origins and avant-garde self-consciousness. In the next fifteen years, Benny's writing would record its fraught growth, and as a document of the British perspective on jazz history, *Drums in My Ears* is unique. It describes a period in which original masters such as Coleman Hawkins and Sidney Bechet were still alive and working in the same field as a younger generation whose standard-bearers would lead the revolution of the Sixties. Benny's 'was the generation which saw jazz grow from a cultural backwater ... into a great flourishing cultural stock exchange', and his own efforts were part of that shift.[3]

It is true that Miles Davis was already committed to the experiments involving the abandonment of the hitherto obligatory frame of harmonic progression from discord to resolution, true also that names like Sonny Rollins and John Coltrane were familiar to all students of the music. On the other hand, both Louis Armstrong and Duke Ellington were still young enough to have produced some of their finest work only a year or two before, Armstrong with 'Satch Plays Fats', Ellington with his Shakespearean vignettes, 'Such Sweet Thunder'. Players like Dizzy Gillespie and Jay Jay Johnson, Cannonball Adderley and Oscar Peterson were still regarded as extreme moderns ...

Many of the dominant figures from the pre-war Swing Age were still not only alive but kicking. Lester Young and Billie Holiday, Coleman Hawkins and Johnny Hodges, Sidney Bechet and Billy Strayhorn, Jack Teagarden and Henry Allen – none of these had qualified yet for memorial albums. Art Tatum and Clifford Brown had been dead only two years, Charlie Parker three, Django Reinhardt five. As for the shocking suggestion, accepted in more recent times without the batting of an eye, that jazz might after all turn out to be a finite art, almost nobody had considered the possibility. In 1958, jazz was just emerging from the disastrous internecine wars caused by the Bebop revolution of the mid-1940s, or rather by the critical reaction to it. Only now was the heat beginning to go out of the argument. People still listened, and wrote, and thought, however, in terms of the rigid compartments of jazz so obligingly but so misleadingly supplied by critics. Like Caesar's Gaul, or the old Victorian novel, jazz was divied into three parts, Traditional, Mainstream and Modern, although as there was nobody who could define any of these terms to anybody else's satisfaction, certain difficulties presented themselves. There was Duke Ellington, for instance. He had recorded 'Black and Tan Fantasy' in 1927, 'Take The 'A' Train' in 1940, 'Star-Crossed Lovers' in 1957, so presumably he must be Traditional, Mainstream and Modern at the same time. And a player like, say, Illinois Jacquet, although far more derivative than, say, Bix Beiderbecke, must be considered the more modern of the two simply because Bix died in 1931, when Jacquet was only nine years old.[4]

His ear for sincerity matched only by the enthusiasm with which he rooted out charlatans from the musical and critical ranks alike, Benny wrote not only with the perception of a man who not only knows his subject from the inside, but also the candour of one who felt allegiance not to fashion but to the spirit of the music. He was not opposed to innovation in jazz, but to all forms of fraudulence. The problem was that in a music where 'the rate of evolution was so hysterical that in fifty years it had moved from Primitivism to Sentimental Revivalism',[5] many critics and quite a few players became enraptured not by quality, but mere novelty. His unusual frankness was often the cause of unwitting controversy, as with his disdain for Brubeck and the MJQ in the late Fifties, but viewed from the end of the jazz century, his analyses were usually correct. A reverence for the giants of the past who still bestrode the stages of Europe was one thing, but the way he picked wheat from chaff with fastidious precision was a much rarer talent. His tastes were certainly catholic. In 1959, he wrote a new sleevenote for Miles Davis's radical 'Kind Of Blue', the record that did so much to change jazz's harmonic perspective for ever; managed to find musicological consolations in the 'perfect embalming job'[6] of New Orleans Trad that was George Lewis's New Orleans Band; and traced remnants of 'the old masterful felicity'[7] in Lester Young's latest.

The stakes were to rise through the Sixties, as the music underwent the successive assaults of gentrification at the hands of the dinner-suited MJQ, before being academicised by the avant-garde. But Benny never lost his ear for a good player, or the ability to judge what worked and what didn't. As late as 1966, he was describing Sonny Rollins' latest and most florid explorations as 'an extraordinary thing ... a great rubbish dump sprinkled with exquisite pearls of wisdom',[8] and could find even John Coltrane at his most abstruse admirable for his 'remarkable opening of the saxophonist's Pandora's box' and for 'genuinely extending the frontiers of improvisation ... without resorting to methods of musical barbarism'.[9]

By the mid-Sixties, the barbarians of pop were at the gates, while the old clubs were closing. As he observed, 'Now is the winter of our discotheque'. Benny's decision to pack away his saxophone was beginning to look like a wise one, but his defence of jazz's spirit was unflinching, especially when the threat came not from the barbarians at the gate, but from those within, as with his merciless pursuit of the huckstering Ornette Coleman. At Ronnie Scott's Club in 1967, Benny endured Coleman's tortuous saxophone playing, which was the monstrous fruit of many years' practice, and then watched in disbelief as Coleman produced equally incomprehensible noises from first violin and then trumpet, neither of which he had played until recently:

> He is not, however, without shrewdness. By mastering the unique trick
> of playing the entire chromatic scale at any given moment, he has
> absolved himself from the charge of continuously playing wrong notes.
> Like a stopped clock, Coleman is right at least twice a day.
>   To me the most remarkable thing of all is the sycophancy of his
> audiences, who sit in awed silence throughout each number, and then
> applaud like a barbarian horde hailing the fall of a great city. Unques-

tionably, Coleman is of the avant-garde, but I cannot help wondering how many people have noticed he is wearing no clothes.[10]

Many of the acts that Benny reviewed for the *Observer* were at Ronnie Scott's Club, originally in Gerrard Street and latterly in Frith Street. Although they had not played together since the débâcle of Ronnie's big band, they were still close, so much so that in the summer of 1959 they took their girlfriends on holiday together to Majorca, where Scott made an unlikely new friend:

It was in Majorca that he became part of the most incongruous friend-ship in the literary history of the century. Somehow, he met the local celebrity, the poet Robert Graves, who enjoyed talking to other creative artists and thought he liked jazz. Every summer, Ronnie would appear at the Palma Jazz Festival and spend his leisure time drinking and swim-ming with Graves. The old boy talked a great deal about Bacchus, Dionysus and Bunny Berigan, kept comparing Ronnie with Orpheus, and would from time to time take a drag on the kind of cigarette that has no printing on it.

They swam together every day, and when the visits to Majorca stopped, Graves turned up one night in the Gerrard Street club, surrounded by jazzmen eager to argue the case for and against romantic love. It comes back to me that Ronnie phoned me at two o'clock in the morning to say, 'Bobby's in. Why don't you come down?'[11]

On 31 October 31 1959, Scott's club opened in Gerrard Street, a watershed for British jazz. Benny traced the genesis of the club back to one of the nine-piece's early engagements:

The first time I ever heard Ronnie Scott mention the idea of a jazz club was in the bandroom of the Orchid Ballroom, Purley ... Scott and I were sitting in the bandroom, slowly changing into what were laughably known as our street clothes, and pondering the implications of the box-office returns. For the last five minutes, we had been trying to work out how many times nine went into £14 6s. Such mathematics are not good for the soul, so I was astonished when Scott remarked that he intended investing his share of the profits from our orchestra into a jazz club.

'What profits?', I asked.

'It won't always be like this,' he said. 'Not every date will turn out to be like this one.'

As it happened, he was quite right. On the following Thursday, we worked at Acton Town Hall, where this time the mathematics resolved themselves into nines into £11 10s 6d. Not surprisingly, it took Scott more than six years to realise his ambition by taking over a ramshackle cab driver's retreat in Gerrard Street, ripping the place apart, and installing himself as the main attraction in a seven-nights-a-week jazz club.[12]

Apart from the mountainous challenge of running a business predicated upon Modern jazz, there were a raft of headaches that came with the operation, including legal ones. At first, the club was licensed to sell nothing stronger than tea, a shortcoming which considerably reduced its profits. When it came to getting a licence, it emerged that before alcohol could be served, a 'Wine Committee' of three responsible members had to be formed. Hoping that his literary reputation might help their cause, Scott and his partner Pete King asked Benny to join them as the third member. Benny was despatched to Wembley Police Station, to make a statement as to why the club should want to serve intoxicating beverages. 'What is the purpose of this club?', asked the duty sergeant. 'It's to try to get rhythm sections to play in time,' said Benny with a straight face as the sergeant copied him word for word.

The club became an immediate focus for the 'Grouchovian lunacy' of the jazz world, and rapidly acquired its own mythology, from the arrival of Art Baxter wearing a Coke bottle on his genitalia, to the unopened bottle of champagne in the back office, given to Scott and King when the club opened, to be drunk after their first profitable year. Benny was on hand to record some of the legends:

In its early days the club was obliged by the licensing laws to close at midnight, and so Scott offered the premises free to a small group of actors and actresses who came along every Monday after twelve to be instructed in their art by Lindsay Anderson. Predictably, Scott cast himself as a parody of the waiter in 'You Never Can Tell', dispensing lemon teas to Maggie Smith, Cokes to Georgia Brown, coffee for Daniel Massey and George Devine, and carrying everything through in a mock-

Shakespearean voice strongly reminiscent of Sir Donald Wolfit, except, of course, that Scott is a much better actor than Wolfit. The guise of tragedian even splashed over into Scott's daytime routine, and was only discarded when the proprietor of the local betting shop suspended credit when Scott kept asking him, 'Prithee, knave, what fanciest thou in the half-past meridian at Sandown Park this afternoon?'[13]

Then there was the long-running saga of Scott's irate upstairs neighbour, who ran a garment sweatshop and believed his productivity was being undermined by strange noises emanating from daytime rehearsals in the basement. In 1963, the matter came to court, and the court despatched a man with a noise meter to measure the validity of the complaint. Scott and Benny stood with him in the upstairs corridor, while the machine registered little else than 'our own heavy breathing'.[14] The strange noises in question being measured that afternoon were those of Ella Fitzgerald rehearsing 'Whatever Lola Wants' with the Oscar Peterson Trio. Back in court, the judge was not convinced, telling the secretary who was the plaintiff's sole witness that 'Some people like jazz. They might consider you lucky to have it while you work, without paying for it.' Eventually, an out of court settlement was reached. Scott's lawyer asked for life membership as part of his payment. 'Whose life, yours or mine?' replied Scott.

Despite the ravages of time and VAT, the club is still in Frith Street. I was eight years old when Benny first took me there, and 23 when we played together on its stage. Although they saw each other only intermittently after Benny moved away from the nocturnal world of the clubs, whenever he met Ronnie in later years, 'It was always as though we had been enjoying life together only yesterday.'[15] When Ronnie died in December 1996, Benny was profoundly shaken. Apart from the loss of a friend and mentor, Ronnie's death, with its intimations of his own demise, made Benny reappraise his youth. His verdict was mixed. He was proud of having played what he felt was a modest part in the development of jazz in Britain, and as ever was retrospectively frustrated by his own self-consciousness. Approached by a publisher to write a memoir of his time on the road with Ronnie, Benny found it a hard book to write, because writing about Ronnie's youth was in effect writing about his own youth, while Ronnie's death threw a long shadow over Benny, who by now had been playing cat-and-mouse with cancer for twelve years.

226

At Ronnie's funeral, Benny was the first to speak, if only because his skills as a broadcaster might help him broach a subject as terrible as the death of his idol. It was a freezing day in early January, and the location was the common last stop for expiring jazz men, Golders Green crematorium. What seemed like the entire jazz world was there, so many people that speakers had to be set up in the chapel's doorway to relay the service to the crowd who stood outside, impervious to the weather. Standing at the lectern before the packed hall, Benny began, 'This is an address I hoped I'd never have to make', and went on to tell the story of how, by hiring him four decades earlier, Ronnie had made the rest of Benny's life possible. Friends and musicians continued to file up and pay their respects until proceedings had to be closed because of the queue of coffins forming outside the chapel for the next bookings.

Looking at the small knot of grey-haired men who gathered afterwards, it was hard to equate these bowed, modest figures with the musician-ogres they had been in the Fifties. Apart from being an inspirational player, Ronnie had also been *die gunzer macher* (the great facilitator), whose ambition and willpower had made Modern Jazz feasible in Britain. It was also hard not to feel that that day's gathering was honouring not only the passing of one of our great musicians, but also the passing of one of the symbols of a vanished world that lived on only in the memory of those who were there. The world of immigrant Jewry, of wartime London, of Geraldo's Navy, of Ronnie's nine-piece, of a Bohemian Soho carved up by Albert Dimes and Jack Spot. Not only Ronnie's world, but my father's world. As Benny said to another packed house a few months later at Ronnie's memorial service at St Martin-in-the-Fields, 'Nobody dies until everyone who knew the man no longer remembers him ... Ronnie is someone who was loved, so he will never be forgotten.' Benny felt that Ronnie's death had served final notice on his own life, and because his friendship with Ronnie was so tied up with Benny's youth and youth's own assumptions of immortality, he never came to terms with it. I know that as an atheist, Benny was hoping for the same afterlife of human memory that he reserved for Ronnie. Coming home that cold January day, I had an uneasy feeling that I had just attended a rehearsal for Benny's own funeral, which would also be a rite for that lost time, observed by the same old men.

Benny had last met his old friend earlier that year, when, as we were beginning the second set of a gig at Pizza On The Park, Benny was ambushed onstage for 'This Is Your Life' by Michael Aspel, Acker Bilk, Laurie Holloway and Denis

King. Benny's immediate reaction to being presented with the famous red book was, 'About bloody time!' He was hijacked and taken to Television Centre, where faces from every aspect of his life were waiting. Foremost among the many old warhorses from Benny's playing days was Ronnie. When Ronnie came through the doors to that familiar fanfare and a round of applause, there was a moment of absurdity, one of Time's cruel jokes. In recent years, both men had found their playing style hampered by the unforeseen dental consequences of ageing. Just audible on the broadcast over the applause as two embraced was Benny asking his friend, the companion of his youthful wanderings, 'How's the teeth?', and Ronnie laconically replying, 'Alright.'

By 1959, everything was changing. Archer Street's heyday had passed, and rock'n'roll had supplanted Modern jazz as the new thing. The musical companions of the early Fifties were becoming scattered by the passage of time. Like Benny, Pete King had virtually stopped playing, in his case to concentrate on running Ronnie's club. By achieving his ambition of opening his own club, Ronnie had entrenched himself against the changing times, and begun the process that would convert him from touring musician to musician and nightclub host. Some, like Harry Klein and Lennie Bush, stuck steadfastly to jazz in the teeth of changing tastes. Others such as nine-piece members Jimmy Deuchar and Ken Wray were thinking of moving to Germany in pursuit of an audience. Bernie Stanton was now a married man, looking for the extra-musical business ventures that would soon make him rich. Joe Harriott had begun to plot his adventurous but lonely course as an avant-gardist, while Dizzy Reece had gone to New York. And Plotski was, hopelessly, still Plotski.

Benny had made his escape in time. For three years, he had striven to disentangle himself from the life of a freelancing musician, and enter that of a freelancing writer. Kenneth Tynan had provided the decisive shift in that balance. In 1959, two other symbolic events happened. In March, Lester Young died in New York's Alvin Hotel, a few months short of his fiftieth birthday. And in August, Benny met Toni Kanal.

Toni 20

In true showbiz fashion, they met on a TV shoot. It was for another rock'n'roll show, *Steamboat Shuffle*, shot on a boat moored at Teddington. He was playing in the band, and she was one of the dancers. When Benny noticed the ravishing dancer with a black pony-tail all the way down her back, he was unsure how to approach her, and sought professional assistance from the band's singer Kenny Lynch, who duly laid the groundwork by beginning to chat up Toni, and then fading discreetly when Benny happened to pass by. She had seen *Oh Boy*, but did not connect the man before her with the Blind Saxophone Player. The Kenny Lynch gambit worked, and, if the family legend is to believed, it was love at first sight. By the end of the year, Benny had proposed, pouring lemon tea over his future bride in the process. For no other reason than she thought it was the sophisticated thing to do, Toni accepted immediately, but said they should wait a year before actually getting married. When Benny proposed in the New Year of 1960 he was thirty-two, and she was eighteen, and had recently graduated from RADA.

Born Ray Antoinette Franklin, Toni was from Bognor Regis, not far from Benny's beloved Brighton, although like him she had been born in Yorkshire. She was the second of four children born to her mother Betty, who had twice been left a widow with young children. Toni came from a more rarified stratum of Jewry. Her background was not the stereotypical Russo-Polish one of tenements and tailoring that Benny had known, but the broadly cultured one of assimilated Central European Jews. Her Romanian great-grandmother had been a concert pianist, her Galician and German grandfathers were businessmen, a great-aunt was the freethinker Charlotte Haldane, and although Betty had been compelled to take in lodgers to make ends meet, she had never lost the manners of her Hampstead childhood. From these origins, it might seem that Toni was a product of the very 'Jewsoisie' that Benny derided, but she had none of the tedious conventionality that had always bored Benny.

Toni was more Bohemian than suburban. She dressed like a beatnik, took her cat on the train on a leash, and was utterly set on being an actress. For Benny, who had wanted to be an artist, but had often lacked the confidence to carry his resolution through, Toni was an inspiration, even if she was fourteen years younger. For Toni, whose pilot father had been shot down just before her second birthday, Benny was also a revelation, an older man who seemed to have no awareness of how special he was. He moved in an exotically different world. When he picked her up from her RADA graduation, he was with fellow jazz critic Eric Hobsbawm, and the dizzying nightly tour of the jazz clubs with Benny was an entry into the inner circle of the profession.

They complemented each other in that each was a strong male or female figure for the other. For the next 38 years, Toni was to devote her life to Benny, suspending her promising career as an actress in order to administrate his life and run their family. Benny was to view this devotion with bemusement. Although he was used to women who would sublimate themselves utterly in their husband's or sons' lives, he found it incredible that this woman in particular had chosen his of all lives. He was profoundly grateful. By the age of 32, he was beginning to feel left on the shelf, and the consolations of early success as a journalist were not enough to make him happy with the present or the future, which though it might be promising, looked very lonely. Despite his success, he was still living with his parents in the squalid basement of Howard House, and would presumably continue to live there with them until all concerned were carried out feet first.

Instead, through Toni's energetic agency, his life became quite a different matter. Away from the influence of his domineering parents, Benny would blossom through the Sixties in a way at which he later marvelled. The Benny of 1959, for whom sandals and berets were the limit of sartorial experimentation, was very soon sporting the purple shirts and ties that Toni bought him. The purple didn't stop there. Most of Langley House was decorated in various shades of it. For children who had never known anything else, it seemed nothing exceptional, but the surprise was that Benny revelled in it. Toni gave him the courage to be unconventional, and the confidence to be a writer, instead of a journalist. Shortly after meeting her, he started writing a proper book, an extended study of jazz's development that would become his first book, *The Reluctant Art*.

Just as Benny had felt ambivalent about many aspects of the musical life at the time, so he was to develop an ambivalent relationship with his own past in later years. After pop music had washed away the world of his youth, he was not averse to musical nostalgia, although his reveries stopped well short of social nostalgia. He was not a believer in 'the good old days'; even in the Fifties a jazz

musician had to play turgid foxtrots in mediocre dance bands to make a pass-
able living. Certainly, he felt nostalgic for a different era, but I don't think he felt
nostalgic for the person that he had been. He might eulogise Frank Sinatra as a
romantic from 'a gentler time'; might refer back with incredulity to the sporting
exploits of Denis Compton; and might retell a story from Hollywood's Golden
Age; but the self-conscious, self-critical frustrations of his youth were handicaps
that Benny had been trying to shake off for years. The dramatic difference
between the Benny of 1955 and the Benny of 1965 was in no way a process
wrought against his will. In effect, Toni set him free. Free from his own self-
imposed limitations, free from guilt for not giving enough of himself to his
parents, free to leave the nightlife for writing and London for the country, free to
become the person that he had always dreamt of being. The reason why his children found their father's earlier incarnation so hard to visualise at times was
that in some ways the man of the Seventies and Eighties was an entirely
different person from the man of the Fifties. Benny always said that Toni had
been his salvation, and I see no reason to differ.

With Toni's arrival in Benny's life, the final pieces of the jigsaw fall into place.
In 1960, there began two associations that would continue for the next 38 years.
The first of them was with the BBC, which, in a rare outbreak of perceptiveness,
had asked Benny to deliver a weekly jazz programme for its Third Programme.
In these demotic days of *EastEnders* and newsreaders who speak 'Estuary
English', it is hard to imagine that there was a time when anything but the most
cut-glass accent was unacceptable on radio or television. After all, the
announcers and compères represented the Corporation, and in 1960 the Corporation was still the patrician institution of John Reith's original vision, which
though it may have talked much more intelligently than it does today, also talked
down to its audience. Benny was the first man with a working-class, regional
accent to be given a programme that allowed him to speak as a specialist from
a position of authority usually reserved for plummier and less able men.

To work for the BBC was an honour. Benny was a child of the Thirties, the
great age of radio in which the Broadcasting House building around the corner
from Cleveland Street had stood paramount, the cornerstone of a global network
that was the etheric corollary of Empire. The lobby of that building states this
intent; it is as much a conscious mimicry of the civic virtues of ancient Athens
as the pediment of the British Museum. As a boy, when I went with Benny to
watch him record a programme, he would occasionally pause in the lobby, and

check my Latin by asking me to translate the sentences high on the wall above, a lofty statement of intent by someone called *Iohanni Reith*. His engagement by the BBC was the first time that Benny had entered the hitherto forbidden world of what is known as the Establishment. There were to be many others, including membership of his beloved MCC, and a seat on the board of his equally beloved Open Air Theatre in Regent's Park, where Toni had played Hippolyta in *A Midsummer Night's Dream* in the early days of their marriage, and where we had seen his musicals performed. But none would be quite as exhilarating as his first work for the BBC.

In the early days of his work for the Corporation, he calculated that if he ran home fast enough to Cleveland Street, he would be there in time to catch the end of the last record, and hear his name announced after the show. He was to carry on working for the Beeb right up to the end; in his bag when we took him to hospital for the last time was his script for the next Sunday's *Art of the Song-writer* show. When in an act of Eighties philistinism, a new station controller attempted to displace him from his Radio 2 slot, his two million listeners were outraged, there were complaints in the press, and a protest march up Regent Street. Chastened, the controller renewed Benny's contract, and the show continued. Taken collectively, his Sunday show is perhaps the largest single collection of history, anecdote and analysis of the popular song. For reasons so asinine that they are best left unexamined, the BBC did not have a policy of keeping archive copies of the shows. When we decided to collect them together and present copies to the National Sound Archive for the study and pleasure of future generations, we had to obtain cassettes from fans who had illegally taped the show every week, including Bob Monkhouse. This casual vandalism was not unique to BBC radio. In the Sixties, Benny worked on the famous *Jazz 625* series, advising which musicians should be filmed, and covering the best of jazz at that time. Only a few tapes have survived, and all by accident rather than design.

A few months after Toni had accepted his proposal of marriage, Benny met the third of the triumvirate of patrons who would do so much for his working life:

It was in the summer of 1960 that I wrote my first liner note for Norman Granz. He had brought a dazzling Jazz At The Philharmonic company to London, and at the press reception sought me out. He asked me if I were Benny Green. I said I was. He then said he had read an adverse comment I had made about one of his own liner notes, and added, 'I suppose you think you could do better.' Trapped in a comically absurd situation, I had no choice but to reply, 'Yes, I could.' Then we both laughed, and he drifted off. When the tour was over, he phoned me from the airport, and invited me to write the liner note for one of his new albums. I accepted, and that was the start of the process which lasted until the final day of his entrepreneurial career, when I wrote my last liner note for him.

During those years, I must have sampled thousands of albums, thousands of musicians playing thousands of compositions, including dozens of variations of 'I Got Rhythm'. Sometimes the liner notes required deep research, sometimes they required no research at all. At the Montreux Festival in 1975, I would sit in the bandroom every night watching the show on a TV screen, then go back to the hotel and write the liner. At the time, I thought this set of notes was scrambled, but I read them the other day and decided that they were no worse than the notes I had chiselled out, phrase by phrase.

All those disparate performances, the big bands and the small groups, the vocals, the trios, the duos, the solo recitals, had one virtue in common. There was not one among them that was not good. Most were excellent, some were brilliant and memorable, a few made jazz history. It comes back to me that when I was sent, early on in the process, the tapes of Oscar Peterson with Sonny Stitt, I went crazy with joy that such saxophone playing could be found on the planet. My reaction has not changed. I was a bachelor then; now I have grown-up sons who have learned enough about the world to have 'borrowed' the album on an unspecified lease. I remember Oscar in the Soviet Union, the marvellous Basie-Peterson duets, Oscar again in 'Night Train', Harry Edison and Zoot Sims, and Tatum, Tatum, Tatum, all sorts of greatness scattered over the years.[1]

For over 30 years, Benny was to write sleeve notes for Norman Granz's Verve and Pablo labels, and was nominated for a Grammy award in 1976 for his work on Art Tatum. Each note was a miniature essay on the artist, the songs and jazz itself. The subject matter was the finest in the world. Building from his success with Jazz At The Phil, by the Seventies Granz had the most powerful roster in jazz, recording and/or managing the likes of Ella Fitzgerald, Oscar Peterson, Count Basie and Duke Ellington. An elegant man whose suits were made at

Anderson & Sheppard in Savile Row and who counted Picasso among his friends, Norman had unusual refinement and kindness for a man in the music business, as well as rare principle. He was the first to insist that his mixed-race touring parties would all stay in the same hotel when touring the southern states of America, and he looked after his artists well, paying good money to musicians who had been ripped off for years. At heart, he was a passionate fan of the music. It was that passion which drove his choice of artists (he made a star of the previously unknown guitarist Joe Pass), and it was the recognition of a similar passion that led him to hire Benny.

Over the years, Benny and Toni became good friends with Norman and his wife Grete. As children, we would receive lavish gifts in the post at Christmas, and when Norman's tours came to London, the whole family would be given the best tickets. It was an unbelievable education. Before the age of ten, I had seen Basie, Ella and Oscar several times, inspirational nights that never leave the memory. During the half-time interval and after the show, we would follow Benny backstage to meet them all. Belying her talents, Ella was a nondescript old lady who bore no resemblance to the charismatic swinging star we had just heard. Joe Pass was as composed and concentrated as his guitar playing. Oscar, too, was like his playing, a great torrent of emotion, joy and wit, almost frightening in the flesh. The twinkling-eyed Basie was easier for a child, small and dark, and smelling of sweet cheroots.

To us, it seemed normal, but I realise now how fortunate we were. Those nights shaped our lives. I first became aware of the guitar when it was in the hands of Basie's sidekick Freddie Greene. He kept strumming, but against the wailing brass, he was totally inaudible. My father told me he was there to keep time. One interval backstage, Leo found himself standing at a urinal next to a giant from the Basie band. 'What do you think of the show?', he asked Leo. 'Not bad,' said Leo. The man reflected on this and, doing up his flies, said, 'I thought it wasn't bad, either'. I still shiver when I recall the sound of Basie's band of louche geriatrics tearing into 'Jumpin' At The Woodside', while in the row in front of me a blind man with tears running down his face kept shouting deliriously, 'Bill Basie, Bill Basie!'

As with his work for the BBC, Benny felt privileged to be an amanuensis to Norman and his amazing company. They were a collection of some of the finest musicians of the century, and to be given license to write about them was a dream come true. And working for Norman opened unimaginable doors, making Benny's name synonymous with jazz writing around the world. In 1962, when Frank Sinatra was in London on a world tour, Benny found himself playing Boswell to Sinatra's Johnson for several days, an experience he always cherished:

The London promoter handling the event was Harold Davison ... I was Harold's writer of programme notes. Each note took the form of a three-thousand-word essay on the hero of the hour, whoever he or she might happen to be. Now, it seemed, I was required to write an essay on Sinatra. It was, of course, a labour of love. I admired everything that Sinatra did, musically speaking, and had no interest in his private life. I was one musician looking at another, and I knew him to be the definitive saloon singer of our century. This meant that I worked extra hard to inject some Sinatraesque humour into my essay ... Two days later, Harold telephoned to say Sinatra had enjoyed reading the essay and would like to meet me. I was aghast. Meet Sinatra? What would I say to him? Why should he be interested in a semi-rusticated jazz musician like me? But the roller-coaster had already been set in motion. I was to go up to a side entrance of the Savoy Hotel in Savoy Hill, and wait. At two p.m., a brown Bentley would draw up at the exit and Sinatra would emerge from the hotel and get into the back of the car. I was to follow him in. I followed all of these instructions, and suddenly I was sitting in the back of a car talking to Sinatra. I felt terrible. Earlier, I had lunched with 'Jazz At The Philharmonic' impresario Norman Granz. Two million-aires in one afternoon was too heady a mixture for me.

Sinatra must have sensed my predicament, for he began putting me at my ease. He started chatting about Nelson Riddle and to ask about the various Americans due to play in London. After about five minutes he was my old pal. It was extraordinary. We were driving out north of London to a Blind Children's Home, one of the charities he was endowing with the proceeds of his concert. Long before we had arrived at the home, we were laughing and gossiping like old buddies. The truth is, I got lucky. From a twist in the conversation, it quickly emerged that we both had common ground in our passionate involvement with boxing. Sinatra loved the fighters, and he told me that he had tried to get a bill through Congress which would mean that one third of every fighter's purse would be confiscated so that on retirement each fighter would be able to make a new start. The bill never went through, and Sinatra had to be satisfied with getting the old-time heavyweight Tami Mauriello a job as doorman at MGM. At one point, Sinatra showed me the knuckles of one hand; you could see the bone had been broken. Sinatra had sustained the injury as a kid in an amateur featherweight argument. It was clear that when he displayed the break he was displaying his battle honours.[2]

Back in Sinatra's suite at the Savoy, Benny noticed a large pile of sheet music, and asked Sinatra what it was:

He said that these were the songs from which he would select the programme for the album he was making in London, 'Great Songs of Great Britain'. He then asked if I would care to write the notes for the album, and when I said I would, he said, 'You can come down to the studio, three nights, midnight to three, so you can see what's happening.'

The studio was in west London, and when I arrived, it was to find about a hundred privileged souls standing against the wall of the room awaiting the performance to begin. Sinatra was instantly relaxed the moment he began mingling with the musicians in the orchestra. He was home at last. On the second night, he told about a dozen of us to stay behind, so that we could accompany him to 'The Trat' in Romilly Street for supper. It was noticeable that he took care to sit me next to him on his left, and Kenneth Alsop on his right. We were the only two writers in the company. He did little more than taste the succession of dishes, but talked to Kenneth and me of all manner of things. He had recently read a novel of Sinclair Lewis's called *It Can't Happen Here*, about a fascist takeover in America. He sounded worried by the possibility that the fantasy might come true. We also talked of the Michelangelo film which had been going the rounds ... After a while, I excused myself. Sinatra said, 'The night is young, what's the problem?' I explained that I was a newly wed, and that the wife was at home in bed with a chill. 'Get on home,' he said. 'See you tomorrow night.'

On the final night of the recording, I was standing among the crowd pressed against the studio wall, when Sinatra made his entry. As he passed down the line he noticed me, stopped his entourage and came over to me. 'How's your lady?', he asked. I was dumbstruck. Why would he remember a thing like that? I told him she was feeling better. 'Good,' he said, and proceeded on his way. At the end of the recording he invited me to pose with him for some photographs. A pair of them hang on my walls to this day. There was one last piece of unfinished business. I had written up the extraordinary events of the past few days, and I felt I ought to tell him as much. I knew of his reputation with intrusive journalists, and had no desire to break the rules. I told him I had written about my time with him, and asked if he had any objection. This was his reply: 'If you can make some bread, go ahead and sell it.' I then asked if he wanted to see what I had written. This was his reply: 'Write whatever you want, Benny.'[3]

To write whatever he wanted. That was Benny's dream, and it seemed that Toni's arrival in his life had suddenly made anything possible. At the close of 1961, a publisher offered him fifty pounds for the manuscript of *The Reluctant Art*. Having 'made it' as a musician, he had 'made it' all over again as a writer. A few weeks later, the seal on his happiness was set by his marriage to Toni.

It was January 4th, 1962. Snow was on the ground, and the bride had chilblains from putting her feet on a radiator just before the ceremony. The Reverend Rose was the rabbi presiding, and the best man was Bernie Stanton. In their wedding photos, they looked blissful. In the last photo in the album, Benny is with his friends from his life as a musician. George Melly looks almost camera-shy, Pete King and Harry Klein look respectable, Bernie Stanton almost so, a cigarette cupped in his right hand. A smiling Ronnie Scott is raising a shot glass to the camera, with his other hand on the shoulder of Manny Plotski, whose head is thrown back in careless laughter at some unknown joke. Benny's face is radiant, happier than in any photograph from the previous 34 years.

It was the beginning of a new life.

Epilogue: Regent's Park

The last stop on our journey from Cleveland Street is Cleveland Row, in St James's. The name is almost similar, but the neighbourhood could not be more different. St James's is wealthy and aristocratic, a mixture of clubs and pieds-à-terre for country dwellers. Benny would never be aristocratic, but by his sixties he was wealthy enough to buy a small flat here, in a quiet street in the shadow of St James's Palace. After three decades in the country, it was delightful to stay a night or two in the heart of the city he loved, sallying forth in the morning towards the bookshops of Piccadilly swathed in his green overcoat, with a brown felt hat set at a jaunty angle, its brim snapped downwards, looking like a cross between an inter-war man of letters and a Hollywood gangster. This may have been the desired effect. On our gigs, Benny would always say how in Thirties movies, the only way to tell the happy-go-lucky musicians from the villainous gangsters was that the musicians snapped their brims upwards, and the gangsters downwards. From being a jazz man, he had become a primarily literary one.

In the years after his marriage to Toni, his extra-musical career accelerated. Her arrival had opened the creative floodgates, by giving him the confidence whose lack had always dogged him. By 1965, when his first child was born, he was becoming a television personality, co-hosting the arts discussion programme *Three After Six*. His first novel, a satire on his early days as a journalist, *Blame It On My Youth* came two years later, and *Fifty-Eight Minutes to London* two years after that. By then, the newspaper and magazine columns had started. Beginning with *Show Pictorial* and sundry sports magazines, in the Seventies he progressed to regular spots in *Ideal Home*, *The Spectator*, *The Listener*, the *Daily Mirror*, along with countless other occasional pieces. In that decade, his authoritative knowledge of the popular song was recognised by Radio 2, who in 1976 sent him to Hollywood to interview the survivors of the Golden Age of the Thirties and Forties, from Dorothy Lamour to Ira Gershwin. In 1979, he began the *Art of the Songwriter* series for Radio 2 that would run for the next nineteen years.

Through television, his voice became familiar to millions. Inevitably, London was a recurring theme. There was a three-part series on the post-war changes

239

in the city, *London: Not Quite the Place It Was*, and an early evening quiz show, *Sounds Like London*. There were guest appearances, from afternoon quiz shows like *Cabbages and Kings* to *Parkinson*, where Parkinson told the story of his first sighting of Benny in that Barnsley dressing room, and Benny played with the house band. In these years, his routine was relentless. Taking breaks through the day to stroll around the house and find out what his family were doing, he would begin work at 9:00 a.m. and then type all day. In the evening, he would read and make notes for the next day's writing. Even in his sixties, the morning after we had returned late from a gig he would be at his typewriter as usual, while Leo and I were still sleeping.

And so it went on for 35 years, by which time there was a mountain of finished work, sheaves of magazine and newspaper clippings, and a whole cupboard filled with copies of his books. Asked to calculate his output for *Desert Island Discs*, he estimated that at a minimum rate of 1,500 words a day for 40 years, he had written more than twenty million words. Apart from the welter of journalism, there were books on Shaw and Wodehouse, Alan Jay Lerner and Fred Astaire, the great songwriters and the seaside postcard. There were introductions to half a dozen more, from H. M. Tomlinson's Conradesque *Gallion's Reach* to Hugh de Selincourt's *The Cricket Match* and Hesketh Pearson's *Whistler*. In a mammoth labour of love that took the best part of a decade, he had boiled down the annual *Wisden Almanac* of cricket records into three volumes of the best matches, with his own erudite annotations. There were histories of both cricket and Lord's, and half a dozen more books on the sport, until he had 30 books to his name. Above all sports, cricket was the one most intimately tied to his Marylebone youth, with its stolen games in Regent's Park. Even at the height of his work, he would somehow find time to pass whole summer days watching televised Test Matches or County Finals.

When Leo and I began to play professionally in the early Nineties, Benny was prodded by his own inquisitiveness to dust off his saxophone. It had been so long that in the compartment which had once been packed with chocolate and apples there was a torn piece of handwritten sheet music from the Fifties, a tune called 'Big Ben', written for Benny by Harry Klein. And so there began the decade-long Indian summer of Benny's comeback. With it, like so much disturbed sediment there came the heightened memory of his youth. The act of playing, the focus of all that passion and practice, brought him into sharper contact with whom he had been all those years ago. There was the same familiar ambivalence about it

240

all, the same relief that Ronnie Scott, Kenneth Tynan and Norman Granz had rescued him from a life of frustrated obscurity, the same disbelief that Toni had made him capitalise on their opportunities and his own talents. In his old age, I think he was reconciled to his earlier self. His return to the saxophone in the company of his sons was a major cause of that peace, just as it was a major source of happiness for us.

There are countless nights that come to mind when I think of our gigs, but one in particular stands out, touching as it does upon Benny's relationship with his past, and our relationship with him. It was in July 1994, on the night of Justin's wedding party in the garden at Langley House. Ray Gelato's band were roaring, and Benny, Justin, Leo and I were all playing with them. It was Count Basie's 'One O'Clock Jump', an endless blues in which each repeated chorus increases the pressure with a new riff, piled on top of the others, until a climax is reached, where instead of harsh blues licks, the horns play a chromatic cascade, a glissando that is at once an upping of the ante to even greater heights of audacity, and as beatifically calm as the eye of a hurricane. On the original recording of 1937, when it seems as if there is nowhere left for the thundering, rattling giant of Basie's band to go, there appears a high, wailing clarinet, playing the most joyous bluesy phrases at the top of its register, steering the song home on a final exultant flourish. As we played our rendition I was standing in the middle of the group, in front of the rhythm section and behind the horns. It occurred to me as the saxophones began their glissandi that with the production of that ace from our collective sleeve, we had exhausted our options.

It was then that I heard the clarinet. The same glorious, abandoned phrases, at the same epic point in the arrangement. I looked around, but couldn't see one. But I was sure that I could hear one, even over the deafening noise of eleven musicians playing at full tilt. By now, others on stage had started to look around for this ghostly clarinettist, a spirit who seemed to have been summoned from the long-dead Basie band by the passion of our reverent homage. And then this phantasmagorical swinger appeared. From behind the stack of speakers on the left hand side of the stage there came Bernie Stanton, clarinet in hand, his brow furrowed and cheeks puffing, a smile hidden somewhere on a face crumpled with effort. As Bernie moved towards the stage, Benny, still playing, turned towards his friend. It was as if no time had passed at all. It could have been 1949, and they could have been young men just into their twenties, exhilarated by the start of their journey into life and music. Like the understandings that pass between

241

friend and friend and fathers and sons, great music is wordless and timeless. On that night, the paths of Benny's life crossed in rare harmony: past and future, music and family. In retrospect, I began to realise then that perhaps the man he had been in his early life was not dissimilar from the father that I had known. Part of him had never stopped being the young man he had been all those years ago, and when he returned to playing jazz as an old man, he realised that he never wanted to stop being that person:

> When finally I married and retired from the musical life, the switch from one kind of work to another (I became a full-time writer) was so violent that it took a little while to become accustomed to it. Looking back on it, I realise now that for what I was doing, travelling up and down Britain with a saxophone, you have to be young and thoughtless. Were I to attempt it now, they would be carrying me out by the handles within a fortnight. But it was an amazing way of educating yourself. Frank Sinatra once described the touring life as 'a cross-country college', and I am still absurdly proud that I graduated all those decades ago.[1]

And then, on a hot morning in the summer of 1998, I found myself at the crematorium in Golders Green, the same place that we had come to eighteen months earlier to say goodbye to Ronnie Scott, with the same kind of informal service. Names and faces from his life appeared from the car park, until there was a huge crowd. Having just flown in for some concerts, Tony Bennett came straight from the airport to pay his respects. When we went inside, he sat with my mother, an unexpectedly generous gesture which made me realise how widely loved and admired Benny had been. After Justin had broken the ice, anyone who wanted to came up to the front of the packed hall to speak to the congregation, until once again time became tight. I read the Kaddish for Benny, and he was played out by a group featuring his collaborator John Dankworth, Ray Gelato and Bobby Orr from our gigs, and Leo's godfather Lennie Bush, veteran of Ronnie's nine-piece.

They played Johnny Mercer's 'Dream', a favourite from our gigs which Benny would preface with the story of how, having taken his saxophone to a wedding at which Mercer was a guest of honour, he had played 'Dream' in its composer's presence. Mercer had walked right up to the lip of the stage, and had stood there throughout Benny's performance, listening intently. Afterwards, Benny asked Mercer what he thought. Mercer replied gnomically, 'I'll tell you one thing, Elvis Presley couldn't do that.' Benny was perplexed by this, even more so when he realised that at the time of the remark Elvis Presley had been dead for several years.

Later, we scattered his ashes in Regent's Park. When Toni and Benny had settled on this arrangement, they had not realised that it was technically illegal, and so carrying it out involved a fair amount of crawling around the shrubbery to avoid the park keepers. After some considerable and farcical subterfuge, we were able to distribute him beneath some lavender bushes in one of the park's most secluded spots, a sheltered bower originally constructed for the 3rd Earl of Bute, who had requested 'a space fit for contemplation'. I went there on a quiet afternoon in the first spring after Benny's death, when a blizzard of cherry blossoms was blowing around the Inner Circle, and the lavender was coming back to life after the long winter. If you sit there on a summer evening, just audible from behind you are voices from the stage of the Open Air Theatre. Ahead, from the unseen spaces that roll towards Marylebone and Cleveland Street, you can hear disembodied echoes from casual cricket matches, each hurrying to end their game before the fading of the light.

Notes

All number references (as, e.g., 2/216) refer to articles originally written for *Ideal Home Magazine* (IPC).

1. Greenwell Street
1 *Last Empires*, Intro pp.1-2
2 3/61–2
3 3/46
4 3/62
5 3/32
6 'Watch The Screen!', p.2
7 3/22
8 3/27
9 3/62

2. Cleveland Street
1 2/174
2 2/185
3 'Aunt Rose', unpub.
4 3/6
5 2/229
6 'My Yiddishe Momma' (Yellen, Pollack)

3. Davey
1 2/65
2 2/93
3 3/55
4 3/13-14
5 'Aunt Ginnie', unpub.
6 2/234
7 3/45

4. Uncle Henry
1 'Uncle Henry', unpub..
2 Ibid
3 Ibid
4 5/37
5 'Uncle Henry'

6 Ibid
7 Ibid
8 3/70
9 'Uncle Henry', unpub.
10 Ibid

5. This Sporting Life
1 *Last Empires*, Intro, p.1
2 Ibid , Intro p.2
3 3/61
4 3/46
5 3/46
6 3/25
7 3/11
8 3/25
9 3/25
10 3/26
11 3/26
12 'Uncle Henry', unpub.
13 'Aunt Ginnie', unpub.

6. Clipstone Street
1 2/217
2 2/217-218
3 3/40
4 3/39
5 3/4
6 3/39
7 'Regent's Park', unpub.
8 2/161
9 3/23
10 3/23
11 3/7
12 3/8
13 'Aunt Ginnie', unpub.

7. Country Life
1 *Britain at War*, p. 5
2 Ibid, p. 5
3 Ibid, p. 5

4 'Aunt Ginnie', unpub.
5 *Britain at War*, p. 6
6 Ibid, p. 6
7 Ibid, pp. 6-7
8 Ibid, pp. 6-7
9 Ibid, pp. 7-8
10 Ibid, p. 8
11 Ibid, p.9
12 Ibid, p.9
13 Ibid, p.9
14 Ibid, pp.10-11

8. The Return of the Native
1 *Britain at War*, p.11
2 2/123
3 *Britain at War*, p.12
4 3/48
5 3/47
6 2/203
7 Subsequently the Whisky-A-Go-Go of Benny's playing days, and now The Wag.
8 'Aunt Ginnie', unpub.
9 1/225
10 5/249
11 5/249
12 5/249
13 5/249

9. Fitzroy Sqare
1 Britain at War, p.13
2 'Boys Club', unpub.
3 Ibid
4 Ibid
5 Ibid
6 3/9

7 3/20
8 'Ronnie Scott', *Guardian* obit.
9 Kenneth Griffith: *The Fool's Pardon*, p.339 and p.349

10. Salad Days
1 *The Fitzroy*, Dec. 1943, p.2
2 Ibid, March 1944, p.9
3 2/124
4 *The Fitzroy*, April 1944, p.23
5 2/60
6 3/37
7 5/68
8 3/37
9 2/133
10 2/133

11. Blame it on my Youth
1 2/133
2 2/133
3 2/134
4 2/65-66
5 *Swingtime In Tottenham*, p.46
6 *The Fitzroy*, February-March 1949, p.17
7 *Swingtime In Tottenham*, pp.21-22
8 Ibid, p.27
9 Ibid, p.26
10 Ibid, p.28
11 Ibid, pp.29-30
12 Ibid, p.30
13 Ibid, p.33
14 Ibid, p.34
15 Ibid, pp.34-35
16 Ibid, p.45
17 Ibid, p.46

12. Swingtime in Tottenham

1 *Swingtime in Tottenham*, p.51
2 Ibid, pp.50-51
3 Ibid, p.51
4 Ibid, p.51
5 Ibid, pp.52-58
6 Ibid, p.60
7 Ibid, p.60
8 Ibid, pp.77-78
9 Ibid, p.77
10 Ibid, p.79
11 Ibid, p.72
12 Ibid, p.73
13 Ibid, pp.75-76
14 Ibid, p.93
15 Ibid, pp.93-94
16 Ibid, p.99
17 Ibid, pp.101-105

13. Fifty-Eight Minutes to London

1 *Fifty-Eight Minutes to London*, pp.25-27
2 1/217-218
3 *Fifty-Eight Minutes to London*, p.80
4 Ibid, pp.50-51
5 Ibid, p.155
6 2/185
7 2/185
8 At that time, the London Swing Club was run by the parents of that other virtuoso, Victor Feldman, who later played drums and vibes with the celebrated Scott nine-piece that Benny played in. Now, the club is the 100 Club, where Benny saw Leo and me playing on numerous occasions. Among the pictures on the club's wall, there is one from the early Nineties, of Benny, Ronnie, Acker Bilk and others recording an episode of *Jazz Score*, a radio quiz where the questions served only to stir from the memories of the participants endless rounds of hilarious and slanderous story-telling.
9 'Ronnie Scott' obituary for Phil Osborne, p.1.
10 2/197-198

14. Archer Street

1 Unknown
2 2/198
3 2/17
4 2/17
5 2/17
6 1/219
7 1/219
8 1/21
9 1/21
10 1/23
11 'Roy Fox', p.2
12 Ibid, pp.3-4
13 Ibid, p.4
14 Ibid, p.4
15 Ibid, pp.4–5
16 Ibid, p.5
17 Ibid, p.5
18 Ibid, pp.5–6

15. Geraldo's Navy

1 'Ronnie Scott', unpub.
2 *Guardian* obit., 1/29
3 'Ronnie Scott', unpub.
4 Fordham, p. 59
5 *NME*, 24 April 1953
6 Ibid
7 Various *NME*s

16. Ronnie

1 'Ronnie Scott', unpub.
2 1/97
3 2/71-72
4 Fordham, p.67
5 *Daily Mirror*, 3 January1981
6 'Keynote', January 1957
7 2/23-24
8 1/98

17. Kenton

1 Fordham, p.75
2 Ibid, pp.75-76
3 *NME*, 18 April 1956
4 *Daily Mirror*, 15 August 1979. (5/1)
5 Ibid
6 *NME*, 18 April 1956
7 *Daily Mirror*, 15 August 1979 (5/1)
8 2/13
9 2/13
10 *Daily Mirror*, August 1977
11 2/198

18. Lord Rocking-ham

1 'Three Sheets For Bill Haggerty' (*Sunday Express*), pp.1-2
2 'Sonny Stitt sits in with the Oscar Peterson Trio', (*Verve*, 1960)
3 *NME* 'I'm having a Dizzy spell!', 1957
4 *Record Mirror*, 8 March 1958
5 'Workout' by Hank Mobley (*Blue Note*, 1961)
6 *Drums in My Ears*, p.14
7 Ibid, p.13. (Also *Record Mirror*, 21 February 1958)
8 *Record Mirror*, 12 March 1958, 'Jazz At The Blackhawk - Dave Brubeck Quartet' (*Vogue*, 1958)
9 Fordham, p.79.
10 *Notes of a Misspent Youth*, pp.4-6

19. Jazz Writer

1 3/58
2 *Drums in My Ears*, pp.11-12
3 Ibid, p.78
4 Ibid, pp.12-13
5 Ibid, p.13
6 Ibid, p.30
7 Ibid, p.24
8 Ibid, p.159.
9 'Afro-Blue Impressions' - John Coltrane (*Verve*, 1977)
10 *Drums in My Ears*, p.160
11 'Ronnie Scott', *Guardian* obit., and 'Ronnie Scott', *Daily Mail* obit.
12 *London: Jazz Decade*, pp.54-55
13 Ibid, p.55
14 Fordham, p.109
15 1/29.

20. Toni

1 'Guitar Virtuoso' - Joe Pass (Pablo, 1997)
2 'Sinatra' for Beth Dudman, pp.1-2
3 Ibid, pp.3-4

Epilogue

1 *Notes of a Misspent Youth*, p.6

Index

247

G

Gambling, 22, 27, 28–9, 51–2, 55–6, 58–60, 61–4, 65, 66, 68, 83, 99–100

Gelato, Ray, 11–12, 75, 241–2

Geraldo's Navy, 139, 179–80, 227

Gerrard Street, 184, 224

Gershwin, George, 16, 152, 162, 179

Gershwin, Ira, 239

Gilbert & Sullivan, 16

Gillespie, Dizzy, 180, 221

God Save The Queen, 135, 220

Golders Green, 227, 242

Gonsalves, Paul, 201

Good, Jack, 216–20

Goodman, Benny, 12, 114

Granz, Norman, and JATP, 185–6; 211, 214, 219; Benny and, 232–5; 241–2

Grappelli, Stephane, 75

Graves, Robert, 69–70, 224

Great Portland Street, 92, 93

Great Songs of Great Britain, 236–7

Great Titchfield Street, 32, 75–7

Green, Benny, as father, 1–10; returns to playing, 10–13, 240–1; 'family history', 14–15; death of, 16, 242–3; as polymath, 16–17; his parents, 21–2; and his grandmother, 22–5 (See: Green, Deborah); his grandfather (See: Green, Joseph); early memories 22–6, 39; loss of childhood, 29–30; in Howard House 32–6; in Cleveland Street, 36–8; relationship with mother, 39–41 (See also: Green, Fanny); relationship with father, 44–53, 67–8, 80 (See also: Green, David); and Uncle Henry, 57–64 (See also: Green, Henry); and boxing, 69–70; and Aunt Ginnie, 72–3 (See also: Green, Ginnie); at BBC, 75, 231–2; at Friday lunch parties, 75; and Daisy Head, 78; his classmates, 76–7, 78–9; at British Museum, 80–3; last Christmas before War, 84–7; evacuated to Moor Park,

91–5; to Cornwall, 96–7; returns to London, 97; in Blitz, 99–100; learns saxophone, 101, 106–8, 117–18, 131–2; at North London Emergency Secondary School, 102–3; as runner, 104–6; at Marylebone Grammar, 108–10, 129; at Boys' Club 111–12, 118–20; *The Fitzroy*, 113, 123–4; early musical efforts and Spigelman, 113–17; and Jewishness, 120–2; literary heroes, 125–7; and Plotski, 128, 138; National Service, 129–31; first gig 133–5; and Weiser, 137; and Stanton, 137–8, 241–2; early gigs with Stanton and Anton Burns, 135–43; gigs with Stanton and Sonny Landau, 145–52; plays *Lady Be Good* solo, 152–3; promotes gig with Stanton 153–5; at Sherry's Ballroom, 159–60; and *Fifty-Eight Minutes to London*, 159–62; at Selsey Bill, 162– 3; in awe of Ronnie Scott, 163–5; and touring, 165–6, 170–2, 195–7, 206–7; with Roy Fox, 172–3, 175–8; with Ralph Sharon, 174–5; love affair with Olive 175–8; at sea, 179–80, 209; in Ronnie Scott quintet 181–3; in Ronnie Scott Orchestra, 184–98; hears JATP, 185–6; writes articles for *NME*, 185–7, 200; as smoker, 192–3; plays prank on agent, 194; tours with Ronnie, 195–7; in Scott's big band, 199–200; with Stan Kenton, 201–4; at Isle of Wight, 204–6; disillusioned with music, 200–1, 209, 228; diverted to Nova Scotia, 209–11; hears Sonny Stitt, 211–12; with Dizzy Reece, 212; at *Record Mirror*, 213–15; with Josh White, 216; in Lord Rockingham's XI, 216– 17, 219–20; and Kenneth Tynan, 217–18, 220–1; as jazz critic, 222–4; and Ronnie Scott's Club, 224–6; loss of Ronnie Scott, 226–8; on *This Is Your Life*, 227– 8; meets Toni, 229; and

Norman Granz, 232–5; and Frank Sinatra, 235–7; marries Toni, 237; in St James' 239; success in 1960s and '70s, 239–40

Green, David (Davey), marries, 21; home, 33; character, 43–5, 101–2; relationship with Benny, 46–8, 51–3; and War medal, 49–51; and Ginnie, 51–2; philandering, 67–8; 92; in Blitz, 99–100; hears Benny play, 184–5

Green, Deborah, as grandmother, 22–5, 65–6

Green, Dominic, childhood impressions of father, 7–10; plays with father, 10–12, 169, 226, 227, 240–2; death of father, 16–17, 242–3; makes enquiries in family, 13–14, 63; tours, 15–16, 165–8; understanding of father, 16–18, 104, 121, 129–30, 241–2; childhood impressions of grandfather, 43–4; at Friday lunch parties, 75; at school, 95, 109; plays football with father and brothers, 103–4; at Oxford, 110; walks in West End with father, 75, 164, 169–70; at sea with father, 179–80; at BBC with father 231–2; meets jazz legends, 234

Green, Fanny, 8, 9, 21; and Benny, 39–41; and Dave, 67– 8, 92–3, 121, 209

Green, Gaby, 8

Green, Ginnie, 23, 30; and Davey, 51–2; and Benny, 72–3, 92–3, 107

Green, Henry as bookmaker, 55–6, 58–60, 61–3; relationship with Benny, 55–7; as driver, 57–8; love life, 60–1; at theatre, 64; at boxing, 70–1

Green, Joseph, 22, 26; at cinema, 27–8; 30; as gambler 28–9, 65–7; 99–100

Green, Justin (Jay), 8, 23, 103, 137, 241, 242

Green, Leo, 8; plays with Benny,

Tunney, Gene, 16
Tynan, Kenneth, 217–21, 228, 241

U

Uncle Mike (Lewington), 71–2
University College Hospital, 32

V

Valentine's Day, 126, 169
Vernon Girls, 216
Verve Records, 185–6

W

Watford, 8
Wells, H.G., 26, 37, 86, 124–6, 129
West Central Jewish Lads' Club (See: Boys' Club)
Westminster, Duke of, 33
When I Fall In Love, 205–6
White, Josh, 216
Wilde, Marty, 216
Wilde, Oscar, 31
William Ellis School, 102–3
Windsor, 36
Wisden Almanac, 26, 240
Wodehouse, P.G., 124, 240

Wolverhampton Wanderers, 36
Woolworth's, Oxford Street, 67
Wray, Ken, 184, 196, 228

XYZ

Young, Lester, 10, 12, 113; *Lady Be Good*, 152–3, 181; in London, 185–6, 190–1, 222, 223, 228